The
NEW TESTAMENT PRINCIPLE
of
KINGDOM STEWARDSHIP

The
NEW TESTAMENT PRINCIPLE
of
KINGDOM STEWARDSHIP

STEPHEN EVERETT

DESTINY IMAGE® PUBLISHERS, INC.
P.O. Box 310, Shippensburg, PA 17257-0310

"Speaking to the Purposes of God for this Generation
and for the Generations to Come."

This book and all other Destiny Image, Revival Press, Mercy Place, Fresh Bread, Destiny Image Fiction, and Treasure House books are available at Christian bookstores and distributors worldwide.

For a U.S. bookstore nearest you, call 1-800-722-6774.

For more information on foreign distributors, call 717-532-3040.

Reach us on the Internet: www.destinyimage.com.

ISBN 10: 0-7684-2649-9

ISBN 13: 978-0-7684-2649-6

For Worldwide Distribution, Printed in the U.S.A.

1 2 3 4 5 6 7 8 9 10 11 / 12 11 10 09 08

Dedication

I dedicate this book to the memory of my late friend, confidant, and co-laborer, Apostle Lorraine Alston. She was always a voice of encouragement in my life and a rock of stability in the lives of many others. She was unafraid to explore cutting-edge truth. Only eternity will reveal the full value of her life as a Kingdom ambassador on this earth. Through the people you fathered and mentored, your legacy lives on. You provided integrity, dignity, and competence to what it meant to be a female son of God. Ann and I will forever love, esteem, and appreciate you.

Acknowledgments

I would like to acknowledge the following local churches and ministries who provided me a friendly, non-threatening atmosphere in which to work out the truths in this book in a communicable format. Your trust and belief allowed me to carefully examine, teach, practice, and promulgate principles the Holy Spirit was revealing to me.

A special thank you to Drs. Daniel and Ernestine Williams, Mother Delores Etchison, and all the family at Present Truth Ministries in Kinston, North Carolina. You were the first ones to examine this message with me, allowing me to hammer out its truths.

To Dr. Willie and Pastor Vera Murray and the family at God's City of Refuge in Newport, North Carolina. You continue to model the integrity of a senior statesman in the Body of Christ. John the apostle would be pleased to call you a "modern apostle of love."

To Don Nori and the Destiny Image Publishers' family. Thank you for publishing prophets. Without you, much that needs to be said to this generation would be unspoken.

Finally, to my teacher, the Holy Spirit, who continues to reveal truth from the Word of God. Thank you for entrusting me to communicate those truths with honesty and integrity.

Endorsements

This book has arrived at a very pivotal time as the church is about to experience one of its greatest moves. God is repositioning the church and bringing it into a place of liberality and freedom like it has never yet experienced. The two biggest stumbling blocks in today's society are fear and greed. The secular world and even those of us in Christian circles make the mistake of allowing these two factors to hinder our giving, investing, and general distribution of wealth. Our thought process: "If I give, I will have less because there is only so much to go around." However, the reality is that giving enlarges our capacity to receive and is a direct result of our love for God. When His love encompasses our hearts, these self-centered thoughts disappear, and we are able to see the needs of others and be a blessing to them. First Timothy 6:18 (AMP) reads, *"[Charge them] to do good, to be rich in good works, to be liberal and generous of heart, ready to share [with others]."* Blessed people bless people.

EUGENE STRITE
World Harvest Outreach
Chambersburg, Pennsylvania

The New Testament Principle of Kingdom Stewardship is an insightful and courageous work offering a divine solution to the plague of poverty and death in the earth. Much needed reform in the church (not just revival) will be generated by heavenly information enabling the church to manifest with Kingdom authority. Dr. Stephen Everett emphasizes "the church in the marketplace is anointed and empowered to decree God's judgments with the intent of producing reformation." Fully embracing the powerful revelation of this anointed study will advance the 21st century church in transitioning to the end of this age.

Pastors Arlan and Mary Sapp

Restoration Church of the Highlands

Sebring, Florida

Upon carefully engaging myself in deep instructive teaching, my heart and my mind could not put this life-changing manuscript aside. What an electrifying explosion of what I believe to be a message from the throne room. My first thoughts: here lies the spiritual key to unlock the jail door of poverty in Christendom.

Dr. Stephen Everett has tapped into the foundation of biblical prosperity and scaled the peaks of Kingdom business without making money the issue. Reading this great word reveals the hand of God in the revelation of the simple truth of *The New Testament Principle of Kingdom Stewardship*. As a dedicated teacher of the Word of God, classified in many circles as "heavy," Dr. Everett has laid the ground works for Kingdom apostolic reformation.

Having traveled many years with Dr. Everett and experiencing the clarion call upon his life, I am on the other side of amazement in the revelatory offerings that God has so graciously and lovingly allowed me to witness as a spiritual son and personal friend to this prophet of God. I personally and aggressively recommend this book as a study guide to financial comfort and absolute obedience to Kingdom business.

When the fog is lifted, the clouds unfold, the dust is cleared and the smoke is gone...what is left is the sweet aroma of Kingdom revelation available to the Body of Christ. Stephen Everett has been used mightily by God to enlarge territory made available for blessing the Kingdom of God.

BISHOP VIRGIL DAMITRI PATTERSON Sr.
Crusade Christian Faith Center
Inglewood, California

While the direction of what is being shared may be breaking new ground in our thinking, it, however, should not be seen as novel, but within the apostolic ethos of the New Testament. Paul's writings clearly reveal the grace of giving and not a legalistic commandment or disposition. This is what should also be the focus of contemporary apostolic revelation. This is what Stephen Everett seeks to direct your thoughts to in this volume. Some of the Pentecostal and Charismatic wineskins and paradigms we have inherited must give way to a more perfect understanding as we move experientially into the Feast of Tabernacles. Many of the legalistic tenets of previous moves of God will have to be left behind as Father shows us a better way.

LOCKSLEY SMITH
Assistant to Minister of Finance
Kingston, Jamaica, West Indies

In every generation, God specifically moves with a fresh "word" from within the rent veil. The highlighting of the Holy Spirit is very vital to the Church in every generation. Consequently we have an unfolding of truth contained within the pages of this book. It is my confidence and conviction that the Lord is speaking very clearly about Kingdom giving and distribution to the Church today. In Dr. Everett's book you will discover a "relevant word." It is my earnest desire that this insightful information will enable you to understand the Spirit's iteration in this hour concerning dimensions of giving and receiving according to God's "due order." I am confident that as you remain open to the Holy Spirit, these truths will quicken you as they have quickened my spirit, my family, and my local church.

Dr. Daniel L. Williams, Senior Pastor

Present Truth Ministries

Kinston, North Carolina

The Lord has anointed Dr. Stephen Everett to release a revelatory word for this time.

After hearing this pioneering word, it has revolutionized the way our ministry operates in the area of receiving and giving. It has provoked us to move in the economy of the Kingdom.

This line-upon-line teaching builds an undisputable message which will challenge the church world's view of Kingdom distribution and re-distribution, causing a paradigm shift in the way they have regarded finances and the relationship of giving.

Rebecca M. Murray, PhD

Portering The Glory International, Inc.

The Old Testament sets the patterns for worship in the Tabernacles of Moses, David and Solomon, the pattern for priesthood in the Aaronic and Levitical orders, and the progression of our redemption in the Feasts of the Lord. The pattern for financial order was also set in the Old Testament and is the only system ordained and blessed by God.

The Old Testament serves as an example and shadow of heavenly things (see Heb. 8:5); when Moses made the Tabernacle, the Lord commanded him to make all things, "according to the pattern." Likewise, King David instructed his son in First Chronicles 22:13, "then shalt thou prosper if thou takest heed to fulfill the statutes and judgments which the Lord charged Moses concerning Israel: be strong, and of good courage, dread not, nor be dismayed." Israel in the wilderness typifies the New Testament Church (see Acts 7:38). The Hebrew word for *statutes* means "appointed custom, manner, pattern, ordinance."

Like a skillful surgeon, Dr. Stephen Everett cuts through the wounds that have plagued our modern-day church with lucid precision. With a gentle hand he leads us to the appointed pattern that will heal and restore the ways of wealth. As a father directing his son, he encourages us to take the necessary steps to reconfigure our mindsets and align us with the purpose of God. Deuteronomy 8:18 heralds, "for it is He that giveth thee power to get wealth, that He may establish His covenant...."

The church today does not lack in number but lacks in power; there are many great visions without the ability to fulfill them. *The New Testament Principle of Kingdom Stewardship* is an anointed map that shows us the way.

DR. WILLIAM D. HINN
Resurrection Life Center International
Ark of Covenant International Network

Table of Contents

Foreword

A kairos moment has dawned upon the global Church, named in some circles as the Apostolic Reformation, advocating the *reformation* and re-formation of existing structures within the Church of Jesus Christ, especially those who have moved away from the exact pattern detailed in Scripture. Associated with it is the clarion call for re-reading of Scripture so that every aspect of the ministry of the Church is brought in alignment with the divine standard promulgated by the righteous Kingdom of God. Ultimately, the objective is to build the Church as an agency through which the Kingdom of God is expressed in the earth. Therefore everything in the structure and ministry of the Church is brought under the spotlight of critical analysis. From within this scenario emerges the need for the financial structures of congregations, believers, and businesses to be adjusted.

Dr. Stephen Everett writes with remarkable insight into the deep-seated problems that have plagued Christendom. He approaches this complex subject from the presupposition that the progressive development of the Church opens the door for new teachings to be unveiled. In this way casting clearer insights into the actual manner in which the Church should function. This is the primary function of revelation—present truth—making visible what has been before the believer but not seen. The unveiling of truth—revelation—is the sovereign work of God and is disclosed at His good pleasure. When it is received and implemented, there is immediate upgrade to existing structures permitting the release of a greater glory from the throne of God.

Presently, fresh emphasis is placed on how to order our financial world so that the blessings of God may flow without restraint. The reformation of personal and corporate financial structures undoubtedly creates the capacity for transfer of wealth from the treasury of Babylon into the administration of the Kingdom of God for distribution to the diverse needs of our troubled humanity.

Proponents of the Apostolic Reformation, like Stephen Everett, assert that there are more accurate ways of serving God with one's finances. The teaching in this book presents a *more excellent ministry of giving* that facilitates the release and distribution of resources. In it is the wisdom of God communicated to the Body of Christ for accessing the wealth of the nations so that resources may be laid at the feet of the apostles for the mobilization of the Gospel of the Kingdom of God in the earth.

I believe this book presents the antithesis to the prosperity culture of giving for the primary purpose of receiving. Everett presents a financial model that may supplant the avaricious gospel of prosperity. In a nutshell, Kingdom distribution succinctly presents the culture of authentic apostolic ministry: it is more blessed to give than to receive.

Dr. Everett is an astute student of the Word of God and a profoundly anointed speaker, having earned the recognition of being a leading proponent of the Apostolic Reformation in Africa and globally. History will witness to the fact that this book was a watermark in contributing to the emergence of a new Church that will selflessly steward the end-time purposes of God in the earth.

THAMO NAIDOO
River of Life Christian Ministries
Pietermaritzburg, South Africa

Preface

Are you tired of being consumed and swamped by life's two predominant races? You're probably wondering, "Two races? I feel as though I'm in *several* races." The two I'm referring to are the mediocre, unfulfilling secular employment race, and the other complex, commit-when-you-can, and convenience-oriented church life race. Many people go nonchalantly to work every day motivated only by money—the one thing King Solomon says answers all things. (See Ecclesiastes 10:19.) After receiving compensation for unfulfilling work, many people pay out-of-control bills on an as-I-can basis. Most of the bills were created by a ruse—alleged need, greed, and desire. Various methods of consumer credit serve as temporary solutions for the lack of actual cash. The credit mentality ambushes and compromises tomorrow's prosperity by encouraging spending today. The cash flow problem becomes so dreadful that some take a second job to pay more bills for new credit to cover the old credit. As a result, people are drowning with more month than money, more debt than dollars. Many feel utterly and mercilessly trapped, tormented, and question how long it will be before everything collapses.

Then they go to church hoping to have a spiritual experience, praying for some relief before facing the next dreadful week of business-as-usual. At church, everything moves like clockwork leading up to the second main event of the service after a highly-charged praise service: *It's offering time! Better known as praise giving by the more spiritually literate!* Internally the downtrodden's comfort meter is sinking fast and they feel flustered because of their prior undisciplined spending habits. Now they must prepare to hear the company line, with all of its artistry, for the billionth time. Excitedly, one of the leaders reminds everyone during offering time how God loves cheerful, prompt-to-do-it givers.

Feeling compelled to give, they place a check or dollars into the calligraphy-enhanced, color-coded, emotionally appealing envelope, praying there's enough money in the account to cover it. At this point, they aren't sure whether they've caved in to organizational pressure, guilt, emotional blackmail, or some form of manipulation and intimidation. Then they glance at some of the more prosperous people who are on tip-toe, waiting for this epic moment to give. Oh yes! Their once brown eyes have turned green with jealousy and envy because of the other's excitement. They are encouraged to sow seed with lavish promises of exorbitant returns. Once more, there was just enough hope or hype in the presentation to keep them sowing. Maybe this time what was shared will work! Eagerly and expectantly, they hope to get a yacht in return, but instead, it's a worthless, uninspiring, scruffy canoe; or, worse yet, their ship never arrives at all.

Unfortunately, this experience conveys modern life with a touch of wry. People are driven by the anti-Kingdom emotion of fear, coddled by covetousness and its voracious twin, greed, which is the polar opposite of love. At this level, there's always the need to amass more *things* to present an artificial face of prosperity. Then, we fight the dreadful consequences of not having enough money to pay for acquisitions, and the parallel need to make more money in order to support everything you thought the initial money would fund. The frightening part of this deception is how much it portrays ordinary Christians in America and other industrialized countries. We're burdened by the self-defeating fact that our current economy permits ordinary people to purchase things only the wealthy could a few decades earlier. Our ability to procure commodities has greatly increased—much to our detriment. Is there a resolution to the problem of consumer gluttony?

The Kingdom of God offers a fascinating, alternative solution to deliver us from this destructive behavior. Uncontrolled spending is an insidious practice that holds many incarcerated to the world of commodities, consumerism, and debt. We are presented with the profound prospect of leaving Adam's world of greed and need, and entering Christ's world of seed with increased godliness and no lack. Our heavenly Father is committed to helping us get out of both races permanently. However, it will be on *His* terms based on the tried, proven principles of His Word. There are some ideals in His Word that are just now opening to our understandings during this third wave of reformation. Many of us have been taught extremely well about various methods of giving in the previous order of restoration and reformation. Many hold the idea that we know everything the Bible has to say about giving—this is an illusion. There is another dimension to giving we haven't fully explored.

Our heavenly Father has begun to remove the scales of cynicism and the mask of scorn and abuse off our eyes so we can observe and learn. Many Christians have placed a protective guard over their minds because of past exploitation and subsequent hurts. Our protective gear can sometimes prevent us from hearing with clarity the Lord's unadulterated voice. The time has come to drop the security shield and become vulnerable again. What do we have to lose, and why such a pertinent prerequisite? We actually have nothing to lose and everything to gain! We will explore ideas that will thrust us into another dimension of Kingdom reality.

New ideas evoke excitement for some and strong resistance from others during initial download. Regardless of what endeavor you're in, or field of study you're challenged by, new ideas meet the same preclusion. Although the idea and the seer are showered with greatness many years *after* its conception, at first both are vilified. In the words of Jesus, *"No man desires new wine at first, for he believes that the old is better!"* (Luke 5:38-39).

Eventually, we find little problem with a new idea as long as it is continually presented in truth, presented intelligently, and in love. Discernment allows us to gauge the condition of our audience's ear and their ability to hear something new. Therefore, we must be careful to protect what we're hearing and prevent it from becoming *a stone of stumbling* or a *rock of offense.* There are a number of examples indicating that new ideas have sometimes been stones of stumbling such as:

- The precious *name of Jesus* (see 1 Pet. 2:9).

- *Speaking in tongues* in the 20th century for many in the existing church.

- The *name* associated with baptism, that eventually produced Pentecostal denominations.

- The term *latter rain* became a note of annoyance to many Pentecostals.

- The concept *submission to authority* provided a knot-on-the-head to many unsuspecting Charismatic groups.

- *Confessing the Word* because it was linked with the Eastern religion concept of positive confession from a humanistic level during the Word/Faith Movement.

- *The banner ministry* provoked some to call it modern calf worship because they could not understand the need for prophetic enactment.

- *Laughter and various manifestations of the Holy Spirit* in many church environments in the 1990s.

Considering this list, there may be various views in this book that may qualify as stones of stumbling. This is neither my wish nor intent. New ideas usually take a period of time to work out. However, it is the will of our heavenly Father to condition our minds to widen our margins of thinking. Why live in a self-limiting fashion, a vegetable garden, when a vast domain with hills and valleys, forests and rivers, orchards and vineyards exist? Unlimitled possibilities are available for those who seek them out. These days of reformation require expansive thinking coupled with bold, daring deeds.

The catalysts of any reformation are willingness to change and effective amendments for ineffectual information, systems, and practices. For instance, all reformations highlight something in the Scriptures that devastate incomplete or erroneous theologies and structures. What we didn't count on was the Lord touching our handling of money and reordering our steps.

We must be ready for the Lord to introduce other terminologies and more mature concepts we may not initially understand or concur with.

Two examples: *the first of the firstfruits* and *Kingdom distribution*. Perhaps you may be somewhat familiar with these concepts but haven't necessarily developed a clear hermeneutical perspective about them. As we each stay focused on the King and His purposes, not one concept or word has the potential to overthrow our faith. We're strengthened to explore, to make quantum leaps, as grace opens us to higher dimensions. Thus, we release back to God what belongs to Him already, indicating we comprehend our roles as stewards in the Kingdom of God. Terminologies are assistants to aid us in placing substance to our faith; they are never intended to become assailants to our joy.

Many individuals have excelled in the principles of finance and reaped great rewards. They applied the law of seedtime and harvest and discovered Genesis 8:22 still works today. Others practiced the same principle and did not learn the secret of distribution and have, at times, found money to be a tremendous burden. Why? I believe Lord Francis Bacon discovered and delivered an important key of explanation. He said: "Money is a great treasure that only increases as you give it away." Anyone who has read the teachings of Jesus knows this is a Kingdom tenet. If we don't learn the secrets of distribution, we will be consistently burdened with financial worries. More than likely, we will climb aboard the ship of consumerism and sail the dark, beastly waters of materialism and acquisitiveness. We will fail to discover that giving constitutes the proper environment that deprives poverty of an atmosphere in which to thrive.

As well as a how-to manual, this book reveals why we must understand economic strategies from a Kingdom perspective. It is a clarion call to all, from those living in million-dollar mansions to those living in more modest homes. Most people want more money without actually understanding its effects and usefulness. When we receive something without the gift of understanding we will more than likely abuse that gift. Americans have become more affluent over the last 50 years as our purchasing power has tripled. Yet, sociological polls show those who consider themselves *unhappy* far outnumber the *happy* folk. Why so many unhappy people? Placing our energies into extrinsic attempts to find happiness through acquiring more *things* or making more *money* will be largely disappointing. Things and money cannot make us happy continuously. Fulfilling our purpose, the issues connected to legacy, and greater obedience to God produces greater happiness in God's Kingdom on earth!

Money is only an extraordinary idea. If you allow it, it can be your god, but it doesn't have to be. The history of it stretches from the unsophisticated days of bartering to today's urbane electronic fund transfers (EFTs). It is no more than what enough influential people say it is, or what societies converge toward as a common medium of exchange. For example, if enough high-ranking people said dirt was money, it would suddenly escalate in value, stimulating usage in the most opportunistic, commodious way. Culture dictates what is deemed valuable. Over the centuries, currency has included everything from cacao beans, livestock, salt, silver and gold, paper, and now, plastic.

Some preachers believe that quantitatively Jesus spoke more on money than any other subject—including eternal life and salvation. If totally true, this type of avowal induces me to raise my eyebrows and ask, "Why?" Is there a Kingdom purpose at stake, and is there a connection to the human heart and money that must be clearly addressed? The answer to both questions is "Yes!" Money magnifies the heart just as anointing magnifies the character or lack of character in a person. If Christ spoke so often on a subject, the bar of its importance is raised immensely. Jesus said every man's heart will follow money. Wherever your money is, your heart will be there as well.

This book presents a compound theme of Kingdom distribution and the order of first things. With the core message including the transference of wealth for the purpose of proper, Christ-centered distribution, your true economic joy and happiness are connected to how well one functions in this ideal. Placing your happiness in a consume-all-I-want container makes your joy extremely vulnerable. True, lasting joy is in the Kingdom! The teachings of the Kingdom develop the God-like traits, strengths, and talents in every Kingdom citizen, pressing everyone to keep the bigger picture in mind.

Such things as love, creativity, kindness, service to others, and gratitude are universal characteristics of Christ's nature. Therefore, what really makes each of us happy and joyful is to be other-people centered. The greatest service and love can only be expressed outside of ourselves. Kingdom distribution permits us to express natural, internal traits and strengths constant with who we have become in Christ. A much more reliable foundation for joy is established when we behave out of our Christ nature instead of filling our lives with commodities. *The New Testament Principle to Kingdom Stewardship* presents the high values of living out of a more favorably developed distribution viewpoint and praxis.

Chapter 1

SURPRISED AND STUMBLING INTO TRUTH

Canst thou by searching find out God? Canst thou find out the Almighty unto perfection? (Job 11:7).

Behold, God is great, and we know Him not, neither can the number of His years be searched out (Job 36:26).

O the depth of the riches both of the wisdom and knowledge of God! How unsearchable are His judgments, and His ways past finding out (Romans 11:33).

Only he who lives in truth finds it. The deepest truth is not born of conscious striving, but comes in the quiet hour when a noble nature gives itself into the keeping of life, to suffer, to feel, to think, and to act as it is moved by wisdom not its own.

—HAMILTON WRIGHT MABIE[1]

I've got priceless wisdom for every person who loves God and seeks to understand Him; He's difficult to figure out, which, at times, is problematic to our flesh. Just about the time you think you've fully searched His ways, He'll flabbergast you! Sometimes He's an enigma. He's known yet never completely known; He's specific and on occasions vague; He's clear, and yet, indistinguishable. He'll reveal Himself, and then mask Himself. No flesh of person has ever glimpsed Him, and He dwells in unapproachable, celestial light. Only greatness allows Him to be this way. I define greatness as God being superlative to anything or anyone without rival or equal. Even if we took a long, hard look, we would be perplexed by His infinitude. He is greater than anything anticipated or assumed. Without exaggeration, this vast universe and all its intricacies only reveal a slight glimmer of His person. Is it really possible to know all of His ways or judgments?

Consider this thought: Do we really possess the mental prowess or lexis to articulate God's greatness in a manner that everyone could understand? Obviously, no! In our best efforts, we stumble along, inept, and make valiant, heroic, but vain attempts. Our most fascinating presentations leave us wondering if we could have improved. Even cultural distinctions impede us. However, if we'll allow ourselves to meditate on God's greatness, then, perhaps we'll remove the limitations of our current revelations about who *God is*, what He contemplates and verbalizes, and what He can or cannot do based on former paradigms of truth. Yes there are permanent foundations that will remain, such as *God is*; however, God certainly hasn't exhausted *His* ability to communicate beyond His last revelation.

New Every Morning

More and more I'm discovering that many of God's 21st century communiqués are different from what He spoke in the 20th century. The ceiling of His communications in the 20th century is only the bottom rung in the

21st century. He only speaks in agreement with the counsel of His own will for a particular time frame. He's not driven to speak based on human need or input, only divine purpose. Greatness allows Him to resist the temptation to unveil certain things before the appointed season. Nothing is premature, regardless of how opportunistically we batter the heavens in prayer. God's unveilings are completely in alignment with His appointments. His appointments even take precedence over all the strident demands we place on Him to show up, speak something, solve our self-inflicted problems, or meet our unrealistic expectations.

When God downloads things into the earth, there is something noteworthy, dauntless, and timely in each disclosure. Whether He speaks or acts, each new revelation becomes the impetus behind change, transition, and Kingdom advancement. Since the Bible has been canonized, many of God's children earnestly believe God stopped talking. They shudder at the thought that there is a proceeding word from God's mouth beyond the first century of Christian development. Because we're a culture driven by performance as much as society, there are times we think we have exhausted a biblical subject through our previous study, only to wake up shocked, stunned, and somewhat mystified that God has never given anyone or any generation *all* of the revelation or application on any particular subject.

Question: Will we ever get beyond our arrogant thoughts that we can know everything about a subject created by our infinite, omniscient heavenly Father? We must wrestle with this question until we realize that all the knowledge we possess would not fill a tiny thimble. To our credit, we have enlarged our knowledge by attending churches, schools, seminars, conventions, universities, and camps. Probably most of these experiences were wonderful, but none were the ultimate experience. Moreover, none of them totally developed us.

The school of sonship development continues until this present moment. It isn't over until a corporate body matures into the image of Christ. We are all a work in progress. We're yet to apprehend fully what we have been apprehended for. If we remain open, there's an ever-evolving door of revelation in the realm of spiritual things. After 36 years of intense Bible study and Christian experience, I'm discovering this idea afresh every day.

It can be challenging to know that some things in our walk with God will come purely by divine sovereignty. Because we are almost always seeking to upgrade our positions in the spiritual pecking order, it does little for us to know our ambitious little hands didn't produce certain things. We unknowingly have dates with destiny that are pleasantly surprising. Our Father chooses to do the marvelous, the unexpected—the things that the human mind cannot conceive, without the Holy Spirit. There's a dictum the Holy Spirit releases to keep us on course. In those instances, we can take no credit for anything—not even the wonderful information we're about to process. It's not even a matter of being studious, inquisitive, or any other spiritual discipline that we ordinarily think merits us the right to hear fresh ideas from God. As some would say, "This is a God-thing!" Accurately, it's a grace proclamation and impartation. Such is the case with the information in this book. I had no idea what the Father was about to lead me into. The following is an account of those initial instructions from the Lord, and the subsequent journey I've been on since.

A KAIROS MOMENT

Itinerate ministry required me to travel to Washington, DC, in early January 2006. It was my first meeting for the New Year. I remember being very excited about this trip because of the impending opportunity I had to share on the Kingdom of God. Though I had been to Washington several times, I hadn't traveled there specifically for ministry since May 1974. During the course of the meeting, I sensed one of those *kairos moments* in which Heaven intervened. *Kairos* means "a divine moment" intervening in an earthly environment producing an opportunity to fulfill destiny. At the time, I did not think this to be something of profound importance—the beginning of a new book, a new message, or any other type of new communication. No, my desire was to hear clearly what the heavenly Father was saying at that moment. Time has taught me not to be assumptive or even preliminarily suggestive about what the Holy Spirit might say.

One speaker at the meeting addressed various approaches in which we could improve on our giving. I immediately had several knee-jerk reactions. Somewhat suspiciously and hoping I wasn't being too cynical, I thought, *That's all the Body of Christ needs is one more high-leveled marketing message by calculating priests on giving.* Within the deliberations of my head, I further thought, *With a new giving plan, we've positioned ourselves for accusations to be levied against ministers for cavorting with corruption.* I justified my thoughts with, *Aren't our collective reputations tarnished enough?*

I must admit that some of these musings were directly related to possessing too much information about past leadership behavior. Tragically, when it comes to giving, we get stuck on the idea of money alone; when giving is more inclusive and comprehensive than just money. I felt chastised of the Holy Spirit and received a mild rebuke, along with an attitude alteration. Sometime between rejection and acceptance of the speaker's message, my heavenly Father shook me out of my personal funk. I opened my heart long enough to hear the challenge the Holy Spirit issued. I now felt more incarcerated by my previous prayers. Like many Christians, there had been various occasions in my past in which I had asked the Lord to help me improve my giving. I desired to elevate from somewhat above normal giving to extravagant grace giving, which incorporates a greater benefaction.

Since giving has been an integral part of my life, this was a rational request, though somewhat revolutionary. I recognized early on that whole-life giving reflected the most accurate standard of the Kingdom of God, though that wasn't always my practice. We should give of our time, talents, and treasures. I had read the New and Old Testaments carefully and had analyzed with great detail the models of the prophets and Christ. Their lives were the epitome of complete giving—spirit, soul, and body. Some even gave the ultimate sacrifice. Since I had followed most acceptable Fundamental/Pentecostal/Charismatic norms in giving, what more could the Master say to me?

HE SAID...

Before the meeting was over, ever so gently, the Holy Spirit spoke to me to distribute my earnings for that trip to two men of God I had known for years. I had never received a command from the Master like this in 36 years. Certainly, before uninformed zeal could kick in, I wanted to know why. Probably a bit of skepticism sparked the inquiry. I did not immediately receive an answer from the Holy Spirit. My analytical mind, accustomed to answers, gave me several restless days. I knew that in order to receive the full grace benefit from this directive and action, it had to be done out of a willing heart and mind. Operating out of compulsion would somewhat taint the process.

My next step was to communicate with my wife, my teammate. While still in Washington, I telephoned her and shared the instructions from the Holy Spirit. When I cautiously uttered to my wife, "Honey, guess what the Holy Spirit has spoken to me on this trip?" She said: "What?" Because she has shared my life for 30 years, she was alert and knew a bombshell was coming. A new idea was about to burst on the scene, overtaking an old, antiquated one. I shared with her what the Holy Spirit had spoken, hoping for a response of support. After listening patiently she asked, "Did He tell you why?" I had no powerful, majestic, thundering revelation answer. In fact, at this point, I had no convincing illumination for myself either. All I knew was that I had heard the Master's voice clearly.

Because I don't believe in blind faith, which to me is nonsense, I needed an answer. The Bible says, *"So then faith cometh by hearing, and hearing by the word* [rhema] *of God"* (Rom. 10:17). If I was to have full faith in this matter, it would be because the word of God was present, and the same word became impartation. I had a motivating word, but my perplexity was left uninterrupted until I returned to Florida and obeyed what the Holy Spirit commanded me to do. I also knew the importance of balancing the *rhema* word with the *written* Word, thus the subjective weighed against the objective. From the Book of Genesis, I found myself in the evening of a new day, steadily progressing toward the morning because of obedience. I concur with the sentiments of George MacDonald: "I find that doing the will of God leaves me no time for disputing His plans."[2]

Upon my arrival home, I deposited my check, and immediately wrote out two checks—one for each of the men the Holy Spirit identified—and mailed them. Because I still hadn't received an answer, I genuinely needed the wise counsel of King Solomon to comfort me: *"Trust in the Lord with all thine heart; and lean not unto thine own understanding. In all thy ways acknowledge Him, and He shall direct thy paths"* (Prov. 3:5-6). When we trust the Lord, it prevents us from becoming casual in our obedience. More often we are discouraged and disengaged from leaning on human understanding. There are many times in our walk with God when we must trust our hearts and not our heads. If I had leaned on human understanding and procrastinated, my analytical mind would have antagonistically disrupted my compliance to the Lord's voice. Don't be hoodwinked—procrastination is a thief! As George H. Lorimer said, "Putting off an easy thing makes it hard, and putting off a hard one makes it impossible."[3] If I had listened to my head, this spirit could have left me in the gutter of despair trying to stagger up the ladder of obedience without success.

I had to remember to model the nature of God, which is love. Love isn't love until it's engaged in responsible giving. In fact, perfect love is refreshment that will destroy the debilitating powers of fear, which causes us to withhold. God loved the world, therefore He gave His uniquely begotten Son. The heavenly Father gave His magnanimous gift with liberality and without fear. Subsequently, giving should never be a fearful, difficult thing for us. In fact, it should be rudimentary. After releasing the two checks from my possession, the Holy Spirit immediately spoke, "Now, I'm going to explain to you what you've done." For me, this was comparable to the great Day of Pentecost in Acts chapter 2. I had an experience, and then the explanation came. The Holy Spirit tirelessly and systematically crafted His explanation, step by step, month by month, for all of 2006.

THE JOURNEY

The Holy Spirit prepared me for a journey through the Scriptures that allowed me to progress in my comprehension of whole-life giving. Any instructions on Kingdom giving should ultimately lead us to a desire to completely give ourselves to the Lord. He began to teach me about the *firstfruits principle* in ways unknown to me. It was the order of first things, or seeking the Kingdom first. I discovered it is the Kingdom's principle of substitution, which constitutes complete giving. It was first form in the Old Testament before it became substance in the New Testament. Frankly I was shocked at what unfolded. My previous knowledge of firstfruits was imperfect and inaccurate. This is not a moot point, in which I will explain more thoroughly.

When we entered modern Pentecost, our belief system established the tithe as synonymous with the complete firstfruits. Perhaps most Christians in our era accepted that idea. If a sampling of believers were polled, one would probably find this statement true more times than false. To substantiate that, many practiced tithing, while others struggled with the principle, and therefore, ruled it obsolete for the New Testament believer. Or, "Since tithes applied to crops in its original format, they have no modern or postmodern application."

In my ignorance, I thought I knew all there was to know about tithing and firstfruits. Self-conceit could have made it impossible to learn with greater acumen what I thought I already knew. Why did I think in those terms? Facetiously, it probably came from the lifetime of sermons preached on tithes and offerings—who needed one more message on firstfruits? Knowing my skepticism probably mimicked other people's, how could I convince the church that we have believed incompletely or practiced inappropriately for years? For decades we have resorted to many extra-biblical measures to raise church and pastoral income. We have been governed more by the corporate structure of the industrialized world, coupled with the federal government's requirements, than we have been ruled by the Kingdom of God.

New concepts began to take shape in my spirit, whittling away at old mind-sets. Just as Martin Luther and others, my own personal reformation began. Apostolically, the new concepts I was entertaining had the potential of becoming an implosion as well as an explosion. That seems to be the nature of the apostolic reformation: imploding mind-sets and exploding external structures, replacing them with configurations consistent for the times. If not handled with wisdom, violent opposition from without or from within the church could make this idea combustible or collapsible.

I faced the dilemma to either reveal or remain quiet about what I had been shown. My dilemma was quickly settled, because I discovered others were studying and considering the same concepts given by the Holy Spirit. Thus, there is an unearthing of a vital part of the postmodern reformation. God gives us breakthrough revelation to share responsibly and timely.

Nature and Kingdom realities both testify that when the season demands it, nothing can prevent new revelations from breaking forth. More than one person will know that the time is ripe. Whether we receive the *full* wisdom of the revelation is another story. I asked the Lord, "why this revelation, and why now?" Shouldn't the collective church have known something about the distinction between the tithe and the first of the firstfruits before now? Perhaps there were some informed ones; I just didn't know them.

The heavenly Father took me on a return trip to the Book of Genesis. This is where the foundation of my new understanding began. All truth is in the embryo stage in Genesis. I discovered that the first acceptable model of giving by man to the Lord was connected to the firstfruits principle. Abel gave the firstlings of his flocks and the fat thereof. It certainly makes sense, since Genesis is the document of God's original information.

It is apparent that Genesis chapter 1 details the reconstruction, reorganization, and restoration of planet Earth. Extreme chaos hit the earth and produced mass destruction. There are various schools of thought about why it happened. However, in the midst of a chaotic nightmare, the Spirit of God began to move over the face of confusion and the Word called forth light out of darkness. This interaction of the triune God with disorganized creation produced structure, order, unity, and life. The principle is very simple: the first order of reorganization or reformation is the appearance of light—which equates to revelation or understanding. At this point, light doesn't necessarily need a material body, only a formidable existence, because light will cancel the claims of darkness every time.

One of the ways to look at light is that it is symbolic of the Creator's foresight. The principle of foresight is that light before a thing, releases insight or light into a thing. God will always see the end from the beginning. The prophet Isaiah captures this idea beautifully: *"Declaring the end from the beginning, and from ancient times the things that are not yet done, saying, My counsel shall stand, and I will do all My pleasure"* (Isa. 46:10). It is impossible to build something fail proof if it's not built upon the foundation of knowing the end first. We see God as a master builder construct order through each day's assignment demonstrating He saw the end from the beginning. He allotted Himself certain activities each day. It is impossible to read Genesis chapter 1 and fail to observe this plan of precision—the right action at the right time. Giving attention to the minutest detail, God creates and forms a glorious masterpiece. His proclamation at the end of each day's work, "It was good!" The end of day six releases the hallmark of God's purposeful activities; He creates man in His image and likeness. Image speaks to representation; whereas, likeness speaks to resemblance. God took a snapshot of Himself and the end result was man. Man was given the dominion mandate, and placed in an ideal environment to initiate the dominion process.

In order to fully grasp and appreciate dominion, humankind had to be given a work assignment under the tutorship of the Creator and Maker. Since God created man, He is the only One who could establish the ideal residence in order for man to work out his purpose. God commanded man to keep the Garden of Eden and to subdue the earth. The implication certainly suggests that there may be an adversarial force lurking.

Genesis chapter 3 introduces the *serpent,* that sinister charmer existing to beguile, waiting for the opportunity to pounce. We immediately see the employment of his greatest tool—the magnetism of his mouth. His insidious nature permits him to lie convincingly. He inserts just enough resemblance of the truth to make his conversations palatable to the carnal realm of humans. In fact, he is a master tactician and manipulator. The right moment finally comes for him to unleash his deadly venom on his unsuspecting target: woman or *womb* man.

The serpent stages a conversation with *man with a womb.* The lack of fear on the woman's part to converse with the serpent presents us with the challenge that maybe this was not their first conversation. Without getting into the full discussion of why woman was chosen, it is more important to understand what was being sought. Now that human beings, male and female, were given dominion over the earth, nothing could come into the earth without their collaboration. We must rightly discern that Mr. Adam and Mrs. Adam were the highest level of teammates and reproducers in the earth. Very simply, the serpent needed man! The one who bore the image of God, with managerial responsibilities for the whole earth, had to be derailed. His preference was a womb rather than a seed bearer in which to conceive, commence, and convey his ideas, and thus, releasing a reign of terror in the earth.

The reign of terror began with a carefully connived plan—a conspiracy. The devil, the old serpent of Genesis, the dragon of the Revelation, was the first terrorist. God's firstfruit in the person of womb Adam was charmingly, methodically, and sadistically attacked. The serpent's smooth patter, his whispering nature appealed to her emotions. Man was hit by a weapon of mass destruction. What weapon? The ballistic missile of misinformation! Misinformation was unleashed and detonated on the human race. The serpent's objective was obvious: Adam must temporarily lose his dominion and be placed into a position of misdirection. Adam had to be overthrown. (What the serpent didn't know was that the infinite wisdom of God had already anticipated this event.) The serpent slyly suggested God was holding out on Adam. Adam bit the bait and fell into the trap. He had chosen to swallow a lie and accepted it as the truth. Lust for the forbidden and the spirit of covetousness opened this carnal door in Adam. The seedling for Adam to become a habitual, aggressive taker was now in place.

Humankind, through the spirit of covetousness, lost its true identity, accepted mistaken identity, took on duality, and immediately entered into a state of fear. Adam was in a fog: he no longer knew what manner of man he was. At one point, he was *ish* (high, noble, and royalty); now, he is *enosh* (frail and feeble). Covetousness entrapped man to reach for more than he could responsibly handle and to keep reaching. He violated God's timetable and commandment and created a world he knew nothing about: *need*. Up to this point, Adam had no needs! God had a schedule in which He would share everything with Adam. The serpent's cunningly devised fable and Adam's greed provoked him to get ahead of the schedule. This opened the door to egocentricity, independence, rebellion, selfishness, and many other self-interest maladies.

The moment Adam became selfish, he was clutched by greed and succumbed to poverty. Wherever poverty exists there is lack and disenfranchisement. Selfishness disconnected Adam from his source of wealth, which was Almighty God. When we're connected to God, we're hooked into the One who owns everything! Poverty enters, first as a spirit, and then it becomes a condition of perpetual lack. Poverty always places man in a grabbing and grappling position rather than a faith-releasing and trusting one. It stifles our trust in the integrity of the heavenly Father to handle our lives with wisdom and exactness. As long as God is the head of our lives, we have nothing to worry about. Anxiety comes when we personally take the helm and seek to develop our own best plan for ourselves. Inevitably, we block ourselves from some of the most basic blessings.

Many other negative doors opened through Adam's decision to disobey God, especially the door to self-preservation. Those who have studied human behavior will tell you that self-preservation is the first innate law of the human race. They're actually speaking from a position after the fall of Adam. Nonetheless, I beg to differ! From a Kingdom position, fearing God and keeping His commandments should occupy top tier. When one lives in the mode of self-preservation, one is preoccupied with the instinctive need for survival. Inherently, this mentality contains the seedbed of the spirit of entitlement. Entitlement compels us to believe we *deserve* to have everything we desire, even if it is at others' expense. Carnal man will do whatever is necessary to fulfill his lusts. If covetousness opens the way to a blissful life, he'll be covetous. If violence is the way, then he will be violent, oppressive, and overpowering.

The low end of this: Man moves away from his God-given nature (love), which always blesses, gives, and cares more for others than self. He becomes an aggressive, egotistical taker and a hoarder with a me-first attitude. A way of escape must be provided. The question becomes: How can Adam escape systematic selfishness, avarice, and greed? The answer is in the great reversal. Systematic giving must be established to reform and redevelop Adam to desire a proper giving mentality and disposition. A plan of giving regularly must be decreed encouraging Adam's participation. It must begin with something that is uniquely first, and then, grow into other areas as divine guidance is received. Thus, firstfruits is the entry level to Kingdom distribution. Adam would become productive. He had to learn to be a releaser rather than a hoarder of his production. Distribution was the secret weapon to assist him in his full recovery and restoration until Jesus came. Jesus Christ as the last Adam exemplified completely the spirit of distribution. He gave *all: Himself!*

As the descendants of Jesus Christ, and recipients of His grace, we will give our way out of comprehensive covetousness, greed, and poverty which permeates the human experience, escaping no race or nationality. Everyone has been infected and affected to a degree. Jesus clearly gave us the remedy, the holy inoculation, when He said, *"It is more blessed to give than to receive."* (See Acts 20:35.)

THE PURPOSE BEHIND THE PRINCIPLES

I'm determined to become an extravagant grace giver. Stinginess will not impede my desire nor become my cell of containment. I intend to learn everything the Master has provided regarding systematic giving, whether it's firstfruits, tithes, or multiple offerings. What one labels the giving becomes secondary to the giving. The key: learn the spirit and the heart behind God's activities rather than being controlled or manipulated by the law of it. We must learn to live within the Spirit of God's laws or principles and not under the legalistic oppression of law. Children need laws, responsible, mature believers don't! If Adam debased the creation by taking, we in Christ must empower it through giving. Adam lowered creation through a selfish, entitlement spirit; God raised creation through charitable benefaction.

It is necessary, then, to consider some very important questions, such as:

- What is meant by whole-life giving? What is its purpose?

- In Exodus 23:19 and Exodus 34:26, what is meant by *"the first"* of the firstfruits?

- What was the purpose in developing a firstfruits culture, since purpose denotes usage?

- What was the heavenly Father's purpose in allowing us to share in His material resources, and then commanding us to develop responsible stewardship and extravagant giving habits?

- What was the exact purpose of tithes? Does God really need a certain percentage from us?

- Why have we transferred from the Old Testament and promoted in the modern Church only one aspect of tithing, when there were clearly at least three different practices of tithing?

- Does the New Covenant speak prohibitively against or convincingly in favor of tithing? Or, is there something greater we have missed?

- How were buildings funded in relationship to each of the ones God commanded to be built?

- What is the revelation we each need in our hearts to begin entry-level giving, and then move to a greater maturity, breaking the stronghold of covetousness?

These questions urge us to think. If we don't learn the purpose behind each of these principles, we will abuse them. Abuse is the illegal, illogical, and harmful use of a thing, which is totally contrary to its purpose. For instance, microphones are used to magnify a person's voice. If someone used a microphone to sing loudly in a library, regardless to their reasoning, the person would be using the equipment in a nonstandard, abusive way. We may know all about giving and tithing, but are we using that knowledge in the way God intended?

It is important to understand the profound, uncomplicated truth that Father God owns all things by reason of creation and redemption. In the beginning, He created all things; and in Christ, He redeemed them. He extracted everything out of Himself when there was nothing. His innovative hands scooped inside His endless enormity. What creativity! God is different in that He creates with nothing, while humans need things to be creative. By this definition, God is the only one in the universe who qualifies as Creator. God's omniscience stores information and retains the title to all He creates, even down to numbering the hairs on our heads. This thought is obvious as various writers pondered the enormity of God. We see agreement in the Law, the poetic books, history, and the prophets. All expressed the same sentiment:

> Now therefore, if ye will obey My voice indeed and keep My covenant, then ye shall be a peculiar treasure unto Me above all people: for all the earth is Mine (Exodus 19:5).

> Who hath prevented [anticipated or proceeded] Me, that I should repay him? Whatsoever is under the whole heaven is Mine (Job 41:11).

> The earth is the Lord's, and the fullness thereof; the world, and they that dwell therein (Psalm 24:1).

> For every beast of the forest is Mine, and the cattle upon a thousand hills. I know all the fowls of the mountains: and the wild beasts of the field are Mine. If I were hungry, I would not tell thee: for the world is Mine, and the fullness thereof (Psalm 50:10-12).

> The silver is Mine, and the gold is Mine, saith the Lord of hosts (Haggai 2:8).

> Wherefore David blessed the Lord before all the congregation: and David said, blessed be Thou, Lord God of Israel our Father, for ever and ever. Thine, O Lord, is the greatness and the power, and the glory, and the victory, and the majesty: for

all that is in the heaven and in the earth is Thine; Thine is the kingdom, O Lord, and Thou art exalted as head above all. Both riches and honor come of Thee, and Thou reignest over all; and in Thine hand is power and might; and in Thine hand it is to make great, and to give strength unto all. Now, therefore, our God, we thank Thee, and praise Thy glorious name. But who am I, and what is my people, that we should be able to offer so willingly after this sort? For all things come of Thee, and of Thine own have we given Thee . . . O Lord our God, all this store that we have prepared to build Thee a house for Thine holy name cometh of Thine hand, and is all Thine own (1 Chronicles 29:10-14,16).

Moses, Job, David, and Haggai formed a four-fold cord that can't be broken. The Scriptures require two to three witnesses to establish a thing, and here, we have four. We must remember God is the Owner of all and we are but stewards of His possessions. Press bravely to assail the spirit of covetousness ingrained in the fabric of fallen humanity. Covetous Adam has been replaced by generous Christ. Now that we are redeemed we are beneficent people. We are all called to liberality. It is God's objective to bring all of us into the abundant life and out of the slavish life of greed, ignorance, and selfishness. All of us may draw from His commonwealth, producing a common well-being for all. This precious truth can only be realized by our acknowledgement of, surrender to, and practice of the principles of God's Word. There is no portion of anything within our care that is truly ours, and the rest God's.

Clutch all the money that you consider yours, and remember, God had to create the trees before anyone could extract the paper it was printed on. Humankind has no ability to create gold, silver, or copper for coins. By nature, the more you hoard money, the easier it slips out your grasp. The clothing you are wearing, whether from cotton, wool, skins, or synthetic, God provided the basic components—plants, animals—for each piece. God gave someone the technological wisdom and expertise to create the modern conveniences and toys we enjoy. All are His; He made everything, gives it for our good, and trusted it to us for His service.

I will have accomplished my task if after you read this book you have acquired a more inquiring spirit, and are feeling a bit unsettled about what you thought you knew. If you feel rattled and stretched, good! If you desire comfort and conventionality, reading this book and walking with Jesus will be the most burdensome thing you've attempted. Our walk with Him entails change—changing the assumptions and perspectives about who He is. Change is about walking through open doors, and properly discerning the seasons of God. We have left the door of the modern church and have traveled through the entrance into the postmodern church and world.

Doors are access points into new dimensions of the Holy Spirit. Our current position, or door, can be a barrier or a blessing. In the Feast of Tabernacles, God's current Kingdom economy, as with every experience, some doors open first, and are foundational to every other door we walk through. A definition of *doors* for me is "revelation knowledge." When God gives revelation knowledge, it is indicative of His love and favor toward us. Those who lack revelation knowledge in today's economy will be stymied by outdated information. We need to be constantly updating in order to be efficient in the postmodern reformation. Also, there are enemies stationed at open doors, including ignorance, selfishness, fear, and rebellion, seeking to harass and contain us with phobias, thus impeding Kingdom progress.

Every time we come into a new vista, we have to lay aside deep-rooted, decaying understanding. Its permanence isn't enduring because it is askew to what God is saying in the now. We gain by dying. At first, we will endure uncertainty. But, God will give us the grace that is necessary to be at peace in the new world. The landscape in this postmodern world is filled with enormous possibilities. Revelation knowledge gives wider choices; opportunities for greater union life with Christ. This book thrives with impartation—it is not documentation for collecting offerings. Its objective is not to supply a fresh three-pronged fork for the lust of the flesh, the lust of the eyes, and the pride of life. It is a tool to open God's Kingdom doors.

ENDNOTES

1. Virginia Ely, *I Quote*, (New York: George W. Stewart Publisher, Inc., 1947), 342.

2. R. Daniel Watkins, *An Encyclopedia of Compelling Quotations*, (Peabody, MA: Hendrickson Publishers, Inc., 2001), 536.

3. Ibid., 592.

Chapter 2

An Extraordinary Secret

Then Thou shalt see, and flow together, and Thine heart shall fear, and be enlarged; because the abundance of the sea shall be converted unto Thee, the forces of the Gentiles shall come unto Thee (Isaiah 60:5).

Wealth is the test of a man's character.

—Anonymous

When I was a very young minister, I heard Dr. Derek Prince and other vital teachers address Isaiah 60:5. Dr. Prince used it as a foundational text to explain the redistribution of wealth projected for the Kingdom of God. The world's wealth would be bestowed upon God's people in due season. The rich are babysitting Kingdom money until Kingdom vessels are sufficiently prepared to handle the wealth. This is an intriguing, stimulating idea with multilateral opportunities. I'm sure those with most of the world's wealth would think this extraordinary secret is nonsense. Many Christians are still wondering how and when this will happen. If in our lifetime, what would be its purpose? Fundamental transitions must take place in our concepts about money before we can arrive at an Isaiah 60 destination.

It is important that we see the Kingdom's socioeconomic order different from the humanistic systems governed by men's economic theories. God's thoughts are higher than man's. God's motivation is nobler than man's. God's plans are just and right. Man's plans are usually unjust, egocentric, and mostly lacking in altruistic value. This principle becomes extremely important as we examine the economies of most countries. God has placed wealth disproportionately worldwide. Unfortunately, the citizens of some of the most wealthy countries are among the most poor. Examples include the oil-rich Middle Eastern countries before their awakening to great wealth. After the great awakening, nobility benefited and has continued to do so greatly. In comparison, precious few citizens of those nations profit. Conversely, places such as Hong Kong (China) and Japan became wealthy with cherished few natural resources.

Consider the full import of the Kingdom of God in every nation. Can you imagine trillions of dollars, euros, yens, and pounds coming into the Kingdom of God without centers of greed and avarice controlling people's hearts? I can! The message of wealth redistribution is exciting and prompts us to think beyond our current limited status. It is an extraordinary secret!

Redistribution contains at least two major facets: (1) To divide more of something previously distributed; and (2) To divide something or share something in a different way, e.g., in more equal proportions or among a wider range of people. I thought, *God forbid a bastardizing rerun of socialism's application of wealth redistribution.* Socialist's emphasis on equality stripped people of creativity, motivation, and human rights, and ignored the differences in God-given talents, dedication, and industry.

The Kingdom's principle of redistribution is different from that of Karl Marx and those of his ilk. In God's world, everything is done on the basis of divine intellect and purpose. Everyone has the opportunity to succeed.

The parable of the talents certainly gives us insight into this principle. (See Matthew 25:14-30.) Kingdom distribution is centered on divine justice—a justice that doesn't limit the rights of others, but highly respects the worth of all.

Most of us know who the wealthy are in our city, where they reside, and maybe know of their disassociation with the poor, except to hire them as cheap labor. We also know how disproportionate their financial portfolios are compared to ours. But we probably don't consider the reasons why. Maybe the difference in wealth stems from inherited social advantages, educational opportunities, acute business savvy, or upward mobility opportunities. It amuses me to think that our heavenly Father committed Himself to adjusting the imbalances long before we even knew the difference.

IMBALANCES

In today's world, the idea of redistribution seems far-fetched in view of the powerbrokers controlling economic affairs worldwide. Like Mary when the angel came to her with news about the impending immaculate conception of Jesus Christ, we may ask ourselves, "How can these things be?" It seems doubly impossible from our earthly rather than heavenly perspective. A love/hate relationship with the current expression of capitalism promotes this doubt. Unless people have a real vision for the Kingdom, it is difficult to see beyond the free market system, driven largely by greed and competition. Irresponsible capitalism is the economic structure that creates the world's greatest wealth disparity because of the human engine that drives it. Ironically, I know people who think capitalism and Kingdom economics are synonymous. Time will prove that concept to be in disagreement with the Scriptures.

Note the footprints of capitalism. Probably the vast majority of the world's wealth is controlled by a very small percentage of the world's population.. For example, as recently as March 9, 2007, in the money section of *USA Today*, the tally of billionaires around the globe reached a high of 946. This number is not very high considering the world's population is over six billion people. Their combined wealth grew 35 percent to $3.5 trillion, according to *Forbes* magazine's 2007 rankings of the world's richest people.[1] Leading the list in the United States were Bill Gates and Warren Buffett, who manage to keep getting richer as they give more and more money away. What a powerful Kingdom principle: *More comes as more is given away!* I personally believe the accrual of wealth comes from spiritual, physical, and natural differences and their inevitable consequences. For instance, how do you prevent a Bill Gates, Warren Buffett, or Oprah Winfrey from becoming who they are?

Someone during the 19th century Industrial Revolution years would have asked the same question about Andrew Carnegie, John D. Rockefeller, or R.G. LeTourneau. Nevertheless, if a wider range of people share that portion of the pie enjoyed by the privileged few, redistribution of some type must take place. And, if redistribution occurs without the nature and heart of humankind transforming, planet Earth still has a mess.

God's means of accomplishing total redistribution remains somewhat of a mystery. We're standing at the seashore of history waiting to see how the tide of divine invasion is going to bring this extraordinary secret ashore. There's not even a remote plausibility of this idea fully happening outside of the Kingdom of God. However, once in a while there are glimpses of it when wealthy individuals or foundations provide funding for pocket projects in developing nations. I believe most have good intentions to help those less fortunate. Nevertheless, many are content to keep what they have rather than risk their powerful position in society. Though poverty doesn't always come because of exploitation, some powerbrokers aren't in a hurry to even the balances. In the name of freedom, a bureaucracy develops that protects the few, cementing the poor to their economic status. Once in a while, crumbs trickle down to the disempowered.

Although Jesus taught much about the proper handling of money (see Matt. 6:19-24; Matt. 25:15-30; Mark 12:41-44; Luke 12:16-21; Luke 12:29-34; Luke 16:9-15; Luke 19:12-26), the Kingdom of God is less concerned with money per se than with money as a tool to aid in dominion's responsibility, which promotes the freedom of servanthood. Money is to serve the purpose of the Kingdom rather than men becoming slaves to money. In the beginning, humankind was given great freedom and great tasks with few restraints. In the Kingdom, we use that freedom to serve one another, bless one another, and empower each other. The Kingdom is a *commonwealth*, which means "common well-being of all." Very simply, commonwealths are established for the political, social, and economic benefit of all members; it's not about elitism or poverty. Strong controls by central governing oligarchies are unnecessary and create unresponsive people. In the Kingdom, control at the edges is all that is needed. The heart of humankind under the auspices of the Holy Spirit is the central point of control—the jurisdiction of righteousness.

To me, this is obviously the best plan, because a large majority of the world's population lives in the ghetto of poverty or the suburbs of barely enough. Note these statistics:

- The Gross Domestic Product of the poorest 48 nations (of the world's countries) is less than the combined wealth of the world's 3 richest people.

- The combined wealth of the world's 200 richest people hit $1,000,000,000.000 in 1999; the combined incomes of the 582.000.000 people living in the 43 least developed countries is $146,000,000,000.

- Approximately 790.000.000 people in the developing world are still chronically undernourished, almost 66% of whom reside in Asia and the Pacific.[2]

If we as God's children are to resolve this overwhelming disparity, and conquer humanity's illusive ills created by it, such as waves of criminal activities, there must be a greater sharing of the earth's resources from a Kingdom perspective. Poverty must be eradicated from the face of the earth. About poverty, along with death as an accomplice, the prophet Isaiah says, *"It's the face of the covering cast over all people, and the veil that is spread over all nations"* (Isa. 25:7). Veils block us from seeing the truth in Christ—a truth that declares He has ripped the veil into shreds, crucified Adam, crushed the serpent's head, and demolished the clutches of the world's system.

Isaiah tells us that revelation, unity, the fear of the Lord, and enlargement are keys to precipitate this flow (wealth redistribution). The Body of Christ must be able to see what God is doing—revelation. If we can't see, we won't recognize the signs of God's movements. Unity facilitates spiritual movements. In unity the Lord has commanded the blessing, even life forevermore (see Ps. 133:3). Unity promotes an environment of inclusiveness, and demands diversity just as the holy anointing oil modeled. (See Exodus 30:22-25.) The fear of the Lord grounds us in wisdom. When one has had very little wealth, it requires wisdom to recondition and renew the mind. In fact, wisdom attracts wealth. King Solomon is the prototype of that reality. Enlargement is necessary to broaden our capacities to handle wealth responsibly. The reason most people have so little wealth is their inability to steward wealth properly. Earlier in this chapter, I made reference to the Parable of the Talents. It is a classic example of one individual's failure with opportunity while two others responded to the favorable time of the Lord. He lost the wealth he had been given because he lacked the wisdom necessary to engage the markets of his day and produce gainfully.

According to the Scriptures, wealth redistribution under the Kingdom umbrella is a marvelous thought concealed, at first, and now revealed in the Word of God. It is one of the balances that will glorify and magnify the wisdom of God. There are six other occasions God declares this same thought. For me, it was quite alarming when I discovered them, knowing that seven symbolizes divine completeness and spiritual perfection. In fact, when God established an oath with people, He would seven Himself. Seven is the completeness of his name or nature manifested. All of life revolves spiritually around the number seven. God will completely spoil the wicked and turn the wealth over to the just. Listen to the six other times this thought is postulated.

> *This is the portion of a wicked man with God, and the heritage of oppressors, which they shall receive of the Almighty. .. Though he heap up silver as the dust, and prepare raiment as the clay; he may prepare it, but the just shall put it on, and innocent shall divide the silver* (Job 27:13,16-17).

> *A good man leaveth an inheritance to his children's children: and the wealth of the sinner is laid up for the just* (Proverbs 13:22).

He that by usury and unjust gain increaseth his substance, he shall gather it for him that will pity the poor (Proverbs 28:8).

For God giveth to a man that is good in His sight wisdom, and knowledge, and joy; but to the sinner He giveth travail, to gather and to heap up, that he may give to him that is good before God. This also is vanity and vexation of spirit (Ecclesiastes 2:26).

There is an evil which I have seen under the sun, and it is common among men: a man to whom God hath given riches, wealth, and honor, so that he wanteth nothing for his soul of all that he desireth, yet God giveth him not power to eat thereof, but a stranger eateth it: this is vanity, and it is an evil disease (Ecclesiastes 6:1-2).

And strangers shall stand and feed your flocks, and the sons of the alien shall be your ploughmen and your vinedressers. But ye shall be named the priests of the Lord: men shall call you the ministers of our God; ye shall eat the riches of the Gentiles, and in their glory shall ye boast yourselves (Isaiah 61:5-6).

The collective thought in these verses can't be misinterpreted or distorted. It is profound with irrefutable ramifications. Some people are gathering immensely, but others will benefit. King Solomon, while in a carnal state, felt this was vanity and vexation of spirit. Remember, Ecclesiastes is the book of wisdom from beneath the sun, or humanistic wisdom; whereas Proverbs shines with the wisdom from above, or heavenly places.

Solomon reacted as any rich man would who was controlled by the opportunities and advantages of wealth. He was perplexed with the notion of why squander all the efforts necessary to accumulate riches, wealth, and honor if you must heave it up for someone else to enjoy?

While meditating on the praxis of these verses, I asked the Lord to show me models of this release set forth in the Scriptures. The apostle Paul recorded that *"whatever was written and whatever happened"* provided us instructional and learning opportunities. (See Romans 15:4 and 1 Corinthians 10:11.) The record was quite impressive. From Abraham to Christ, they each experienced the transfer of wealth. Though riches came, it was secondary to the truths God taught each individual about fulfillment in the Kingdom's scenario. Each model presents an alternative to a worldview that scorns the principles of God's Word and promotes covetousness as a general policy.

ABRAHAM: BREAKTHROUGH INTO WEALTH

Abraham, the father of all faithful, is the first model of wealth redistribution. He and his small band journeyed from Mesopotamia until they arrived in what was later called the Promised Land. There's no indication at this point whether he is wealthy or deprived; what's clear from the Scriptures was the command God gave him to forsake all. In antiquity, there was no middle class; this is a modern Industrial Revolution phenomenon. Vast landholders were the known wealthy in ancient times. Upon arrival in Canaan, Abraham pitched his tent and assembled an altar unto the Lord. The importance of this act cannot be overvalued. Altar building was an acknowledgement of God's ownership, His right to be Lord of the hollowed grounds occupied by his servants. In fact, altars will always give

God fresh accessibility to a place along with our mutual cooperation. The Invisible One's presence becomes magnified at the altar.

Abraham dwelt between Bethel and Hai when he came into the land; Bethel was on the west and Hai on the east. *Bethel* means "the house of God," and *Hai* means "the heap of ruins." By principle, we can live life's experiences camped in the twilight zone, the lukewarm region between God's house and a heap of ruins. At this point, there's no full commitment to either. While dithering, wisdom prevails upon us to make sure our gaze is toward the house of God, which is the gateway into heavenly things. There's a scriptural principle that says, *"We become the image of what we behold."* (See 2 Corinthians 3:18.) If we take the alternative view and focus on the heap of ruins, we will, likewise, be transformed into a deformed, devastated condition. That will continually prove disastrous.

The Bible says, *"And there was a famine in the land: and Abraham went down into Egypt to sojourn there; for the famine was grievous in the land"* (Gen. 12:10). As of yet, God hadn't taught Abraham how to handle the difficulty of famine. Therefore, Abraham responded from the insecurity of his humanity—he fled! Until we learn to walk in faith, we flee complexity and the circumstantial conflicts of life. Phobias control us when we're so driven. Interestingly enough, Abraham never imagined he had a date with destiny in Egypt. Abraham would lie and become well compensated! Now imagine that, especially when one of the great moral absolutes in all cultures forbade lying. Abraham spoke a half-truth about his wife Sarah. Subsequently, Pharaoh took her into his house based upon the recommendation of his princes. What Pharaoh didn't know was about to kill him. God plagued his house because he dared embrace another man's wife, who happened to be a developing prophet. Pharaoh recognized his mistake, confronted Abraham, returned his wife, and commanded him to depart from his country.

When Abraham returned to the land, he was very rich. The word *very* emphasizes the importance of Abraham's position and the accuracy of what occurred in Egypt. *"And Abram went up out of Egypt, he, and his wife, and all that he had, and Lot with him, into the south. And Abram was very rich in cattle, in silver, and in gold"* (Gen. 13:1-2). There's no record of how long he dwelt in Egypt. One thing is for sure, he came out blessed by the power of wealth redistribution. Egypt represents the world's system and all of its socioeconomic structures. Learn to live with this idea: Abraham got rich in the world! In today's language: The marketplace provided Abraham great wealth. He wasn't just a little rich, he was extremely rich. Abraham's economic status was transformed from being poor to wealthy by a massive exchange. Now he would face the challenge of whether wealth would be his god, or if the Almighty would remain his God.

There are many significant lessons in this story applicable to postmodern times. Just to have a history lesson without the spiritual application teeter-totters on a missed opportunity. No where does it say, "Abraham ventured into Egypt seeking riches." One *could* say, "He stumbled into wealth!" Some of our greatest blessings in life will be those we stumble into—things about which we have never even thought about. The Bible compels us to seek the Kingdom and watch things be superadded to our lives without anxiety. Equally, it warns against the treacherous desire to get rich, which in itself is a deathtrap.

> *He that hasteth to be rich hath an evil eye, and considereth not that poverty shall come upon him* (Proverbs 28:22).

*But they that will be rich fall into temptation and a snare,
and into many foolish and hurtful lusts, which drown men in
destruction and perdition. For the love of money is the root
of all evil: which while some coveted after, they have erred
from the faith, and pierced themselves through with many
sorrows* (1 Timothy 6:9-10).

The itch to get rich never sank its carnivorous teeth into Abraham's
soul. He didn't covet silver or gold and err from his relationship with
Almighty God. The meeting with the King of Sodom tested this area of his
life. This appears to be one of the most important tests the people of God
face. It is impossible to serve two masters; either we will love one and hate
the other. This parallels the devil tempting Jesus with wealth and power.
Jesus refused and experienced triumph like no other Adam before Him.

Concerning breakthrough into new dimensions in God, the separation from a desire to get wealth is crossing the line of demarcation properly, correctly passing through the transition zone. If the adversary
becomes aware of your price, he'll tease, tantalize, and provide opportunities for temptation. He may sugarcoat the temptation with flattery; however, the objective is to get us to do something inconsistent in our
relationship with our heavenly Father. Abraham knew what H. L. Wayland
discovered: "To value riches is not to be covetous. They are the gift of
God, and, like every gift of his, good in themselves, and capable of a good
use. But to overvalue riches, to give them a place in the heart which God
did not design them to fill, this is covetousness."[2] Preachers who have
known abject poverty are especially vulnerable to this. We must be ever
watchful because everything that appears to be a blessing may not be.
Don't allow the spirit of covetousness to turn you into a harlot or a

hireling. I encourage every man and woman of God to never prostitute or bid oneself to the highest contract. When the night falls, be able to sleep with the Christ in you peacefully because you have honored him with integrity.

> *And the king of Sodom said unto Abram, Give me the persons, and take the goods to thyself. And Abram said to the king of Sodom, I have lift up mine hand unto the Lord, the most high God, the possessor of heaven and earth, that I will not take from a thread even to a shoe latchet, and that I will not take anything that is thine, lest thou shouldest say, I have made Abram rich* (Genesis 14:21-23).

Abraham's retort proved he had separated from the desire to gather wealth. A greedy, avarice man would have welcomed the king of Sodom's invitation to pillage the spoils. However, Abraham knew wealth can't be defined as possession of stuff. I define *wealth* as being in authority over your circumstances so that you are free to obey God at all times. Within the construct of this definition, health is wealth! Many holistic practitioners believe a sound body implies a mind free from fear and its co-conspirator anger, from negative thoughts and other mental injuries. The greatest wealth we will ever possess is the integrity and wholeness of our relationship with the heavenly Father. If we will not succumb to materialism, Father transfers true riches into our lives. For all of us, that means separating from anything that will diminish the vastness of God, deplete us, and fleece us of real spiritual substance. Abraham's separation led to revelation and revelation to worship. When any of us worship the gift more than the giver, we have contradicted the purpose of the gift. Thus, the story of Abraham, the firstfruit of Kingdom wealth redistribution, continues to speak loudly today. Every time we read his story it provides us the opportunity to meditate on how the father of all faithful got this one right.

ISAAC: WEALTH THROUGH INHERITANCE AND INVESTMENT

Before Abraham died, He gave all that he possessed to Isaac his miracle son. Isaac mirrors what it means to be an heir of your father. The Bible says, *"And Abraham gave all that he had unto Isaac. But unto the sons of the concubines, which Abraham had, Abraham gave gifts, and sent them away from Isaac his son, while he yet lived, eastward, unto the east country"* (Gen. 25:5-6). This certainly presents a different picture of the transfer of wealth. Abraham had drawn from the pool of the world's wealth on two occasions besides what his servants had produced: in Egypt (Gen. 13:1-2), and in Gerar (Gen. 20:14-16). Though Abraham was rebuked sternly for lying each time, he leaves each situation wealthier than when he entered. His release of wealth out of his hands demonstrated that wealth did not possess his heart.

The method he employed provides a prototypical genre for us today: *Get rid of it all before you die! If you are interested in advancing the Kingdom, give the plentiful portions to the one who bears the blazing torch of purpose, and has the heartbeat of God.* It is never wise to cater to sloppiness, sentimentality, and favoritism in these situations. A look at modern legal testamentary instruments show, although courts are bound by the intent of a will or trust if validly executed, that public policy strongly favors fairness within distribution when possible, benefiting the family and avoiding favoritism. Much wealth has been squandered because people forgot that wealth was a divine gift from God, which should be directed by the mind of the Lord. People of God must be as resolute as philanthropist Andrew Carnegie in these matters. He said, "Why should men leave great fortunes to their children? If this is done from affection, is it not misguided and teaches that, generally speaking, it is not well for the children that they should be so burdened."[3] God's voice must be heard or the pressures to release God's wealth into the wrong hands will overtake us. Covenant sons must inherit all the heavenly Father has committed to any of us.

When Isaac receives the mantle of generational purpose, he was spared the responsibility of hammering everything out from the anvil of new beginnings. One of the most important truths of generational advancement envelops the idea of *"making your son greater than you have become."* Abraham started his Kingdom walk with a challenging word from God. It manifested as a desire to please God, though he was imperfect. He lived unprecedented passion and obedience, which led to a perfect heart. He obviously gained much and relished the empowerment of his son. His words to Isaac were probably something like my father's words to me, "It's going to be better for your generation than it was for mine." My father was not a prophet, but those words were prophetic.

Isaac observed the model of his father Abraham for nearly 75 years. What a model! Abraham set the trend for his seed to follow. Unfortunately, when things transition from one generation to another, our respectable *and* appalling habits transfer. Likely a familiar spirit may be responsible. *Familiar* carries the connotation of that which is recognizable, common, and decipherable in a family. For instance, there are families known for their humility, and others for their pride; some are known for their generosity, and others by their miserliness. If something has become a familiar, household spirit, someone in the progenitor generation has probably opened the door to it. Because of the hazards of travel in Abraham's day, when it came to self-preservation, he had a problem with dishonesty. This problem attached itself to Abraham and even became problematic in Isaac. (See Genesis 26:6-7.) I am amazed at the similarity of circumstances between Abraham and Isaac when it came to the redistribution of wealth.

Famine hit the land in Isaac's day just as it did in Abraham's day. God spoke specifically to him not to go down into Egypt like his father Abraham did. Therefore, he dwelt among the Philistines and experienced furtherance in wealth redistribution. The contrast is quite striking: Abraham reaped from an already prepared harvest in Egypt, whereas Isaac invested to harvest in Philistine territory. The Scripture says, *"Then Isaac sowed in that land, and received in the same year an hundredfold: and the Lord blessed him. And the man waxed great, and went forward, and grew until he became very great: for he had possession of flocks, and possessions of herds, and great store of servants: and the Philistines envied him."* (See Genesis 26:12-14.) This Scripture aligned with the principle of Genesis 8:22—seedtime precedes harvest. Also, if a person is to reach their greatest level of productivity, that person must listen to the voice of God, plant where He says to plant, refuse to be governed by the depressive conditions of others, and simply wait on God to give the increase. By following these simple rules of engagement, Isaac greatly strengthened his economic position— and so will we today.

Isaac experienced progressive growth, which I believe is the Kingdom pattern for God's children. Isaac became a very great man at the chagrin of the Philistines—they envied him. In this context, greatness does not happen over night. Some would call progressive growth slow, deliberate knowledge, which prepares us for the long run. Because of the click-a-button world we live in, it is hard to appreciate progressive growth. We must ask ourselves, "Have modern Kingdom people progressively grown enough to inflame the ire of today's world system?" Quite frankly, I would say, "No!" If we compare the Gross Domestic Products (GDPs) of nations, which measures the production strength of nations annually, the Church, the holy nation, is not even mentioned. Selfishness, I believe, is the foremost reason we are not fulfilling our potential. As long as we are stuck in the morass of a bless me, taker mentality, we are going to miss the mark.

To further document progressive growth is the right way, there were other great prophets who followed this pattern including: Samuel, John the Baptist, and Jesus Christ.

CONCERNING SAMUEL

And the Lord visited Hannah, so that she conceived, and bare three sons and two daughters. And the child Samuel grew before the Lord...And the child Samuel grew on, and was in favor both with the Lord, and also with men" (1 Samuel 2:21,26).

And Samuel grew, and the Lord was with him, and did let none of his words fall to the ground. And all Israel from Dan even to Beer-sheba knew that Samuel was established to be a prophet of the Lord (1 Samuel 3:19-20).

Note this principle in Samuel's life: Progressive growth released progressive authority in his words. His words eventually became the very mouth of God in the earth.

CONCERNING JOHN THE BAPTIST

And the child grew, and waxed strong in spirit, and was in the deserts till the day of his shewing unto Israel (Luke 1:80).

Note the principle in John's life: Progressive growth released him from days of obscurity to a place of favor. He became the voice of God in the inter-testament period.

CONCERNING JESUS CHRIST

And the child grew, and waxed strong in spirit, filled with wisdom: and the grace of God was upon Him ... And Jesus increased in wisdom and stature, and in favor with God and man (Luke 2:40,52).

Like his predecessors Isaac, Samuel, and John, Jesus Christ was molded in the same pattern of progressive growth. They each were powerful Kingdom transition vessels who grew; they were enlarged, or increased in the amount of the life of God garnered and expressed. Each of them advanced the Kingdom during their time on earth because they increased in wisdom and godly stature. The very nature of transition implicates growth and development. To understand how profound this idea becomes in the Kingdom, it is important to understand other synonyms of transition including: change, changeover, evolution, conversion, shift, move, switch, alteration, and modification. Each word carries the powerful idea that things are improving from a Kingdom perspective, thus advancing society toward an ideal utopia little by little. We are changing from an imperialistic, capitalistic society into a Kingdom culture. The gradual development of this culture evolves because of the genetic material of divine nature first arriving in the person of Jesus Christ, continuing in the Holy Spirit, and identifying a people in the earth to experience this great shift each in their own order.

Isaac teaches us how to behave as children of God with wealth. When the envious (Philistines) choose to violently oppose him over wells of water, he doesn't fiercely react; he relents and releases what is rightfully his out of a peaceful disposition. Contentious, spiteful, hateful, and strife-filled people cannot silence or undo a person of peace. As J. Muller says, "Peace is the masterpiece of reason."[4] Isaac's greatest wealth wasn't his money or any of the tangible assets he owned, it was the serenity of his character, the positive qualities, the fortitude of character he had developed in Abraham's household. Because he had a secure pledge from the heavenly Father about inheriting all (see Genesis 26:2-5), he didn't have to safeguard anything. The guarantee from God held in custody everything spoken until the time of fulfillment. Everything about Isaac exhibits sonship displayed. A son receives the blessing of his father, trusts implicitly in him, and lives a fulfilled life out of his father's bountiful supply.

Christ is the greater son of Abraham (Gal. 3:16). As in the natural, Isaac inherited all from his father; also spiritually, Christ inherits all from His Father. Therefore, He is the legitimate heir to everything God promised Abraham. This speaks much to us because the Bible declares that we are now Abraham's seed, and heirs of the promise. *"For ye are all the children of God by faith in Christ Jesus. For as many of you as have been baptized in Christ have put on Christ...And if ye be Christ's, then are ye Abraham's seed, and heirs according to the promise"* (Gal. 3:26-27,29). There's a wonderful Kingdom connection to this promise. Paul, on another occasion, spoke of the specificity of it: *"For the promise, that he should be the heir of the world, was not to Abraham, or to his seed, through the law, but through the righteousness of faith"* (Rom. 4:13).

The seed of Abraham receives the Kingdom mandate to inherit, steward, and manage the earth. This responsibility must be conjointly accomplished with Jesus Christ as the Head of the mission. With this assignment, we must properly administrate all the earth's resources. From this viewpoint, our perspective of redistribution is a little different. We must grasp that wealth is the least important component of joy. The real importance behind redistribution is the opportunity to change others' circumstances. It is extremely important to understand, then, fiscal responsibility as an heir. Waste is completely unacceptable. As we grow in grace and knowledge, they prepare us for living and life in a Kingdom culture exposed to wealth redistribution. What has been in the hands of Adam's mismanagement must now enter into the safe hands of the children of God.

In the next five to ten years (2010-2020), trillions of dollars will be passed to the next generation. This will be the largest transfer of wealth from parents to children, from foundations to individuals, in the history of humankind. Authority has commonly transferred from one generation to another, sometimes through violence, and other times in peace, but not this kind of wealth. The question becomes, "What will the recipients do with this accumulated wealth?" If men like Bill Gates and Warren Buffett are precursory of the future, much of it will be invested in foundations with humanitarian objectives.

The Church may be a powerful recipient and participant. There is no organism on earth with a more vested interest in humanity as the Church. Our concern not only includes spiritual responsibility, but also, a holistic responsibility for all people. Somehow, out of the integrity of our hearts, we must present ourselves as unselfish global caretakers including every ethnicity, creed, and shade of humanity. When people generously and thoughtfully transfer wealth, we should be the first in line with noteworthy Kingdom causes and strategies of why we are the most worthy to receive a share of the wealth redistribution. I'm finding more and more that people of the previous generation, people of my natural father's generation, think more in terms of placing hard-earned money into institutions, rather than into irresponsible children's hands.

JACOB: SERVANTHOOD AND RETROACTIVE WEALTH

And Jacob vowed a vow, saying, if God will be with me, and will keep me in this way that I go, and will give me bread to eat, and raiment to put on, so that I come again to my father's house in peace; then shall the Lord be my God: and this stone, which I have set for a pillar, shall be God's house: and of all that thou shalt give me I will surely give the tenth unto thee" (Genesis 28:20-22).

Jacob, because of the blessing of Abraham, is the third link in the legal Messianic line. He bears the torch of generational purpose as he leaves the Promised Land. He had no idea he was leaving for 20 years. (See Genesis 28.) His purpose was twofold: (1) To take a wife from among the daughters of his uncle Laban, the Syrian; and (2) to avoid the revenge of Esau, his brother, for the blessing Isaac blessed Jacob with. (See Genesis 27:41-44.)

As Jacob is leaving, he dreams a dream which connects him with his purpose. It is a constant reminder of who he is—the guardian of his identity. The heavenly Father gives him five specific promises, indicating this is a God-centered, sovereign, grace-filled dream. The promises are: (1) to give Jacob the land on which he was sleeping, (2) to be present with him, (3) to keep Jacob in all the places he would go, (4) to bring Jacob back again, and (5) to never leave Jacob. Each of these ideals represents a tangible aspect of the grace of God. Five is the number of grace and the free gifts connected with grace.

The first promise the Father gave Jacob goes to the heart of God placing humankind on the earth. It intrinsically ties into the dominion mandate and the responsibility adjoined to it. The second promise deals with the nearness of God and His desire for habitation and not just visitation. Grace allows God the right of continuance in the human experience by means of the incarnation principle. God continues to live in and through us. The third promise deals with God's ability to preserve and to protect His personal investment in a person's life, regardless of time and experience. Grace reckons God to be the personal Gatekeeper of His people, which suggests divine security. The fourth promise reveals how the heavenly Father redeems what appear to be dead-end streets. It employs the law of circularity. And, finally, the fifth promise provides a firm foundation for all the other promises, which are built on the integrity of God. Grace allows all of us to enter into the rest of God without the anxiety of and frustration about the future.

I am reminded at this point of the many parables, or narratives, Jesus told in order to communicate the infinite, flawlessness of grace. God teaches Jacob something about grace in his dream. Grace enables people to remove themselves from the world of retaliation and enter into God's world of immeasurable forgiveness. In the forum of grace, it seems that God, at times, rewards irresponsible behavior. He gives grossly, unfair wages to those who have not suffered the brunt of the labor. There's a yearning

Father who can't get beyond his penchant for unconditional love. To prove this, He leaves the confines of eternity and enters into the nightmare of the deformed human system, which by the time Jesus appears opposes divine interruptions. Grace reached earth's maladjusted and malevolent.

For example, Jesus ministered to the tax collectors, reprobates, the lepers, and the whores. Jesus said, *"... They that are whole need not a physician; but they that are sick. I came not to call the righteous, but sinners to repentance"* (Luke 5:31-32). Grace operates so powerfully in the life of Jesus, even during His darkest hours on earth, that He counters magnificently out of a grace-full disposition.

Jacob is on his way with some impressive promises as a result of an unplanned encounter with God. During the course of his sojourn, he comes upon Uncle Laban's family in Haran. He is welcomed by Laban, and they eventually enter into a labor contract. Jacob's eyes light upon Rachel and in his heart he assertively pursues her. The Bible says, *"And Jacob loved Rachel: and said, I will serve thee seven years for Rachel thy younger daughter. And Laban said, It is better that I give her to thee, than that I should give her to another man: abide with me"* (Gen. 29:18-19). This is where the story really gets interesting! Jacob isn't aware that Laban has more schemes. Jacob's love prevents his labor from becoming painstaking. He demonstrates that when purpose is attached to labor it can be achieved quickly and joyfully.

On the day of his wedding, Laban beguiled Jacob. He brings Leah, the firstborn, to him, rather than Rachel. It was customary to give the older daughter in marriage first. The lesson learned: familiarize yourself with a different culture, especially if you desire to avidly participate in that culture. Jacob worked seven years before he received Leah, representing the Law economy in which you are recompensed after your labors. However, a deal was struck in which he would receive Rachel also, and work another seven years. This is a priceless representation of grace. You receive a gift, and then, responsibility comes because of the gift.

As Jacob keeps the flocks of Laban, God blessed Laban because of the presence of Jacob. The time came when he finally heard the Lord say, *"Return unto the land of thy fathers, and to thy kindred; and I will be with thee"* (Gen. 31:3). Because of Jacob's initiative, inventiveness, and ingenuity, he had become quite wealthy. The portion of the flocks that were his hire far surpassed Laban's share. He said to his wives, Rachel and Leah, *"And ye know that with all my power I have served your father. And your father hath deceived me, and changed my wages ten times; but God suffered him not to hurt me. If he said thus, the speckled shall be thy wages; then all the cattle bare speckled: and if he said thus, the ringstraked shall be thy hire; then bare all the cattle ringstraked. Thus God hath taken away the cattle of your father, and given them to me"* (Gen. 31:6-9).

This circumstance in Genesis represents an interesting example of wealth redistribution connected to industry and the work ethic. A commitment to servanthood allowed God to decide the wages, which eventually brought great reward.

Jacob returns to the Promised Land after 20 years. (See Genesis 31:38,41.) He was an influential, prominent man by this time. The Bible says, *"And the man increased exceedingly, and had much cattle and maidservants, and manservants, and camels, and asses"* (Gen. 30:43). Containment was no longer part of Jacob's life; he had broken forth in the widest application. The standards by which wealth was measured are Jacob's realities. It is important to understand he didn't get to this position in his life alone. If he refused to find out why this transfer had taken place, it would become a disservice to the purpose of God in his life.

The same is true for us. A season of great wealth release is coming to the Body of Christ. Many Christians are going to be ill-prepared for this transfer because of selfishness and consumerism. We still behave more like slaves to materialism than the Lord's freed people. We must begin to pray in advance that God will give us wisdom and prudence in these matters. If we ask, the heavenly Father will give us wisdom liberally. Once again, if we have been given the mandate to manage the earth, it is important that we do it from a position of positive power. When given the trust to manage earth's resources, that, indeed, is a position of power. Jacob was returning to the land empowered by the grace of God. Though he wasn't perfect in his faith, he was now mature enough to handle some of God's resources responsibly.

SOLOMON: WISDOM AND WEALTH

Solomon's reign was a prophetic synopsis of the new millennium and the postmodern world. His name means "peaceful," which is the nature God predetermined for these times—perfect peace and harmony experienced by all of God's creation. Terms like safety, well being, happy, friendly, welfare, health, and prosperity are within the formation of this peace. If one would consider the word *peace* as a shell or covering, its inner spirit contains each of these ideals. However, it appears the new millennium has begun contrary to this thought. Nations continue to rise up against nations. Warfare driven by lust is everywhere. Someone must announce the hour for ruthless conquerors has vanished. The Church is the messenger of glad tidings of peace, but our voices are drowned by the guttersnipe, vulgar sounds of the old Adamic order. We must come to grips with what is at stake! When there's peace with God, peace with one another, and peace with creation, we'll execute the dominion mandate as it was intended from the beginning.

It's important to understand the turmoil connected with David's transition prior to Solomon being enthroned. First Kings chapter 1 is replete with revelation and saturated with information we can draw from to understand those times. Our adversary, the devil, attempts to avert the purposes of God with several rapid moves. David represents an anointed, dying order that the systems of men erroneously attempt to keep alive. (See 1 Kings 1:1-3.) Adonijah, David's son, reminds us of a counterfeit order emerging like an Ishmael, and exalting himself before the true anointing appears. (See 1 Kings 1:5-6.) Joab is the politically-motivated one who flows with whatever appears to be on the cutting edge of God's ways. (See 1 Kings 1:7.) Abiathar is a carnal, priestly order finally removed, not only in precept (see 1 Sam. 2:27-36), but also in practice. (See 1 Kings 1:7; 2:27.) The heavenly Father took away the first priesthood in order to establish a more perfect order.

Zadok, Benaiah, Nathan, Shimei, and Rei model a five-fold ministry that resists the lust for power and waits for the appointment of the Lord. (See 1 Kings 1:8.) These mighty men are overcomers, and an administration exemplary, waiting the revealing of the new king and his kingdom. Bathsheba represents the church with an oath from the king concerning the manchild from her womb destined for the throne. (See 1 Kings 1:28-31; Revelation 12.) Solomon is the manchild who comes to the throne and rules the nation with great wisdom and authority. (See 1 Kings 1:33-40.)

And he stood before the altar of the Lord in the presence of all the congregation of Israel, and spread forth his hands: for Solomon had made a brazen scaffold (laver), of five cubits

long, and five cubits broad, and three cubits high, and had
set it in the midst of the court: and upon it he stood, and
kneeled down upon his knees before all the congregation of
Israel, and spread forth his hands toward heaven (2 Chronicles 6:12-13).

The foundational key to Solomon's initial success was his humble dedication. Solomon identified with the finished work of Calvary by becoming the embodiment of a living sacrifice on the altar of dedication and arising in newness of life. The measurements of Solomon's scaffold were equivalent to those of the brazen altar in the Tabernacle of Moses. (See Exodus 38:1-7.) Interestingly, the altar and the laver became one in this event, for the word *scaffold* means "laver or hearth." The scaffold is metaphorically a fire/water pot. What a moment of sanctification in Solomon's life! He began his reign on the note of an official committal to the holiness of God. Also, he was rejecting the vanity and activity of the flesh as a governing principle of life. The heavenly Father welcomed his dedication and spoke of Solomon's impending greatness in the Kingdom.

UNINTERRUPTED PEACE

And Solomon sent to Hiram, saying, thou knowest how that
David my father could not build an house unto the name of
the Lord his God for the wars which were about him on every
side, until the Lord put them under the soles of his feet. But
now the Lord my God hath given me rest on every side, so
that there is neither adversary nor evil occurrent (1 Kings
5:2-4).

If Solomon was a tree, his early reign would be identified by a triad of branches, which are traits of the Kingdom's administration: (1) uninterrupted peace, (2) unparalleled wisdom, and (3) unprecedented prosperity. Peace existed because David, Solomon's father, like Jesus Christ defeated every enemy before placing the Kingdom into Solomon's jurisdiction. Peace is freedom from disturbed states of mind, being, and body; it is the absence of mental conflict; the harmony, balance, and serenity that the Holy Spirit produces in a divine invasion.

From a biblical basis, peace is a person (Jesus Christ), and could be symbolized by the rule of Mt. Zion. The prophets Isaiah and Micah declared the rule of Zion will become such an economy of peace that men will be compelled to turn their weapons and technologies of mass destruction into instruments of improvement for all nations. We have yet to see this happen.

Tranquility defines the Kingdom when Solomon inherited it. The word *adversary* is "satan, the attacker, or accuser;" and *evil occurrent* means "impact or impingement by accident or violence." Imagine a society with no devil and no violence! It is one of the most remarkable features of the Messianic Kingdom in its glory. To write a thesis on the concept of millennium, there must be a conceived period of no attacks, no accusations, and no violence in human social intercourse; and in addition, no more sparring with any kind of devil. What a *profound* idea to know that the God of peace has dealt with all our enemies in the person of Jesus Christ. David could have spoken the same sentiments to Solomon as Jesus spoke to the disciples: *"Peace I leave with you, my peace I give unto you: not as the world giveth, give I unto you. Let not your heart be troubled, neither let it be afraid"* (John 14:27).

You may think I'm extraneous, a bit bizarre, and mistaken by saying

God has no enemies. Most people would say, "Maybe God doesn't have enemies, but I certainly do!" And there are Scriptures referring to our enemies. But I choose to respond with, *"Greater is he that is in you than he that is outside of you."* (See 1 John 4:4.) Christ, the peace of God, lives in every believer. There may be those who are doggedly determined to bring about your demise; however, a choice must be made. Do we, within ourselves, identify them as enemies or friends, reacting out of the Christ nature or out of our memory of Adam's knobby nature? I'm amazed that the Master treated those who were convinced he should be vilified as friends. He even spoke peace (shalom) to the raging sea, which is the greeting you give a friend.

The issue remains: How do we interpret things inside ourselves? The balance of things outside of us is never bigger than the definition we give it inside. The only times we see Jesus choosing to exercise righteous indignation and confrontation were with religious spirits in people. We must properly identify the real enemies in every case; and it's not human flesh.

> *For though we walk in the flesh, we do not war after the flesh: (for the weapons of our warfare are not carnal, but mighty through God to the pulling down of strongholds;) casting down imaginations, and every high thing that exalt itself against the knowledge of God, and bringing into captivity every thought to the obedience of Christ; and having a readiness to revenge all disobedience when your obedience is fulfilled* (2 Corinthians 10:3-6).

Surprisingly, this text doesn't speak of the everyday, run-of-the-mill battles of most Christians. This passage refers to apostolic warfare and subsequent battle strategies. The enemy most Christians face is erroneous ideas; the flawed judgments people hold about the finished work of Calvary. Any idea that opposes the full knowledge of God, which is Christ, must be ruthlessly with lion-like aggression destroyed through our obedience of completely conforming to God's conclusion. We only qualify to revenge disobedience through the model of obedience we become. Any other form of revenge or retaliation constitutes the wrath of man, which works not the righteousness of God. When Jesus could have reacted from the son of Adam side and retaliated against His murderers, He chose to behave like a son of God and forgave them all.

The church of postmodernism, which rejects much of what the modern church has become, must comprehend and apprehend the perfect and complete victory of the *finished work* of Calvary. If we compared ourselves to the powerful witness of the church of the first century, we would appear dreadfully anemic. Jesus, our heavenly David, defeated, dispossessed, and disposed of every spiritual giant just as David defeated the giants of the old covenant. He defeated them and crowned and clothed them with disgrace and shame to be worn for the rest of eternity.

Just as Joshua had his captains place their feet on the necks of five kings in his day (see Joshua 10:22-27), Jesus placed His feet on the necks of these five "kings," and hung them in Himself when He sacrificed His life:

1. Jesus defeated the triumvirate of *death, hell, and the grave.* They had been the ruling three in the public administration of Adam's deformed order. (See Philippians 2:5-11; 2 Timothy 1:8-9; 1 Corinthians 15:25-27.)

2. Jesus defeated the *devil,* destroyed the *works* of the devil, and delivered those overpowered by him. (See Hebrews

2:13-14.) The devil manifested on the cross as one of the malefactors. (See Luke 23:39.) He moved in his usual expression—a malicious spirit of accusation.

3. Jesus, as the last Adam, defeated *the former essence of the old Adam—the sin nature.* He was God's quintessential victory statement over all who preceded Him. The first Adam also manifested on the cross and begged to be remembered, and He was! (See Luke 23:40-43.)

4. Jesus defeated the *world system* that was in Adam's flesh by walking above it and maintaining fellowship with his God and Father. (See Romans 6:10, 12-14; 1 John 2:15-17.)

5. Jesus defeated every expression of the *spirit of poverty*—impoverished health, finances, relationships, etc.... There's no area of poverty left untouched or unexposed in the presence of Jesus Christ. He was complete victory over all Adam's madness. (See 3 John 2; 2 Corinthians 8:9; Deuteronomy 8:18-20.)

UNPARALLELED WISDOM

Wisdom does not show itself so much in precept as in life—in firmness of mind and mastery of appetite. It teaches us to do as well as talk, and to make our words and actions all of color.

—SENECA[3]

And Solomon said unto God, Thou hast shewed great mercy to David my father, and hast made me to reign in his stead. Now, O Lord God, let thy promise unto David my father be established: for Thou hast made me king over a people like the dust of the earth in multitude. Give me now wisdom and knowledge, that I may go out and come in before this people: for who can judge this Thy people, that is so great? (2 Chronicles 1:8-10).

Historically, Solomon was first and foremost known for his wisdom, and then for his administrative skills and order. He was a wonderful prophetic type of the Lord Jesus Christ who was the coming of wisdom—the Just One, the Man of Justice. The Bible says about Solomon:

And he spake three thousand proverbs: and his songs were a thousand and five. And he spake of trees, from the cedar tree that is in Lebanon even unto the hyssop that springeth out of the wall: he spake also of beasts, and of fowl, and of creeping things, and of fishes. And there came of all people to hear the wisdom of Solomon, from all kings of the earth, which had heard of his wisdom (1 Kings 4:32-34).

Solomon had expertise in many valuable subject areas. It revealed his dominion in the avian kingdom, the plant kingdom, the animal kingdom, and the sea kingdom. Father God initially gave Adam dominion in each of these realms. (See Genesis 1:26-28.) Solomon brought together spirituality and science. I believe postmodern believers must do the same. Even the great commission demands this demonstration. In it, we are given dominion over the spiritual world, the language world, the animal world, the chemical world, and the world of disease. (See Mark 16:15-18.) When we look at the facts that the seas are being over-fished and polluted, species of animals and birds are disappearing, arsonists are destroying forests, and there are ecological disasters in the tropical rain forests, we realize that there is a great need for a corporate church of wisdom to rise up again.

Wisdom is the God-given ability to perceive the true nature of any matter and implement the will of God as the final solution. It is particularly important in the execution of justice, fairness, and impartiality—that which is necessary to build a commonwealth. If there is any weight the whole of humanity suffers under, it is the weight of partiality in one form or another. In our postmodern world, when just people are empowered, their wisdom will help terminate the reign of partiality which breeds violence. Remember, violence doesn't subjugate itself to one people group or a particular nation; it is everywhere. However, violence committed by the poor and disenfranchised is a cry for justice. Please understand I am not indicting all poor people as criminal elements. I truly understand what it means to be economically poor without being a criminal. However, in order to gain attention, some poor people will commit vile, vitriolic acts until they become secondary by nature. Then, a counterproductive culture is produced, called prison life that is atypical to everything the Kingdom of God is about.

Nothing has relevance until we see it in Christ, magnifying the Christ-centered principle that all Bible hermeneutics should be governed by. Will we choose to see everything from an in-Christ perspective? Christ was made unto us wisdom. (See 1 Corinthians 1:30.) From a Tabernacle of Moses glance, one of the four pillars before the Holy of Holies could be called wisdom. We need wisdom to live accurately out of the Holy of Holies. Christ imparted Himself into the church by His Spirit. Therefore, we have received the *spirit of wisdom* of which a word of wisdom may flow out of at any time. This wisdom is also obtained and released through the jurisdiction of the fear of the Lord. (See Psalm 111:10.)

When Paul prayed the great apostolic prayer for the church at Ephesus, he placed the Spirit of wisdom before the Spirit of revelation. (See Ephesians 1:16-22.) This unfolds the truth that wisdom really is the principle goal. However, if we see accurately within the season of God, wisdom enables us to interpret correctly what we are seeing. Also, wisdom coupled with revelation has the ability to blind us to what we once beheld. After the scales of our former sight falls away, we see God in a purity we've never seen before. There's something about a handicapping condition that opens us to God like nothing else can. In fact, we're conditioned to see with a pure heart after such an encounter.

The great value of wisdom delivers us from the evil man, or the man of sin (see Prov. 2:12), which is also called the beast nature in the New Testament. Additionally, we are delivered from the immoral woman, or harlot system. (See Proverbs 2:16.) The harlot system released out of the first Adam became a seductress and evolved into Babylon the great. Mr. Adam and Mrs. Adam became the metaphors of what Solomon saw— they fit these descriptions perfectly. Through powerful seduction, humankind was lured from the elegance and excellence of a preeminent position of security in the heavenly Father. Wisdom's security has the empowering effect to affirm us and preserve us. The basic security connection with our heavenly Father is made and we become settled and satisfied in His words. Wisdom tells us the Father's words are sufficient and satisfactory.

UNPRECEDENTED WEALTH OR PROSPERITY

And God said to Solomon, because this was in thine heart, and thou hast not asked riches, wealth, or honour, nor the life of thine enemies, neither yet hast asked long life; but hast asked wisdom and knowledge for thyself, that thou mayest judge my people, over whom I have made thee king: wisdom and knowledge is granted unto thee; and I will give thee riches, and wealth, and honour, such as none of the kings have had that have been before thee, neither shall there any after thee have the like (2 Chronicles 1:11-12).

The heavenly Father established a proper paradigm in response to Solomon's prayer: first wisdom, and then, riches and wealth. The presence of wisdom invites unbelievable abundance. It becomes dangerous for people to have prosperity without wisdom. Most of the modern examples of lottery winners attest to that fact. Wealth releases internally first (see 3 John 2). Poverty is just the opposite: it is the result of an external thief coming upon you. (See Proverbs 6:11.) *Wealth* or *prosperity* means "to flourish, to succeed, to thrive, and to grow in a vigorous way." In the Kingdom, prosperity directly relates to humility, which agrees with and obeys the Word of God. (See Joshua 1:8.)

As exampled in Joseph and other great leaders, the Lord will humble us before He raises us. Prosperity is an attitude of excellence manifesting as the released hand of God in blessing. Globally, there is to be such a distribution of wealth that he who gathers much or little will lack no thing. Because Solomon asked for the principle thing, wisdom, God promised him riches, wealth, and honor like no other king would experience.

Solomon's wealth subsisted in the core of his wisdom or information systems. The queen of Sheba and others from the East experienced the proliferation of his wisdom. I believe this to be comparable to our times. In the past century, the major source of wealth was measured in land, labor, and capital. Things are changing! The most important capital now is our creativity, our spiritual capital, and our cognitive genius. As most churches and businesses in the postmodern world are learning, skillful trainers of people are expensive. However, it is horrendous and cata-strophic to leave people untrained in a global market. Corporations will pay thousands of dollars to those who can impart the proper wisdom and information to their employees.

The principle of first the natural, and then, the spiritual may apply here: If knowledge is a prime resource of the emerging economies of the 21st century, it will be more so in *spiritual* economies. The Feast of Pente-cost produced highly spiritual people with spirituality exceeding knowl-edge in many cases. The Feast of Tabernacles must produce a balanced, ambidextrous body—those who are spiritual and knowledgeable at the same time.

> And when the queen of Sheba heard of the fame of Solomon concerning the name of the Lord, she came to prove him with hard questions. And she came to Jerusalem with a very great train, with camels that bare spices, and very much gold, and precious stones: and when she was come to Solomon, she communed with him of all that was in her heart. And Solomon told her all her questions: there was not any thing hid from the king, which he told her not (1 Kings 10:1-3).

Word of Solomon's fame traveled abroad rather quickly. The multimedia of his day was word-of-mouth, from town to town, hamlet to hamlet. He had proven wisdom, which generated an unprecedented model of Kingdom understanding and prudence. Very simply, wealth redistribution came to him because of what he knew and could discern. Today, if people aren't formally trained in the schools of medicine, jurisprudence, finance, or psychological expertise, people probably won't pay to dialogue with them. In Solomon's case, he was reimbursed handsomely for his counsel.

The industrial world, the descendant of the Industrial Revolution, measured a man or corporation's value by tangible assets, such as cash, land acquisitions, buildings, machinery, exports, and accounts receivable, not necessarily knowledge. Today, as in Solomon's day, value is measured in many intangibles including: spiritual, academic, and interpersonal competence; business savvy and innovative ideas; and longevity of relationships.

I have many friends whom the Holy Spirit has developed with such credentials. Like John the Baptist, they have been developed in the desert of obscurity waiting for their time of showing. If I were to call their names, they would no longer be obscure. There's a common denominator in each of these men and women: they are not greedy, selfishly motivated, or building kingdoms for themselves. Their desire to see the Kingdom come and God's will be done on earth is pristine. They are primed for spiritual promotion and rapid wealth redistribution.

First Kings chapter 10 proves Solomon acquired great possessions without conniving or hoodwinking anyone; the God of glory blessed him because he was David's son. Initially, the blessing comes because of the continuation of covenant. Every promise God made to David rested in

Solomon. Nations kept bringing him stuff! (See 1 Kings 10:10-22.) We are blessed because of Jesus Christ; and nations will bring us stuff as well.

I foresee the postmodern industrialized world coming to the church for solutions and answers. They will bring their wealth if the right information is in the church's database. The apostle Paul eloquently stated God's divine intention for the church: *"to the intent that now unto the principalities and powers in heavenly places might be known by the church the manifold wisdom of God, according to the eternal purpose which He purposed in Christ Jesus our Lord"* (Eph. 3:10-11). Destiny has predetermined that the powers that be will behold God through the church. She may appear a bit crusty right now, however, all of Jesus' predictions about her aren't fully processed yet. But, just wait! When she develops according to divine determination, she'll be the present wonder of the world.

> *So king Solomon exceeded all the kings of the earth for riches and for wisdom. And all the earth sought to Solomon, to hear his wisdom, which God had put in his heart. And they brought every man his present, vessels of silver, and vessels of gold, and garments, and armour, and spices, horses, and mules, a rate year by year* (1 Kings 10:23-25).

THE NATION OF ISRAEL: WEALTH TRANSFER ON A CORPORATE LEVEL

> *And the Lord said unto Moses, yet will I bring one plague more upon Pharaoh, and upon Egypt; afterwards he will let you go hence: when he shall let you go, he shall surely thrust you out hence altogether. Speak now in the ears of the people,*

and let every man borrow of his neighbor, and every woman
of her neighbor, jewels of silver, and jewels of gold. And the
Lord gave the people favor in the sight of the Egyptians.
Moreover the man Moses was very great in the land of Egypt,
in the sight of Pharaoh's servants, and in the sight of the peo-
ple (Exodus 11:1-3).

Thus far we have spoken about wealth distribution and redistribution on an individual level—from countries to prophets and kings, or from fathers to children. To expand our picture, it is necessary to shift gears. In the Scripture passage from Exodus, the nation of Israel, as the natural seed of Abraham, holds the promise of wealth distribution in opposition to their current status. God's sovereignty, through the instrumentality of Jacob, led them into Egypt. (See Genesis 46:5-7.) During the event of covenant-cutting, the Lord God spoke to Abraham:

And he said unto Abram, know of a surety that thy seed
shall be a stranger in a land that is not theirs and shall
serve them; and they shall afflict them four hundred years;
and also that nation, whom they shall serve, will I judge:
and afterward shall they come out with great substance
(Genesis 15:13-14).

A course has been established by the heavenly Father's far-sighted prerogative. Abraham's future seed would know the pain of disenfranchisement, the sting of tyranny before coming into a place of great wealth and acceptance. This time would continue for more than four centuries. God's plan would reverse their impoverished, refugee condition. Though afflicted as menial servants, sons of the soil for years, they would exit with a new identity, as kings and priests—a holy nation.

Israel had no idea of the God-centered purpose behind wealth redistribution. They received four centuries of back wages with interest and penalties to help build God a sanctuary in their midst. Automatically, the wealth is elevated from a selfish, I-deserve-this commodity to a greater distribution principle. God ultimately required the newly freed Israelites to discharge the money out of their hands into His, trading an inferior purpose for a superior one.

When we constructed our ministry buildings in Jacksonville, North Carolina, we experienced something similar. Most of us had been freed from the clutches of sin and spiritual slavery, thus our funds were channeled to build God a house. Because we all participated from the highroad of willingness, we accomplished wonderful things in a relatively short season. God blessed us to build the necessary edifices to conduct Kingdom business in our community. Israel brought the Tabernacle to full construction in nine months because of willful obedience to the Word of the Lord.

God's longstanding plan has always nurtured the idea that a corporate people would be conformed to the image of Jesus Christ. That people would be healed of any hemorrhaging identity issues acquainted with the grief of slavery, the angst of displacement. In the prolific words of the apostle Paul, they would move from uncertainty to a guaranteed surety: *"Having predestinated us unto the adoption of children by Jesus Christ to Himself, according to the good pleasure of His will, to the praise of the glory of His grace, wherein He hath made us accepted in the beloved"* (Eph. 1:5-6). Without contradiction, these verses establish us in an incredible identity and finality. Just like natural Israel, we are God's children because it pleases

Him. He loves us, just because! We are no longer alienated, godless Gentiles running amuck without Christ. Praise God! We are members of the commonwealth of Israel with covenantal promises, with hope, and with a loving heavenly Father.

Our participation in the commonwealth positions us for wealth redistribution. It will be impossible for God's settled conclusion in this area to malfunction. Also, God's purpose has little to do with hit-or-miss, dependent on what we do or don't do; but it is a sure thing flowing steadily from His initiative. And God's initiative may be summed up in one word: *grace*!

> *And the children of Israel did according to the word of Moses; and they borrowed of the Egyptians jewels of silver, and jewels of gold, and raiment: and the Lord gave the people favour in the sight of the Egyptians, so that they lent unto them such things as they required. And they spoiled the Egyptians* (Exodus 12:35-36).

The Egyptians readily gave the Israelites their wealth. What a marvelous conclusion to years of aches and pain. Israel's obedience to the word of the Lord loosed the favor of God personified in the Egyptians. When the cups of the modern and postmodern Amorites are full, the Church of Jesus Christ will undergo the same caliber of massive wealth shifts. Trillions of dollars will be spoiled out of the hands of ambitious, covetous, power-hungry people. They may gather it from all of their schemes, but the righteous will use it to build the Kingdom.

Our responsibility, right now, is to humble ourselves before the mighty hand of God and prepare to present Him in a different form. We must allow Him to shape us and squeeze every bit of the desire for wealth out of us. The demise of our flesh and newfound freedom, will benefit the nations greatly. Our deliverance will prevent us from repeating history, which is an unprejudiced reporter of human events and facts. The aggressive *taking* disposition of Adam's bankrupt world of greed will be entombed forever by a generous, big-hearted people.

The Church, through the power of wealth redistribution, will aid the poor of this world with expanding opportunities. She is the only organism qualified by the wisdom of God to do so, transcending many generations. It will mirror free markets to the degree that all people will have goods and services multiplied effectively because of multiple gifts and talents in the human race. There will be risks-takers constantly expanding our horizons, creating new enterprises and investing the gains from them for the common good of all. The competitive edge to outclass one's neighbor will no longer be a motivating force.

Humankind will think in terms of how can I more perfectly serve and bless my brother and sister? Our standard motivation will be the righteousness, harmony, and justice the Kingdom of God has produced within us. With that comes a social justice and social responsibility which conforms to the idea of the importance of all people. Contrary to what we see now, the culture of the Kingdom of God will change the earth.

ENDNOTES

1. http://www.usatoday.com/money/2004-09-23-forbes-400-richest -list_x.htm, accessed 2/1/08.

2. http:www.nativevillage.org/Messages from the People/21st poverty_facts, adapted from: http://www.globalissues.org/TradeRelated/ Facts.asp, accessed 2/15/08.

3. Virginia Ely, *I Quote*, (New York: George W. Stewart Publishers, Inc., 1947), 358.

4. R. Daniel Watkins, *An Encyclopedia of Compelling Quotations*, (Peabody, MA: Hendrickson Publishers, Inc., 2001), 556.

5. Virginia Ely, 360.

Chapter 3

A New Leadership Model

*When the country is in chaos, everybody has a plan to fix it -
but it takes a leader of real understanding to straighten things
out* (Proverbs 28:2 TM).

The final test of a leader is that he leaves behind him in other
men the conviction and the will to carry on.

—Walter Lippmann,
column in tribute to
Franklin D. Roosevelt,
April 14, 1945[1]

When the nation of Israel crossed the Jordan River, and entered the
Promised Land, they transitioned with a new leadership model and a fan-
tastic promise: *"For ye shall pass over Jordan to go in to possess the land
which the Lord your God giveth you, and ye shall possess it, and dwell
therein"* (Deut. 11:31). Moses, Mr. Everything, was dead. (See Joshua 1:1.)
He had to die in order for Israel to understand that the system that he represented could never bring them into their inheritance. God's inheritance
was a gift to them, and could never be merited based upon the works of

the flesh, or performance-based religion. It was a promise that came to them strictly by grace. The Message Bible says,

> *God said to Joshua, Today I have rolled away the reproach of Egypt. That's why the place is called The Gilgal. It's still that. The People of Israel continued to camp at The Gilgal. They celebrated the Passover on the evening of the fourteenth day of the month on the plains of Jericho. Right away, the day after the Passover, they started eating the produce of that country, unraised bread and roasted grain. And then no more manna; the manna stopped. As soon as they started eating food grown in the land, there was no more manna for the people of Israel. That year they ate from the crops of Canaan* (Joshua 5:9-12).

Several details are important to understand about Israel's transition. Gilgal was Israel's first campsite after crossing the Jordan River and main headquarters during the early campaigns of conquest. God abolished in the minds of the Israelites the reproach of all idolatrous Egyptian worship and lusting for Egyptian products remaining in their hearts. The new generation had to submit to circumcision. They were formally reinstated into covenantal relationship with the Lord. God annihilates Egypt's wicked and intimidating memory.

I find it startling that it took Israel 40 years to shed this humiliation after observing such mighty exploits by a sovereign God. Pharaoh nor his hosts could stalk and overtake them anymore. Gilgal was to be an audiovisual of this fact; they heard the voice of God and they witnessed the fact of their final deliverance from their past by entering the land at this spot.

God could have chosen other places but it wouldn't have the same impact on their collective consciousness.

The Church in the Kingdom compares to Israel in the Promised Land. We came into the Kingdom at the point of the Cross. Our Gilgal, in which our sinful reproach was rolled away. The apostle Paul said, *"Giving thanks unto the Father, which hath made us meet to be partakers of the inheritance of the saints in light: who hath delivered us from the power of darkness, and hath translated us into the kingdom of His dear Son"* (Col. 1:12-13). Contextually, we're speaking about an event that occurred almost 2,000 years ago and made possible by the blood of Jesus Christ. Our light, or revelation, will determine how clearly we see this truth. Revelation knowledge determines whether this truth is *right now* for a person or *later*. In the Kingdom, the influences of darkness have lost their mobilizing power to produce fear and ignorance.

I'm still perplexed that we bear any of the reproach, the harassment of the old man, the old world, and the old system, especially when we consider how remarkable a deliverance we had in Christ. We've had small victories in every dimension since that time, but nothing in comparison to what should have had. As stated earlier, Jesus defeated every foe, triumphing victoriously over each of them. Yet poverty and death reign on all continents as though undefeated. It's time that these twin reproaches are eradicated off the face of the earth by Jesus' brethren. Church, the time is now!

PASSOVER FREEDOM

Israel celebrated the Passover when they began as a free nation and so do we celebrate our freedom in Christ our Passover. (See 1 Corinthians

5:7.) Passover means that a death has been exacted to meet the legal demands of a righteous God. Wherever the presence of the death victim is, the destroyer must pass over. Israel passed over for the purpose of conquering and dispossessing enemies. We have passed over because Jesus has conquered and dispossessed all enemies through His death, burial, resurrection, and ascension in our stead.

Immediately, something tremendous happened to Israel: the transitional food which sustained them for 40 years immediately halted in the Promised Land. In the modern and postmodern world, after eating the truth of the Kingdom of God, nothing from the previous orders will satisfy. The culture and maturity of the Kingdom will not bear us behaving as young children and adolescents. We must grow up! The heavenly Father provides us initially with crops we didn't plant. That's grace. He is so excited about bringing us into a place of productivity that He will allow the soon-to-be vanquished occupants of the land to make preparation for our arrival. And He will guarantee no crop failure in the year that the cup of their iniquity is full.

I can identify with the heavenly Father changing our portions. New seasons demand different handfuls on purpose. I was a strict, fundamental-believing person, cutting my teeth on pre-millennial doctrines and hermeneutics. However, the wisdom and grace of God brought me into an experience I was taught no longer existed: the baptism of the Holy Spirit with the evidence of speaking in tongues. Naturally, I was amazed! And what I soon realized was extremely important—I could no longer be satisfied in my previous experiences in God, and the diet consistent with that season of my life.

A great shift happened, moving several of us from a fundamental culture into a Pentecostal culture. Most things about the Pentecostal culture were very different, even shocking. How we approached our relationship with the Lord changed the most. We were partaking of new food which compelled us to encounter God more accurately. I have since found that every transition has produced a difference in the spiritual rations prepared by the Father for us. Be careful how you pray for change. God, in His divine wisdom, will change everything, maybe not all at once, but He will change things.

Joshua's Leadership

Leaders are chosen on the basis of purpose. Every God-ordained purpose has numerous seasons, signifying, incidentally, that there will be many leaders. A certain leader may be effective in one season and totally neutralized in another. So it was with Joshua, the second generation leader of the children of Israel. It is crucial to understand why he was chosen instead of one of Moses' sons. So often modern leaders treat God's business as though it is their own private family business and fail to replace themselves with true spiritual sons. Not so in the case of Moses. Joshua was thoroughly prepared by Moses for conquest, with skills tailored for the times. The peculiarity in the familial anointing (the tribe of Ephraim) of Joshua was more important than we realize. The things of purpose in one's background really matter. Along with the mentorship of Moses, he was prepared to lead the children of Israel into the land as God's captain and executive administrator.

Moses and Joshua had different leadership styles. Moses is a strong, iconic-like figure seen alone in context to leadership; whereas Joshua begins with a team of leaders, and he is clearly seen most of the time within the context of a team structure. Moses' family tree was Levi; Joshua was from the tribe of Ephraim. *Levi* means "joined;" *Ephraim* means "doubly fruitful." Moses bore the same name throughout his lifetime; Joshua's name changed to more perfectly identify with his unique calling. (See Numbers 13:8,16.) Moses received one-on-one fathering from God Almighty; Joshua received fathering and mentoring from Moses, and then God.

In the initial stages of Israel's deliverance, Father God had to have someone so joined to Him in order to accomplish what needed to be done. That person would be in constant communion with the Lord. Because of the rigors of the assignment, and the battering of constant questionings and criticisms, the leader had to stay close to God to remain relevant. Thus, Moses knew God in the most exceptional way.

> And God said, *"Hear now My words: If there be a prophet among you, I the Lord will make Myself known unto him in a vision, and will speak unto him in a dream. My servant Moses is not so, who is faithful in all Mine house. With him will I speak mouth to mouth, even apparently, and not in dark speeches; and the similitude of the Lord shall he behold: wherefore then were ye not afraid to speak against My servant Moses?"* (Numbers 12:6-8).

As great as Moses' anointing was to deliver the people out of bondage, it was equally inept to deliver them into their full inheritance. When men are leading alone, followers are governed by both their strengths and weaknesses. It would require a corporate anointing to lead the people into the Promised Land. Thus the importance of Joshua and his leadership team.

Joshua was a descendant of Ephraim, a descendant of Joseph. (See

Genesis 48.) Joseph was Jacob's eleventh son and his wife Rachel's firstborn son. The sovereign plan of God elevated Rachel's firstborn to receive the firstborn portion of Jacob's inheritance and demoted Leah's firstborn, Reuben. (See Genesis 48:21-22.) Later, when Jacob established Joseph's sons, Manasseh and Ephraim, to be accounted as his sons, he, in effect, gave Joseph the firstborn, or two portions.

Before his death, Jacob elevated Ephraim to the firstborn position ahead of Manasseh, even though he was younger. (See Genesis 48:12-20.) Thus, Ephraim becomes the lead tribe among the sons of Israel. The primary leader of the tribe of Ephraim would become the leader of the nation once they entered the Promised Land because of the leadership assignment. Actually, the legalistic code of the law of inheritance is violated twice. Both sons were born during a time of fruitful production in Egypt. (See Genesis 41:50-52.) Joseph had a production/distribution anointing that transcended his generation into Joshua's, which was vital when it came to dividing and distributing the Promised Land to each tribe and family. (See Genesis 41:53-57 and Joshua 11:23.) This was a marketplace anointing. Moreover, the marketplace anointing on Joseph was now on Joshua. Perhaps we could safely conclude this was an economic anointing. So, then, Moses modeled intimacy and Joshua distribution. Moses was the gatekeeper of intimacy and Joshua distribution leading to prosperity.

THE MARKETPLACE ANOINTING

The magnitude of the marketplace cannot be underestimated when it comes to executing the dominion mandate and the rites of Kingdom inheritance. In every age, the marketplace has needed Kingdom influencers—

people to be salt and light, as Joseph was. Salt is an *unseen* influencer; its presence is noticeable, but not necessarily seen. (Marketplace intercessors could very well fit this role.) Light is a *seen* influencer. (Business, government, and educational leaders fit this role.) Marketplace anointing was designed to touch first individual homes; second, the city; and third, the world. True marketplace leaders understand the significance of this order.

Webster defines *marketplace* as "a place in which a market is set up; the business world; and the arena in which works, opinions, or ideas are debated and exchanged." In early New Testament days, marketplaces were often located just inside the city gate where streets converged—the clustering place from all directions. In the Old Testament, the marketplace was a place of selling merchandise (*commerce*). Among the Jewish people, a market was strictly a commercial center, while among the Gentiles it was associated with other functions of public life.

A Greek *agora* or a Roman *forum* was an open area surrounded by commercial buildings, temples, a hall of justice, and government buildings (*government*). People would gather to exchange information and opinions and to mingle socially (education and social interaction). A rostrum or *bema*—a raised platform—also stood in the marketplace from which public officials could address assembled crowds and even render judgments.

The marketplace anointing plays a significant role in the creation and redistribution of wealth. It was purposed to release the Kingdom culture to counteract the corruption that has pervaded the business, government, and educational[2] fields. In the United States, billions of dollars annually are funneled into each of these fields, but much is wasted on bureaucracy and produces unsatisfactory results. For example, although millions of dollars are provided to the field of education, we lag behind our Asian counterparts in science and engineering.[3] In business, the U.S. was once a great exporter, now we import more than we export.[4] That is certainly a recipe for failure. Something has to change—fast!

The church in the marketplace, just as Jesus in the marketplace, is anointed and empowered to decree God's judgments in this arena with the intent of producing reformation and eliminating waste. Reformation will address imbalances, which are abominations before God. Markets are the battlegrounds in cities and nations. Whoever controls the markets has control over the city and, in effect, the nation.

For instance, there are powerful individuals and families in small developing nations who control quite a bit of the Gross Domestic Products in their countries. Their opinions and economic strength give them power. Godly marketplace ministers as Kingdom envoys have the power to release the ministry and word of reconciliation, helping solve much of the imbalance in today's world.

There is a teaching circling Christendom that promotes business people as kings and Ephesians 4:11 ministers as priests; business people as apostles to the marketplace; and priests as apostles to the sanctuary. I believe that teaching is inconsistent with revealed truth. Peter said,

> *But ye are a chosen generation, a **royal priesthood**, a holy nation, a peculiar people; that ye should shew forth the praises of Him who hath called you out of darkness into His marvelous light* (1 Peter 2:9).

John further confirmed,

> *Unto Him that loved us, and washed us from our sins in His own blood, and hath made us **kings** and **priests** unto God*

and His Father; to Him be glory and dominion for ever and ever. Amen (Revelation 1:5b-6).

If we each apply proper hermeneutics, the New Testament unifies kings and priests and it doesn't promote separation. This endorsement shrewdly filters an outdated Old Covenant idea into the New Covenant without the expanded revelation of the New Covenant. We find the separation of powers in the Old Testament, which I believe is a safeguard for the nation against unprincipled leadership.

Again, I believe we are dealing with the fancy footwork of the carnal mind seeking to ooze corruption and hybrids into the purity of grace. Jesus was a king and a priest and He ministered effectively in the marketplace *and* the sanctuary of people's hearts. The third witness to this truth again from the inkhorn of John. He writes, *"And hast made us unto our God kings and priests: and we shall reign on the earth"* (Rev. 5:10). Let it be established irretrievably that we are *all* kings and priests in Christ!

Finally, Joseph's anointing that Joshua received reminds me of the eleventh hour church working in the marketplace vineyard. (See Matthew 20:1-16.) Remember, Joseph was Jacob's eleventh son! The Dispensation of Grace created a multidiversified workforce established upon the principles of equality and inclusion as the Kingdom of God advances from one generation to the next. God created the earth and owns it as His vineyard with man working and developing it to its fullest potential as a wise steward.

The vast majority of the work will be done in the marketplace. More hours of our lives are spent in the marketplace than in any other venue. For the sake of advancement and continuity, no person or group of workers remain forever as the focal point of divine expression. Each group must take what has been revealed to them, establish it through empowering others, and thus reach into future generations. This is a powerful form of the distribution of the wealth of knowledge. Henceforth, we have a combining of purpose, destiny, and legacy.

TRANSFORMATIONAL LEADERSHIP

There is a crisis in church leadership. If you don't think so, just look at all of the complications churches are facing today. Leaders fear change, and resist it. Albert Einstein hypothesized correctly when he said: "Everything has changed but our ways of thinking, and if these do not change we drift toward unparalleled catastrophe." Joshua faced change and couldn't mimic what he had seen for the past 40 years. It was really a new day when God transitioned Moses. Our conception of leadership must change also as the current models become obsolete, lacking the flexibility and dexterity for today's generation and Father's objectives. If we remain status quo, we risk irrelevance and also isolating ourselves from the cultures we live in. The hierarchical, dualistic version has run its course, which resembled the corporate industrialized world more than it did the Kingdom of God.

The old pecking order is dissolving, opening an opportunity for us to rediscover how the apostles, under the auspices of the Holy Spirit, led the church in its embryonic stage. We must review the authenticity of the church's calling to be a Kingdom of God replica in the earth. Instead of leadership sects fashioned more after Hollywood stardom, we need leaders who are difference makers and provide sources of empowerment.

In the past, we've had our generals, our heroes and heroines, our Samsons and Deborahs. They were needed at those bleak times in human history because of the orientation of Kingdom affairs. Their lives became points of reference to divine initiatives to awaken people to God's doings.

Because the people were burdened by the heavy loads of their conquerors, these leaders had to be great confronters and initiators. They had to command organizations with top-down directives in the early stages of their administrations. This type of leadership may last for a short period; however, it is never intended to be permanent because of man's addiction to power and propensity to use it wrongly. Apart from a constant work of the Holy Spirit in our lives, the best of us will forget the purpose behind power, which is to serve others more effectively. If adjustments aren't made, then, leaders will often fail at what their initial assignments were: *FREEING PEOPLE.* Instead of creating societies of freedmen, this environment will often produce puppetry, fear, distrust, and competition that nixed partnerships and mutual aid in both leaders and followers.

There are many examples in the twentieth century of leaders who ruled by absolute authority and complete suppression of subjects. The cult formed around Jim Jones' leadership in Georgetown, Guyana is one of the most memorable in modern history. Compliance and obedience are the standards indicating commitment to them, which truly isn't commitment at all if it's forced. Anyone within the community with different ideas was considered rebellious, heretical, and depending upon how many people they infected with their contrary opinions, schismatic. In the Kingdom, leaders must become magnanimous enough within themselves to realize varying ideas may be the healthiest thing to promote fuller growth and development within the community.

After ministering as a senior pastor for 20 years, I have found that the kind of controlling leadership model I just described will ultimately be counterproductive to Kingdom objectives, especially if it lasts too long. There has to be a revitalization of leadership models and approaches in the postmodern world. Genuine commitment to these models must be given freely; it generates spiritual courage, imagination, insistence, and knowl-edge-creating organisms. People feel a co-ownership with the vision. There are very few men or women who possess strength in all these areas. Therefore, it will take a diversified leadership unit, just as in the first cen-tury, to lead the church. The apostle Peter may stand, his voice may be the most forceful; however, he needs the other 11 to stand with him to be viable and effective. In my case, I may stand, but I'll need my wife, Ann, to stand with me. The power remains the same though the vessels laboring with God change through time. The postmodern Joshuas may have the baton; but they need teams sharing the task in order to create dynamic futures for the Body of Christ.

LEADERS

"Who do we desire to lead us into the future of God's purposes, especially with so much wealth and influence at stake?" From a political vantage point, the United States of America and many industrialized countries worldwide are asking the same question. Do we yearn for solid leaders with high-quality, stabilizing judgment, or do we accept more exploiting leaders leaving trails of waste? Are we going to just *join* something (Moses/Levite company), or will we connect with that which is *fruitful* (Joshua company)? Though we are duty bound to honor our apostolic her-itage and history, are we going to allow the limitations of previous genera-tions to stifle us—blocking us from exploring these questions?

We will continue to honor Joseph's bones and the stones out of the Jordan River; however, they must not prevent us from marching forward into the promised land of the Kingdom. As we ponder the complexity of these questions, the self-assured are going to encounter problems. We must sacrifice the old to get clarity for the new. It may have been the anointing in a shepherd's staff that delivered us initially, but it will necessitate Ark-bearing priests for stage two.

Because massive wealth redistribution is on the horizon, we're going to need leaders who aren't swindlers and charlatans, or aren't gullible to con artists. They must have the spirit of distribution woven into their internal fabric as Joshua did. This brings me to the necessity to address modern *seed faith* manipulations. Even though the message of *seed faith* is a powerful biblical truth the tendency to misuse that truth is prevalent in many places.

Where is the danger? It is twofold. It starts with preachers who use this truth as a means to get people to commit financial resources to their ministries without a covenantal relationship with the person. Through manipulation and appealing to people's needs, these preachers rob God's people with false promises. The other problem is the people who give to these ministries. They have been taught that their needs can be met by simply depositing money in another person's bank account. They do not understand the truth of maximizing their potentials through wisdom and work to achieve the financial blessings that God has for them.

This cycle of deception must be broken. For that to happen we will need a new style of leadership in the Kingdom of God—a leadership that will teach God's people how to become influential in the marketplace.

Joshua was such a leader. Though a commander of the Lord's armies, Joshua's greater task was to divide the conquered lands among the tribes according to the word of Moses, which is also a marketplace ministry. Today's men and women must be Bible-based people who will beg for the Body of Christ as Joseph of Arimathea did, and then venture into the markets. Leadership of this quality isn't about politics, self-assured confidence, poise and knowledge—it is about character! It's about who bears the marks of Christ in their body with a rock-solid Kingdom outlook.

The world loves its own, and hates us. Their outlook doesn't include the Kingdom. More Christians are being martyred today than any other religious persuasion worldwide.[5] When godless men realize trillions of dollars will flood into the church, we'll need people like the apostle Peter who can't be bought by sorcerers desiring to participate in the new order just to get wealthier and maintain control over their small empires. If covetousness be found in our hearts, we will definitely have a price tag around our necks.

THE GIFT OF BEWILDERMENT

Joshua had many outstanding leadership traits; however, there's one that defies reason and identifies him with many progressive, postmodern leaders. When he first began his commission, he was just as bewildered as any new primary leader. The previous leadership paradigm did not accomplish the goal of reaching their destiny; so he needed to rethink leadership. As he recalled the victories achieved under the guidance of Moses, he had no strategy to take Jericho. How would they overthrow that insurmountable walled city? He hadn't traveled this road before, though he had spied out the Promised Land 40 years earlier. Things had drastically changed!

Bewilderment is an unpleasant, unglamorous gift in the Kingdom of God. When we're baffled and puzzled about what to do, or what direction to take, it becomes a mode of transportation to drive us directly to our heavenly Father. Postmodern people are rejecting many of the leadership tenets and models that have governed the modern world. For one, my generation accepted leaders because of the authority of their positions. Today, postmoderns would rather have leadership connected by personal, established relationships. They seem to resent pecking-orders, and will only yield to leadership when it is earned. Just because a bishop said it, doesn't make it the gospel anymore.

There's a rediscovery of what the apostle Peter stated: *"The elders which are **among** you I exhort, who am also an elder, and a witness of the sufferings of Christ, and also a partaker of the glory that shall be revealed"* (1 Pet. 5:1, emphasis added). When evaluating this statement, the word among really stands out. Speaking bluntly, the new breed of postmoderns love leaders who are beside them rather than over them. This aligns with the idea that we are all taking the trip together as kings and priests, pondering the question of the journey more than just seeking answers.

In this case, every member of the Body will have something to offer during the course of the journey. Leadership, to some degree, is in everyone. Because every single cell carries the DNA of both parents, then every member of the Body of Christ carries the DNA of the Godhead. All members of the Godhead have leadership qualities. It is foolish and presumptuous to think leaders have more of God in them than other members of the Body of Christ; they just have a different function. When this happens, an unspoken assumption prevails that leaders should be required to manifest more of Christ's life than anyone else, regardless of what may be their God-given niche. This, without contradiction, blocks the Body of Christ from maturing.

We must die to these ideas springing out of hierarchal models developed in the modern world and influenced by the industrialized world's corporate structure. Our job is to develop and strengthen bona fide communities of faith until we all mature. We can ill afford to keep one another in the damaged goods department of *has been* because of wrong concepts. Let's begin to look for new ways to cultivate our relationships, beginning with redefinitions of the governmental gifts of Ephesians 4:11 as they pertain to a postmodern world. (Please, at no point am I saying destroy the tools Jesus gave to help mature the church. Then I, of all men, would be guilty of destroying the hand Father God gave to feed us.)

Maybe, the word *coach* would be a good place to start to incorporate all of Ephesians 4:11 ministers. A word history in *Webster's II New College Dictionary* reveals that a coach was used as *"a tutor or a trainer"* in allusion to the speed of stagecoaches and railway coaches. A coach in the university parlance was an instructor who brought his students along at the fastest possible rate. The simple idea of this word is to convey special people from where they are to where they need to be. I can't think of a clearer way to describe of the governmental gifts Jesus gave to His church. The apostle Paul said it this way: *"Not for that we have dominion over your faith, but are **helpers** of your joy: for by faith ye stand"* (2 Cor. 1:24). A coach is a helper. To me, this is one of the many descriptions of the governmental gifts of Ephesians 4:11.

> *And He gave some, apostles; and some, prophets; and some, evangelists; and some, pastors and teachers* (Ephesians 4:11).

There are also other considerations we must make about these ministries. We came out of the modern church era handicapped in our understanding about two of the Ephesians 4:11ministers: the apostle and the prophet. Unfortunately, there existed two extreme, polar-opposite understandings about them: some sincere groups underestimated their importance; whereas others overestimated their importance. For example, some brethren sincerely believe the apostolic and prophetic functions ceased to exist after the first century. There are others who freely hand these titles out to everyone. Both extremes are imbalances of the truth, which says, *God gave some* to these ministries, not all; and they were to last until the church came into the unity of the faith and maturity in stature. Evangelists, pastors, and teachers will never fully accomplish this assignment alone. It takes all five functions of the ministry of Jesus Christ.

Presently, there is something safe and refreshing about leaders who don't have all the answers. They refuse to place on the armor of the modern church's misrepresentations, and would rather have an insignificant slingshot empowered by the Holy Spirit. I find myself bumping into many young leaders fitting this description. These men and women aren't writing books on leadership yet because leadership as a spiritual gift is still being hammered into them. Most of them are not self-deluded, domineering, egotistical maniacs manipulating God's people for selfish motives either. And they aren't fulfilling some insecurity need through the exercise of raw power. They really have a heart for people!

Once again to the apostle Peter about these type of leaders: *"Neither as being lords over God's heritage, but being examples to the flock"* (1 Pet. 5:3). My interpretation: "These leaders must lead by example for God's people to follow them." I did not say *be* an example, but *by example*. In this way they earn their respect from others.

I'm often asked the question, "Where is the church headed?" It's unnerving to people when I respond, "I don't know completely—because no man of God knows that; but, it's not where Pentecostal Pre-Millennial futurist eschatology told us the church is headed!" I can only offer people one thought: *Follow me as I follow Christ.*

If we follow the duly ordained pattern of God's church in the wilderness, natural Israel, we're moving into the Feast of Tabernacles. What will this feast look like? I'm not sure, no more than the first disciples were when they waited for the Day of Pentecost to arrive. The primary reason this scenario is unnerving is because we prefer structures we can comprehend and control. We'd rather have someone leading us who knows exactly what to do. We were so anesthetized to the old methodology of doing things we feel unsafe, tremendously insecure in some of the new wineskins. And when we do, we want some alpha male character to stand up and say, "Don't fret! I've got things under control!"

Bewilderment is factored in by God just to let us know we are not in control. Every postmodern leader should realize that Father God has absolutely annihilated our self-assurance, our illusions about complete knowledge of His doings. He's done it through the spirit of bewilderment.

Joshua is a wonderful example of a leader of the land acquisition/redistribution model. As a type of postmodern leadership, he desired to follow the Lord wholly. He wasn't a university-trained apologist, administrator, career minister, solo act, or theologian; he was relentless in his pursuit of God's prudent purposes. He was not self-centered or self-seeking. He was driven to distribute the land between the tribes. The Message Bible says, *"Joshua took the whole region. He did everything that God had told Moses. Then he parceled it out as an inheritance to Israel according to their tribes. And Israel had rest from war"* (Josh. 11:23). Joshua is properly motivated in that he caused others to inherit before he received an inheritance himself. How selfless! How many people will seek the good of others before themselves?

"When they had made an end of dividing the land for inheritance by their coasts, the children of Israel gave an inheritance to Joshua the son of Nun among them: according to the word of the Lord they gave him the city which he asked, even Timnath-serah in mount Ephraim, and he built the city, and dwelt therein" (Joshua 19:49-50).

Land distribution is one way to measure wealth redistribution. This isn't the first time the land was occupied, so Joshua's actions and the reciprocal actions of the people represented redistribution.

Joshua, a son of God, inherited with the people, which speaks of Christ, the Son of God, inheriting with His brethren. (See Romans 8:16-17.) Sonship and inheritance completely jell in the New Covenant. The son is the heir and the inheritance is the Kingdom of God. The Gospel of Luke tells us, *"Fear not, little flock; for it is your Father's good pleasure to give you the kingdom"* (Luke 12:32). Jesus Christ and His brethren were given the title deed to planet Earth. All sons have an inheritance with the other sons. The inheritance is incorruptible, undefiled, reserved in the heavens, and cannot fade away. The Holy Spirit is the earnest of the inheritance until the redemption of the purchased possession. The New Covenant, ratified by the death, burial, resurrection, and ascension of Jesus Christ, established the foundation for the inheritance to be eternal. (See Hebrews 9:14-15.) If we viewed the inheritance from a Feast of Tabernacles, Most Holy Place position, the death, burial, resurrection, and ascension would be the four pillars the veil hung on until Christ came and rent the veil apart. After Christ experienced each of these, there remains no longer any veil other than the one over the unredeemed human mind. (See 2 Corinthians 3:15-16.)

APOSTOLIC TANDEM OF
MALE AND FEMALE

It would be neglectful of me not to speak of a new Joshua leadership model emerging in this third wave of reformation. In fact, I would be remiss if I didn't speak of the original leadership team sent to planet Earth by our heavenly Father to manage His resources, to administrate His estate. In the postmodern world, the greatest distributors of wealth will be male and female rightly related to one another displaying the image and likeness of God. Before we look at the prophets and priests of the Old Testament, and the varied apostles of the New Testament, realize that man and woman were God's first apostolic team. Their jurisdiction was Earth and all that was on it. Jesus restored all God's original ideas and made them pragmatic and feasible.

Now we must view man and woman together as Kingdom rulers and move away from the illusion that structural and governmental efficiency must come through an all boys' club, which identifies the meltdown of a deformed condition. It is time for male Adam to realize that female Adam was reconciled and restored as well. They stand side by side in the purposes of God. In the postmodern world, this team is best suited to dispense and redistribute the earth's resources. They walk as one because of the tremendous dealings of God in the current Day of Atonement. Their qualifications as dispensers of wealth will center on the elimination of competitiveness found in egotistical men that compels them to outdo rather than serve others.

A beautiful example of this male and female team concept was Aquila and Priscilla. We're introduced to them in the city of Corinth. The Message Bible says,

"After Athens, Paul went to Corinth. There is where he dis-covered Aquila, a Jew born in Pontus, and his wife, Priscilla. They had just arrived from Italy, part of the general expul-sion of Jews from Rome ordered by Claudius. Paul moved in with them, and they worked together at their common trade of tent making" (Acts 18:1-3).

Think of it! A male/female team worked in alliance with apostle Paul. In the Scriptures, Priscilla is mentioned first three times, and Aquila is also mentioned first three times. It's hard to get more balanced in a rela-tionship than that! Eventually, Paul sailed for Ephesus along with Aquila and Priscilla. It is in Ephesus where they (Aquila and Priscilla) engage in some of their greatest marketplace ministry. They are introduced to a young man named Apollos.

A man named Apollos came to Ephesus. He was a Jew, born in Alexandria, Egypt, and a terrific speaker, eloquent and powerful in his preaching of the Scriptures. He was well-edu-cated in the way of the Master and fiery in his enthusiasm. Apollos was accurate in everything he taught about Jesus up to a point, but he only went as far as the baptism of John. He preached with power in the meeting place. When Priscilla and Aquila heard him, they took him aside and told him the rest of the story (Acts 18:24-26).

I see veracity, strength, and a security level in Aquila and Priscilla that's incontestable. It is very clear they are not competing against each other or any of these other modern afflictions plaguing today's preaching couples. They had no ministerial handle placed in front of their names, such as bishop, apostle, prophet, evangelist, etc. Labeling, or pigeonholing, a person according to a particular function may damage or limit the wholeness of relationships.

What happens when relationships break down? Do we remove the title as though the function was never there? What happens when the Father desires to use someone in a way other than their title demands? What if the bishop needs to deacon for a moment just as Christ did in John chapter 13? Can we jump down from our pedestals long enough to do what needs to be done for the Kingdom?

Aquila and Priscilla's freedom allowed them to speak with someone who could have used education and eloquence as a shield from other people. At times, without necessarily meaning to, well-educated people have a way of intimidating those they think are inferior. However, unobtrusive Aquila and Priscilla possessed something Apollos needed; their courage transcended his scholastic letters. Because Apollos taught no apparent error, denied no essential element of the faith, taught the truth as he understood it, they were able to instruct him with tact and correct apparent deficiencies.

Many associates in my earlier years of spiritual development had little education; however, they had anointing and spiritual understanding. Aquila and Priscilla had accurate revelatory information Apollos needed to be more exact in his teachings. They captured a teachable moment, something beyond educational theory and classroom experience. As valuable as the information was to Apollos, the people delivering the information were actually priceless. They must have presented themselves reliable, trustworthy, and totally believable. Apollos changed for the better with spiritual exactness about the

Christ. Change isn't difficult, as long as the change agents can be trusted. I see tandems like Aquila and Priscilla as the new Joshuas of the postmodern era. Priscilla and Aquila:

- Had a harmonious, complimentary marriage, which is one of the most spiritual environments couples can create.

- Practiced union life with the Lord and were one with Him.

- Were co-laborers in a secular occupation, thus blending the sacred and the secular.

- Were one in their friendship with other ministries, and networked with them for the good of the Kingdom.

- Were unified in their profound knowledge of the Scriptures.

- Were one in the service of the Church.

ENDNOTES

1. R. Daniel Watkins, *An Encyclopedia of Compelling Quotations* (Peabody, MA: Hendrickson Publishers, Inc., 2001), 416.

2. http://www.ed.gov/about/overview/budget/index.html, accessed 2/2/08.

3. http://www.eastwestcenter.org/news-center/news-releases/ spotlight-on-seminars/, accessed 2/2/08.

4. http://www.globalpolicy.org/socecon/crisis/tradedeficit/tables/ trade.htm, accessed 2/2/08.

5. http://www.chick.com/bc/2006/martyred.asp, accessed 2/2/08.

Chapter 4

NO MORE COMMODITIES OR CONSUMERS

*And when thy son asketh thee in time to come, saying, what
mean the testimonies, and the statutes, and the judgments,
which the Lord our God hath commanded you? Then thou
shalt say unto thy son, we were Pharaoh's bondmen in Egypt;
and the Lord brought us out of Egypt with a mighty hand:
and the Lord shewed signs and wonders, great and sore,
upon Egypt, upon Pharaoh, and upon all his household, before our eyes: and He brought us out from thence, that He
might bring us in, to give us the land which He sware unto
our fathers* (Deuteronomy 6:20-23).

Israel journeyed from Egypt through four phases to become the productive nation they eventually became in the economy of God: (1)
Pharaoh's *commodities*; (2) wilderness *consumers*; (3) wealth *creators*;
and (4) wealth *circulators* or *distributors*. Two of them were positive and
two negative. We will explore the ramifications of each from a Kingdom
perspective. They experienced the transfer of wealth in two major ways:
(1) a sovereign redeployment of wealth, and (2) the extracting of wealth
through labor investment in their inheritance.

As stated previously, the Promised Land for them symbolized the Kingdom for us. The church (Israel) of the old covenant in the Promised Land speaks allegorically to the church of the new covenant in the Kingdom. Both groups received the Kingdom as gifts. Every inheritance children receive from parents is a grace gift. It was in the Promised Land that the nation of Israel became participants in sovereignty and reached a place of economic strength and competence never imagined. God gave them the land; that's sovereign activity. Whether or not the land produced to its peak level of productivity would depend upon their obedience to God's commandments and statutes and their work ethic.

Each of us will be able to identify with these four phases in one degree or the other.

All may not be the descendants of historical slaves; however, all people were subjugated to Adam's enslavement to sin. The Bible says, *"For all have sinned, and come short of the glory of God"* (Rom. 3:23). It matters not the pigmentation of your skin, or the socioeconomic status you've achieved. All were in Adam; and Adam became a slave to the world system he was supposed to have dominion over. Symbolically, Israel's deliverance is that of a corporate Abraham; just as Christ is the deliverance of corporate Adam. We've been delivered to become productive distributors of the Father's wealth. Our deliverance was necessary in order for the initial dominion mandate to be restored.

Pharaoh's Commodities

Therefore they did set over them taskmasters to afflict them with their burdens. And they built for Pharaoh treasure cities, Pithom and Raamses. But the more they afflicted them

*the more they multiplied and grew. And they were grieved
because of the children of Israel. And the Egyptians made the
children to serve with rigour: and they made their lives bitter
with hard bondage, in mortar, and in brick, and in all manner of service in the field: all their service, wherein they made
them serve, was with rigour* (Exodus 1:11-14).

Exodus chapter 1 pinpoints the historical fact that the children of
Israel have been in Egypt for several hundred years. They entered as guests
and became slaves. Joseph's reputation made it easy for them to live there
at first though the Egyptians hated shepherds. The Bible says a new king
arose who had no relationship with Joseph, and he terrorized the children
of Israel. He was motivated by the fear of their potential, especially if war
broke out. There are certain containment measures that are placed in the
system to control and regulate them. Israelite turncoats were chosen from
among their ranks in order to administrate this assignment. The Scripture
calls them *taskmasters*, which means "those who supervise hard labor
demandingly." These Egyptian officials had supervision of the labor gangs
of the enslaved Israelites. Just beneath them and in charge of the actual
work were the Israelite gang-masters who had no mercy for their fellow
brothers and sisters. No doubt they were awarded particular favors from
the Egyptians.

Israel was Pharaoh's free labor force. They built cities to contain the
abundance of wealth they were accruing for him. Israel was a commodity.
Webster defines *commodity* as "something people value or find useful.
Something that's conveniently useful or capable of yielding commercial or
other advantages." In my understanding, a slave fits the definition of a
commodity with precision. Slavery is about amassing economic power. It

is a system that guarantees the enslaved will suffer in involuntary servitude. Mental anguish continually assaults the slaves' psyche even in the midst of physical productivity.

Of all the attitudinal and emotional diseases a person suffers during enslavement, the most hideous and detrimental is bitterness. I define bitterness as unfulfilled revenge. It's important to understand the psychosomatic effects of bitterness; then, we'll comprehend why God required them to deal with this scourge immediately after they were delivered out of Egypt. Israel needed to be at peak-level when it came to creativity and productivity as they entered the Promised Land—residual bitterness would hamper them. The Bible says,

> And when they came to Marah (bitterness), they could not drink of the waters of Marah, for they were bitter: therefore the name of it was called Marah. And the people murmured against Moses, saying, what shall we drink? (Exodus 15:23).

This particular stopover surfaced in the predetermined plan of God for Israel to confront their bitterness swiftly. The heavenly Father never intended them to be blinded by bitterness and the unhealthy host that usually accompanies it. I imagine most people have looked into a body of water and have seen their reflection on a bright, sunny day. Though reflections may be a bit distorted, they generally tell the truth. Reflections bend light from a surface to form an image of an object and manifests or mirrors the resulting image.

Your reflection is who you are. When God was ready to reflect Himself, He said: *"Let us make man in Our image and after Our likeness"* (Gen. 1:26). In Far Eastern or Asian culture, this would be called the power of the mirror, symbolizing self-knowledge. Buddhism is one of the prominent Eastern religions that embrace this concept. Reflections bring us to startling, unpretentious truth because the light (revelation) throws back a true image. At that point, acknowledgement of the condition is the only appropriate response. Excuses for what has been revealed will only impede progress, prolonging denial and driving the dagger of bitterness deeper into our souls.

BITTERNESS

When Israel said, "They were bitter," the Lord showed Moses exactly what to do. *"And the Lord shewed him a tree, which when he had cast into the waters* [that which manifested the condition of the people], *the waters were made sweet..."* (Exod. 15:25). This is a powerful illustration of Jesus, the Tree of Life. When He was thrown in the bitter waters of human experience, humanity was healed and made sweet. In fact, it was absolutely essential that Father God placed His holy seed in the womb of a woman called Mary. It bore witness to a divine invasion into the bitterness of humanity to birth the answer to humanity's troubles.

Bitterness is almost always amalgamated with resentment and hatred, which is toxic waste in the human body, soiling every cell. After 400 years of enslavement, it's not difficult, from a human level to perceive their infested bitterness. Since Father God's sovereignty led Abraham's seed into Egypt, and He will never lead us wrong, why did the bitterness become so painful? Everything commences with a thought. Injurious thoughts lead to damaging words, which lead to destructive attitudes and paralyzing emotions. If they remain with a person long enough, resentment and hatred will develop, eating up a person internally and then manifesting externally through harmful actions and behaviors.

The only remedy—the Word of God. Godly thoughts will prevent the formation of toxic, mordant emotions. We may counteract nagging, disparaging thoughts by speaking powerful, positive words from the Scriptures. The place where we should begin is to walk in love and forgiveness. In addition, if we choose to remain in an attitude of gratitude, thankfulness becomes a healing balm as well.

There are many stories in the Scriptures verifying the debilitating effects of bitterness. King Saul was bitter at David while his administration declined, ultimately dissipating. Ahithophel, David's counselor, was embittered with David because of his lack of integrity with Bathsheba, his granddaughter. Absalom, David's son, was bitter with his brother and his father for Amnon's rape and David's improper prosecution. Ahimaaz, a descendant of Zadok, was bitter during the administration of David because of his desire to run prematurely with undeveloped tidings.

David had many bitter people around him, though he was a man after God's own heart. Each of these men was destined for greatness only to be quashed by the toxicity of bitterness. They would have been inducted into the Kingdom's Hall of Fame if bitterness had not destroyed them. Bitterness prevented each of them from reaching their highest level of productivity.

The story of Naomi, in the Book of Ruth, is another candid illustration of how bitterness putrefies the soul. Famine, or lack, led Elimelech, Naomi's husband, and his family into the land of Moab away from Bethlehem-Judah. *Bethlehem* means "house of bread" and *Judah* means "praise." When someone leaves the bread (the Word of God) and praise, nothing good happens. Elimelech and his two sons eventually died in the land of Moab, the consummate metaphor of *no change* (see Jer. 48:11), leaving their wives widowed. Father God began to visit

Bethlehem-Judah with rain, and it became productive again. Naomi heard about this and desired to return to the land. Her daughter-in-law, Ruth, returned with her.

When they returned to Bethlehem, the whole town was buzzing profusely about Naomi. They all wanted to know if this was really Naomi after all these years. But she said, *"Call me not Naomi (My pleasant one), call me Mara (bitter): for the Almighty hath dealt very bitterly with me. I went out full, and the Lord hath brought me home again empty: why then call me Naomi, seeing the Lord hath testified against me, and the Almighty hath afflicted me?"* (Ruth 1:20-21).

It is extraordinary what bitterness can do to a person if left unchecked. It will leave your countenance downtrodden and the internal organs toxic; but, more than that, a person will absolutely hinder their ability to grow in grace. Grace gave the land visitation; bitterness blocked Naomi from fully participating in grace's endowment.

The greater part of this story reveals that the outsider—Ruth—received what was rightfully Naomi's portion under the Levirate law. (See Deuteronomy 25:5-10.) Bitterness prevented Naomi from the possibility of opening herself to Boaz's pursuit, the near kinsman, which was her legal right. Naomi was drowning in yesterday's sorrows. What she forfeited with Boaz, Ruth was able to claim. Ruth married Boaz. What a story! Ruth is the inconsequential outsider whose life turns out to be essential in revealing the outworking of God's purposes among humanity. She comes to this strange land unassumingly. However, God's sovereignty placed her directly into the Messianic line. Boaz and Ruth had a son named Obed, who was the father of Jesse, and Jesse the father of David. Naomi could have had this honor but bitterness made her infertile. Bitterness makes people non-productive.

When I meditate on modern history, I feel obligated to consider why there is so much bitterness among minorities. Why do minorities comprise the majority of prison inmates? Why is there so much Black-on-Black or Hispanic-on-Hispanic crime in America? Many minorities have feelings of low self-worth, desertion, rage, apprehension, depression, and defenselessness. They feel victimized, true or alleged, by a criminal injustice system, whose well-documented biases destroy minorities everyday. Certainly, wallowing in unchangeable history contributes significantly to this condition. Does injustice within a dysfunctional legal system masked with prejudicial policies favor the majority? Of course it does! Or does unresolved, embedded bitterness trace back to slavery and economic disenfranchisement? Without hesitation—yes! Along with the godless disparities of an unjust system, I believe we must consider all possibilities to take steps to correct the wrongs.

Painful stories of impudence are passed down from one generation to another. Stories must be communicated to the next generation as God told the fathers in Israel to do. (See Deuteronomy 6:20-25.) However, when it is passed on from a place of economic disempowerment, it passes more painfully and detrimentally.

National and international data corroborates what I thought was true. I have gone with ministry teams into prisons and became alarmed at the things I saw concerning the prison population.

> The figures reveal the continuing, extraordinary magnitude of minority incarceration and the stark disparity in their rates of incarceration compared to those of whites. Out of a total population of 1,976,019 incarcerated in adult facilities, 1,239,946 or sixty-three percent are black or Latino, though

these two groups constitute only twenty-five percent of the national population. The figures also demonstrate significant differences among the states in the extent of racial disparities."[1]

Would you dare to think of the drain on the economy it takes to house almost two million criminals, along with the construction costs of facilities? How about the drain on wasted talents, unused because of unacceptable behavior?

Nations originally established as 'New World' colonies seem to share a common thread—that aboriginal and indigenous peoples have among the highest incarceration rates of their countries' prison populations. And as is the case with African American prisoners, the reasons for such figures continue to be hotly debated. In Britain, almost twice as many black people are in prison as at the universities. Muslims of mostly Moroccan origin constitute the overwhelming majority of prisoners in France, home to Europe's largest Muslim population. In Australia, Aborigines have the single highest imprisonment rate of any ethnicity, and make up more than a fifth of the prison population. In New Zealand, fifty percent of the approximately 6,000 inmates identify as Maori, and Pacific Islanders about twelve percent, most of them classified as low or medium security inmates.[2]

Inequality of incarceration is a global problem, not just a North American one. Without making this incendiary or biting, it's imperative to comprehend what institutionalized slavery and racism do to people and the corresponding bitterness left in those so subjected. Unless one has been the subject of such pain, or the descendant of former subjects, it is difficult to really understand. Israel experienced it in Egypt and so have many other peoples throughout the centuries. In modern times, speaking of the last 300 years, South African apartheid was probably the closest to what happened in America, though all of Europe and Asia bought and sold slaves. For example, in the British Empire, William Wilberforce led the charge to abolish slave trading at the beginning of the 19th century. The facts of history and the stinging results are inarguably destructive from each system. However, we can ill-afford to allow things to remain in the corrosive, bitter state these systems left them in.

FORGIVENESS

When Jesus taught on forgiveness, He gave all of us the keys to recoup from the horrific disease of bitterness. Jesus taught that anger is a form of murder in its raw state if left unresolved. He spoke to those who were angry without a cause and those who were angry with a cause. It suddenly hit me that if races of people have been disenfranchised for a prolonged period, they become vulnerable to the evil axis of resentment, bitterness, and anger. There's only one remedy: reconciliation and forgiveness. (See Matthew 5:21-24.) Jesus taught we must forgive everyone's trespasses from the heart. With cardiovascular (heart) disease being one of the greatest killers of humankind (excluding congenital defects) I believe there's a direct link to bitterness and a lack of forgiveness.

In the laboratory of human experience, bitterness is the seedbed for wrath, anger, clamor, evil speaking, and malice—the polar opposite of forgiveness. If we follow apostle Paul's admonition, bitterness will find no place in us. Bitterness envelops the love of God in our hearts and progressively turns our hearts into gall. Like a polluted river, bitterness will corrupt every place it flows. Paul said, *"Let all bitterness, and wrath, and anger, and clamour, and evil speaking, be put away from you, with all malice: and be ye kind one to another, tenderhearted, forgiving one another, even as God for Christ's sake hath forgiven you"* (Eph. 4:31-32).

Israel experienced the grace of forgiveness through the Passover lamb and so must all former enslaved people. Otherwise, the solid blueprints for economic enrichment will probably distance themselves from us.

Minorities in North America particularly, must pay attention to Paul's counsel because we are yet to achieve full economic empowerment in the scheme of vital human rights. It is not because we lack cognitive capabilities, creative capacities, or interpersonal aptitude. I believe it comes down to a few things: lack of opportunity because of built-in containment measures in the system, and disempowerment measures, such as greed, selfishness, and bitterness, where there is opportunity. Of the measures listed, I still believe bitterness is the most acute of them all with dire consequences.

The writer of the Hebrews says, *"Follow peace with all men, and holiness, without which no man shall see the Lord: looking diligently lest any man fail of the grace of God; lest any root of bitterness springing up trouble you, and thereby many be defiled"* (Heb. 12:14-15). Bitterness is like a thorny seed that will choke and wither God's life within you. Just as Jonathan discovered by revelation that Saul was the one who troubled the land, bitterness is the current troublemaker.

Many people have stated, "I love God with all my heart, but why can't I get ahead?" Maybe we all should search our hearts to see if any residue of bitterness remains. Being bitter about the unalterable past will change nothing. Our adversary the devil knows that if any of us remain in bitterness, he does not have to accuse, attack, or for that matter, even agitate us. Bitterness alone will keep us imprisoned, mortified, and lethal. Nursing animosity and clutching wrongs prohibits us from living an exultant, productive life. The following is one of the most sobering quotes I have read about anger or bitterness: "To be angry is to revenge the faults of others on ourselves."[3]

Every time someone strikes a neighbor out of bitterness and anger, that person is actually striking himself. The Master charged us with two great commands which absolutely obliterates the spirit of anger and revenge:

> *"Thou shalt love the Lord thy God with all thy heart, and with all thy soul, and with all thy mind. This is the first and great commandment. And the second is like unto it, thou shalt love thy neighbor as thyself. On these two commandments hang all the law and the prophets"* (Matthew 22:37-40).

Love mixed with grace gives us the power to absolve all grievances and to release all bitterness. And remember, if we choose to live in the prison cell with bitterness, we will negate the powerful, productive person we could become.

CONSUMERS IN THE WILDERNESS

> *And the children of Israel did eat manna forty years, until they came to a land inhabited; they did eat manna, until they came unto the borders of the land of Canaan* (Exodus 16:35).

The wilderness represented transition for the children of Israel. Transition was the linking process between Egypt and the Promised Land. Manna was considered transitional food—something alien and unfamiliar to them. The Hebrew definition means "What is it?" and expresses the wonder of the Israelites at God's bizarre provision of food. It further represented the fact that the Israelites were not producing in the land yet and probably would have rejected the manna if possible. Since they weren't producers, they were consumers. Webster defines *consumer* as "a person who acquires goods and services." For six days Israel would collect the appearing manna, which the Scriptures plainly say was a miraculous event. Jesus affirmed it was miraculous in John 6:32 when He contrasted it with Himself the true bread from Heaven. The psalmist said, *"Though He commanded the clouds from above, and opened the doors of heaven, and had rained down manna upon them to eat, and had given them corn of heaven. Man did eat angels' food: He sent them meat to the full"* (Ps. 78:23-25). The faithfulness of a loving heavenly Father knew exactly what His children needed. It was another step in teaching them to live by faith and not by sight in a supernatural lifestyle.

As important as manna was in assuring the children of Israel that God took responsibility for their provision, it further stated they hadn't yet arrived at their destiny. They circulated in the wilderness for 40 years and never fully learned to walk by faith. The writer of the Book of Hebrews says, *"But with whom was He grieved forty years? Was it not with them that had sinned, whose carcases fell in the wilderness? And to whom sware He that they should not enter into His rest, but to them that believed not? So we see that they could not enter in because of unbelief"* (Heb. 3:16-19). God was displeased with their murmuring, unbelieving, consuming ways. It is a fact that many consumers express very little appreciation for the blessed state they are in. Because they are disengaged in developing their own provisions, an ungrateful spirit defrauds them. The vast majority of first-generation Israelites became carnal-minded takers for 40 years, rotting in a cesspool of unbelief.

> But with many of them God was not well pleased: for they were overthrown in the wilderness. Now these things were our examples [types], to the intent we should not lust after evil things, as they also lusted. Neither be ye idolaters, as were some of them; as it is written, the people sat down to eat and drink, and rose up to play. Neither let us commit fornication, as some of them committed, and fell in one day three and twenty thousand. Neither let us tempt Christ, as some of them also tempted, and were destroyed of serpents. Neither murmur ye, as some of them also murmured, and were destroyed of the destroyer (1 Corinthians 10:5-10).

Moses, in a moment of prophetic candor, cautioned and instructed the second-generation Israelites to remember the lessons from the previous 40 years. He said,

> And thou shalt remember all the way which the Lord thy God led thee these forty years in the wilderness, to humble thee, and to prove thee, to know what was in thine heart, whether thou wouldest keep his commandments, or no. And He humbled thee, and suffered thee to hunger, and fed thee with manna, which thou knewest not, neither did thy fathers know; that He might make thee know that man doth not live

by bread only, but by every word that proceedeth out of the mouth of the Lord doth man live. Thy raiment waxed not old upon thee, neither did thy foot swell, these forty years (Deuteronomy 8:2-4).

It's important to note that the heavenly Father proved the children of Israel and provided for them. It argues for an interpretative context in which the Father brings closure to a way of thinking that contributed to them becoming consumers. Everything they walked through was mandatory if a new way of thinking would significantly affect them. The Father knew the interplay of factors necessary to prepare them to become Kingdom producers. Thus, they experienced reduction and preservation simultaneously.

SEEK FIRST HIS KINGDOM

Webster defines *consumerism* as "the economic theory that a progressively greater consumption of goods is beneficial." In order for there to be consumption, goods, such as food and clothing that satisfy human needs, must exist. It is easy to understand the concept of consumerism from the basic definition of the word *consume* (to take and use up). Adam became a covetous taker in his Garden of Eden experiences. The embryonic foundation of all consumerism was in his choices. Indulgence eventually led to the parody of rampant consumerism.

The Kingdom of God works exactly opposite to this. Jesus taught that Kingdom people could avoid the spirit of consumerism and consumer credulity by trusting the integrity of the heavenly Father to care properly for them. He said,

Therefore I say unto you, take no thought for your life, what ye shall eat, or what ye shall drink; nor yet for your body, what ye shall put on. Is not the life more than meat, and the body than raiment?... Therefore take no thought, saying, what shall we eat? Or, what shall we drink? Or, wherewithal shall we be clothed? For after all these things do the Gentiles seek: for your heavenly Father knoweth that ye have need of all these things. But seek ye first the kingdom of God, and His righteousness; and all these things shall be added unto you (Matthew 6:25,31-33).

As I analyzed these verses, several impressions became obvious. We can either focus on things or focus on the Kingdom—but no one can focus resourcefully on both! Jesus encouraged us to seek right standing before the King in His Kingdom as a priority. Carnal, disoriented, and disconnected people fret and think life is fulfilled in seeking things. Settle it! Things will never compensate for what a relationship with Jesus should accomplish. Things beget more things, casting us into the bottomless pit of uncontrollable desire. In Jesus' world, there are no needs, because God has no needs; He is the proliferation of the idea called unlimited supply.

Jesus equally commanded us to observe the birds of the air and the lilies of the fields for proof texts. I've followed that command many times from the comfort of my home when birds would land in my yard. They are never worried about a meal or special provision; or, maybe, even aggressive behavior toward them. They simply chirp away in praise to the heavenly Father as they harvest the grassy, insect-infused yard for breakfast.

There's no flower I know of that is inharmonious with the proclivity of its DNA. Unlike humans, flowers respond to the natural, coded message the heavenly Father programmed in them. They don't struggle to be obedient or beautiful—they just are! And Jesus compelled us to enter the classroom of life and learn the lesson of provision from them. In a nutshell: We will receive from God exactly what we need without frustration and anxiety. Anything other than that opens us to the ravages of abject consumerism. We may be buying with wide-eyed enthusiasm; however, regardless of the cultural fascination, it is still consumerism.

No one seems to evade the clutches of consumerism without proper Kingdom teaching and knowledge, which continually shifts us into an anti-consumerist position. Our tendency without it compels us to lean back into the old way of thinking. Because I grew up in poverty, I made a pact with myself that I would purchase whatever I desired once I became an adult. I'd never lack again. All of my adult life I would buy necessities and, at times, unnecessary desires. My new birth changed everything. We'll exacerbate ourselves trying to undo the past and relive its lack through our current experiences.

My true worth and identity would never be measured in any of those things. I had to admit that a perpetual buying spree is adversely connected to the spirit of consumerism. Father God prompted me to share some of those things with others. He said, "Do for some young preacher what you wished someone had done for you as a young preacher!" I have experienced joy unspeakable and glory by obeying the word of the Lord. Once again, the Holy Spirit has dispelled ideas associated with wrong thinking, which was birthed out of insecurities and resentments, and ordered my steps down a pathway that leads to a greater maturation.

Without entering the debate of postmodern ethnographers and sociologists, consumerism certainly empowers capitalism in its present context—especially through credit card debt. The original history of the credit card wasn't what it has evolved into today. In fact, these cards were intended for the wealthy because they didn't want to carry cash. Various visionaries saw the profit-making potential in credit cards and extended them to almost everyone. Abuse entered. Today, we have an out-of-control industry just barely above a collapsible state. I personally receive 10 to 15 unsolicited new credit card offers per week. It puzzles me why they continue to come when it is unlikely I or my wife will accept any of their can't-miss offers.

According to the American Consumer Credit Counseling, the total U.S. credit card debt in the first quarter of 2002 was approximately $60 billion. The Motley Fool's Credit Center gave several mind-boggling statistics:

- There are at least 1.2 billion credit and retail cards in North America.

- A full 75% of credit card company revenues come from finance charges.

- The total consumer credit is $1.7 trillion.

- Credit card debt carried by the average American is $8,562.

- Total finance charges Americans paid in 2001 was $50 billion.

- The number of credit card holders who declared bankruptcy last year was 1.3 million.[4]

Any way you look at it, credit mortgages one's future for some hackneyed, self-gratification experience that will ultimately turn into a horror story if left uncorrected. The interest, penalties, and all the other fees that accompany credit card debt could be money invested in the Kingdom of God; instead, it is pilfered away from the Kingdom through legalized robbery. As long as there are producers of goods in free market societies, there will be uninformed carefree consumers of those goods. We, like Israel, must pass through our modern consumer sophisticated jungles to become all the Father has prepared us to be before the foundation of the world. A life lived only as a consumer is far beneath the dignity and the creative powers of a son of God. There is a grace given to us to rise above this virulent disease.

When my son received his acceptance notice into law school, we were faced with an important question: Would we seek other financial sources for support or depend upon our heavenly Father as a resource? At first my son said, "Dad, I don't have the money—what am I going to do?" He had saved money from his teaching job, but it wasn't nearly enough. Before my brain kicked into the gear of reason, my heart responded, "You have a father and a mother!"

Of which, the Holy Spirit immediately arrested my impassioned thoughts for a moment of reflection and rehearsal. He proclaimed, "Listen to what you've just stated to your son! Your son has a father, and so do you!" My response to our son demonstrated something important about parents and children. Fathers and mothers love their children unconditionally and will, without hesitation, invest in their successes. The heavenly Father reminded me that He also invested in our success. He gave us Christ, the fullest exegesis of Himself. We had taught our son all his life to save money, avoiding the excesses of debt and credit. His first vehicle was paid in full without installment debt. Now our teachings were being tried. Because Father God gave us the grace to trust Him, He came through in a powerful way, and our son graduated without the beast of debt further—and further established in the truth that Kingdom seekers are superadded to by Father God.

> *Train up a child in the way he should go: and when he is old, he will not depart from it. The rich ruleth over the poor, and the borrower is servant to the lender* (Proverbs 22:6-7).

> *Point your kids in the right direction—when they're old they won't be lost. The poor are always ruled over by the rich, so don't borrow and put yourself under their power* (Proverbs 22:6-7 TM).

People of the Kingdom must be decisive, prompt, and aggressive in removing themselves from the list of marketable targets for every outlandish money scam that comes along. Without fail, our money can be better used. We have been bilked of billions of dollars long enough by skillful bamboozlers with anti-Kingdom objectives. The spirit of consumerism is antithetical to the divine nature within us. You see, consumer people function totally by the spirit of greed, wanting more and more with very little thought toward saving and investing. In fact, in affluent societies, consumption is a terminal social disorder.

Consumers give away far too much wealth; whereas producers create more wealth. We must stop showing off with commodities while others build solid communities from the profits their businesses market to us. It's now time to dream big and collectively build better communities in our current occupational mode from a Kingdom perspective. Jesus commanded us to occupy until He comes. If we allow the Spirit of grace to teach us, He will lift us above those things that prevent us from working together. Our unity will help us break the damaging control of consumerism. We will teach one another until our outrageous, consuming ways have changed.

It's time to say good-bye to ghettos, the modern plantations of commodities and all the inhumane conditions they breed. Shame upon the landlords of these slum projects who only care about the bottom line. When we see all the graffiti, all the untidiness, all the unkempt streets, homes, and apartments, we're reminded of the locked up rage in former commodities. The outer conditions are nothing more than a reflection of the loathed inner state of the soul. My brothers and sisters aren't inherently evil or inhuman, they simply need the opportunities and encouragement that others have received.

But for the grace of God, I would be in one of these hopeless, merciless situations. The only difference I can see is the Gospel of the Kingdom. It was my emancipation proclamation. With it came proper identity and removal from a slavish condition. The Gospel not only provided freedom, but also all the guidelines for the process of freedom. Step by step for 36 years, I could see my heavenly Father preparing me for production and distribution.

ENDNOTES

1. http://www.answers.com/topic/race-and-crime?print=true, *Race and Incarceration in the United States, Human Rights Watch Briefing*, February 27, 2002, 1.

2. Ibid, 2.

3. R. Daniel Watkins, *An Encyclopedia of Compelling Quotations*, (Peabody, MA: Hendrickson Publishers, Inc., 2001), 34.

4. http://ask.yahoo.com/2004029.html, *Ask Yahoo*: Article written February 9, 2004.

Chapter 5

THE KINGDOM—THE PLACE OF PRODUCTION AND DISTRIBUTION

And the children of Israel encamped in Gilgal, and kept the Passover on the fourteenth day of the month at even in the plains of Jericho. And they did eat of the old corn of the land on the morrow after the Passover; unleavened cakes, and parched corn in the selfsame day. And the manna ceased on the morrow after they had eaten of the old corn of the land; neither had the children of Israel manna any more; but they did eat of the fruit of the land of Canaan that year (Joshua 5:10-12).

The way to wealth is as plain as the way to market. It depends chiefly on two worlds, industry and frugality; that is, waste neither time nor money, but make the best us of both. Without industry and frugality, nothing will do; and with them, everything.

—BENJAMIN FRANKLIN[1]

CREATORS OR PRODUCERS OF WEALTH

The moment the nation of Israel crossed the Jordan River and entered the Promised Land their days of consumerism were numbered. A new generation had arisen with a reconnection to the covenant and with a marvelous task before them. The heavenly Father had marked them with a life-giving promise diametrically opposed to consumerism. They would now become prominent producers and extraordinary creators of wealth. The sadistic army of consumption, greed, covetousness, and out-of-control lust, faced annihilation. They had been a tattered, homeless crew only recently set free from nearly half a millennium of slavery. The transition from being landless slaves to landholding free men and women was daunting. Landholding is the first step in building wealth. In comparison, that's why 40 acres and a mule were extremely important to former slaves after slavery in American ceased.

It's important to review the precursory information God gave Israel before entering the land. A preemptive strike of fear prepared the tenants in the Promised Land for dismissal. (See Joshua 2:8-11.) Two defining moments stood as hefty indicators of Israel's impending victory: the demise of Egypt and the two kings of the Amorites. Father God was opening new possibilities for His corporate children. They had been a consumer generation, and now their collective consciousness was about to arise to a new dimension of strategy and productivity.

One of the most important preliminary promises is found in Deuteronomy 8:18. Deuteronomy is the second giving or a reminder of the same words spoken before. God's plan is failure-proof even if the first group He spoke it to failed. It was always in His mind that the corporate seed experience the same abundant blessings as forefathers Abraham, Isaac, and Jacob. To ensure this, the first generation walked through a 40-year probationary period to empty the nation of pride and to lock in the reality of the goodness of God's grace. Israel was postured for success for one reason—outlandish grace! The emptiness of their hearts was revealed in lack; now, they would be tried in plenty. They were forewarned not to deceive themselves in the midst of wealth.

> *But thou shalt remember the Lord thy God: for it is He that giveth thee the power to get wealth, that He may establish His covenant which he sware unto thy fathers, as it is this day* (Deuteronomy 8:18).

> *If you start thinking to yourselves, I did all this. And all by myself. I'm rich. It's all mine!—well, think again. Remember that God, your God, gave you the strength to produce all this wealth so as to confirm the covenant that he promised to your ancestors—as it is today* (Deuteronomy 8:18 TM).

This thought cannot be overemphasized: The nation of Israel was about to become incredible producers of wealth. Jesus declared that the heavenly Father is glorified when His people bear fruit, which is production. (See John 15:8.) Father God gave them the competence, or ability, to get wealth as proof He was in covenant with them. That ability has never been rescinded, and it remains with them today. Wherever Jewish people are on planet Earth, they are some of the most formidable business people and the wealthiest as a group. In fact, they excel in most endeavors. They knew what it was to be delivered from Egyptian slavery accompanied by abject poverty, a fearsome wilderness crawling with fiery serpents and scorpions, and kings who would have smashed them if possible. They are about to become rich, affluent beyond belief because of the gift of competence. The absence of competence and wealth, then, should make us question whether the covenant is in effect or analogous to another era. If the nation remains in poverty, we must ask ourselves what covenant are they in agreement with in their basic culture.

THE KEY TO WEALTH

The key to wealth (for them and us) is to listen carefully to what Father God says the land will produce best. Certainly they could have been creative and developed other ideas; however, their greatest success was in the Word of God. When Joshua was being commissioned, the Lord said to him, *"This book of the law shall not depart out of thy mouth; but thou shalt meditate therein day and night, that thou mayest observe to do according to all that is written therein: for then thou shalt make thy way prosperous* [to push forward], *and then thou shalt have good success* [do wisely]*"* (Joshua 1:8). The Message Bible says, *"And don't for a minute let this Book of the Revelation be out of mind. Ponder and meditate on it day and night, making sure you practice everything written in it. Then you'll get where you're going; then you'll succeed."* Their success would be in the Word of God and immense production, being transformed into a Kingdom ruling class rather than the ruled. They would become the brokers and merchants rather than the clientele. The Lord further encouraged their success with these words,

> *And the Lord shall make thee plenteous in goods, in the fruit of thy body, and in the fruit of thy cattle, and in the fruit of thy ground, in the land which the Lord sware unto thy fathers to give thee. The Lord shall open unto thee his good treasure, the heavens to give the rain unto thy land in his season, and to bless all the work of thine hand: and thou shalt lend unto*

many nations, and thou shalt not borrow. And the Lord shall make thee the head, and not the tail; and thou shalt be above only, and thou shalt not be beneath; if that thou hearken unto the commandments of the Lord thy God, which I command thee this day, to observe and to do them (Deuteronomy 28:11-13).

Everything about the previous Scripture indicates mass production. The word *plenteous* (SC #3498) carries the meanings "to jut or exceed, to excel, to remain or be left, cause to abound, too much, etc." All the shades of meaning were necessary if they were to comprehend being profitable producers. Webster has defined *producers* as "one that produces a product by physical or mental effort, especially one that manufactures or grows goods and services to sell." Moses assured the people that they would be fruitful if they followed the Word of the Lord. I can hear King David saying, *"Thy Word have I hid in my heart, that I might not sin against Thee"* (Ps. 119:11). I define *sin* as "mistaken identity." In this context, it would be sin to think of themselves as anything other than what God said they were. What products would the Promised Land grow best? Once again, we must read the words of Moses:

For the Lord thy God bringeth thee into a good land, a land of brooks of water, of fountains and depths that spring out of valleys and hills; a land of wheat, and barley, and vines, and fig trees, and pomegranates; a land of oil olive, and honey; a land wherein thou shalt eat bread without scarceness, thou shalt not lack anything in it; a land whose stones are iron, and out of whose hills thou mayest dig brass (Deuteronomy 8:7-9).

The first thing we must declare based upon the spirit of revelation is that the land, or Kingdom, is good. Good refers to high-quality or first-rate in the broadest sense. Many general areas of meaning can be noted: practical, economic, or materially good; desirability or pleasantness; and quality. God, who is essentially, absolutely, and consummately good, gives good gifts to His children. It is His good pleasure to give us the Kingdom. The apostle James captures this thought best when he says, *"Every good gift and every perfect gift is from above, and cometh down from the Father of lights, with whom is no variableness, neither shadow of turning"* (James 1:17). The Message Bible says, *"Every desirable and beneficial gift comes out of heaven. The gifts are rivers of light cascading down form the Father of Light. There is nothing deceitful in God, nothing two-faced, nothing fickle."* The land, the geography and the texture, was the highest gift God could give the people. From this land, the Kingdom would spread to all nations. It contained everything essential for practical life and abundance. In a full New Testament context, that which is intrinsically good and beneficial is provided for through the Cross of Christ. It was the good pleasure of Father God to give us the Kingdom with every spiritual blessing in heavenly places. (See Ephesians 1:3.)

Three Streams of Wealth-Building

I see at least three streams of wealth-building in these verses: *(1) the water industry, (2) agriculture and fruit production (food), and (3) the ore and metallic element industry (various forms of mining).* Two of these were natural resources and the other would come from sweat equity along with the sovereignty of God. Historically, colonization occurred around rivers or other water sources. Most major cities worldwide have a water connection. Even Kingdom colonization occurs where there is water (the Word of God). The agriculture industry revolves around the use of water and three distinct harvest seasons: the barley harvest, the wheat harvest, and the fruit harvest. God may tell us what the land will produce; however, it's up to us to work the land to bring it forth. I call this the human responsibility to participate in sovereignty on the earth. All of the agricultural products would eventually become part of the first of the firstfruits and the tithe offerings.

Water Industry

An important use of water is the development of rivers, lakes, ports, and canals for ship trafficking and transferring cargo. The most important of this group would be building ports located at the edge of a lake, river, sea, or ocean. Today's ports handle billions of tons of cargo annually, and are key components to the global economy, especially for industries where shipments of mass tonnage is necessary, like cars. As more countries engage in international trade, ports will probably continue to grow.

Small business, one of the catalysts behind economic strength in most industrialized nations, accounts for a number of companies that use ports regularly. In addition, ports and waterways play key roles in creating jobs and boosting the economy of a nation. To accommodate the billions of dollars worth of exports leaving a nation, thousands of jobs in many different venues (such as restaurants and new construction projects) are created. Do you think anyone in Moses' day saw prophetically what the Ports of Haifa, Ashdod, and Eilat would become in the 20th and 21st centuries?[2]

Did anyone foresee prior to the 20th century the People's Republic of China having one-fifth of the world's busiest ports by cargo tonnage?[3] After Japan's defeat in World War II, did anyone predict that by the close of the 20th century Japan would have as many busy, major seaports as the United States of America?[4] Access to water is vital in economic development.

In the years of King Solomon's reign, he used the ancient city and harbor, Ezion-geber, at the northeast end of the Red Sea, the Gulf of Aqaba, near Elath. (See Numbers 33:35; Deuteronomy 2:8.) Solomon built ships for trade, especially trade with Ophir.

> *And King Solomon made a navy of ships in Ezion-geber, which is beside Eloth, on the shore of the Red Sea, in the land of Edom. And Hiram sent in the navy his servants, shipmen that had knowledge of the sea, with the servants of Solomon. And they came to Ophir, and fetched from thence gold, four hundred and twenty talents, and brought it to King Solomon* (1 Kings 9:26-28).

King Solomon used the shipping industry and seaport to import gold, which enhanced the economy of Israel and added value to the national treasury. Ophir was the place of abundance. Elath became quite populous in ancient times. Just before the powerful reformation under King Hezekiah, the enemy (Syrians) came in and drove the Jews out of Elath to gain control of this vital seaport. (See 2 Kings 16:6.) Today, this seaport is the port of Eilat. It is Israel's southern doorway to Africa, Australia, and the Far East without having to pass through the expensive Suez Canal.

This port and its modern facilities are especially important to the mining industry because of its ability to handle phosphates and potash. Thus, we see the connection of water and mining to produce wealth. Potash is used to develop fertilizers. According to the Encyclopedia Britannica, listen to the connection of ports and mining:

> *The country's mining industry supplies local demands for fertilizers, detergents, and drugs and also produces exports. A plant in Haifa produces nitrate and phosphoric acid for both local consumption and export. Products of the oil refineries of Haifa include polyethylene and carbon black, which are used by the local tire and plastic industries. The electrochemical industry also produces food chemicals and a variety of other commodities. Oil pipelines run from the port of Eilat to the Mediterranean Sea. Israel has some producing oil wells but continues to import most of its petroleum.*[5]

God knew exactly what He was speaking when He revealed to Moses the three staples of wealth building in the nation: the water industry, the agriculture industry, and the metallic ore industry (mining). For each of us who seek to understand reformation and restoration, these facts are highly important and informative. To give proper preview to what God will do with the multinational, postmodern Kingdom nation, we could look at the economic growth that has rapidly increased in the first Kingdom nation since its rebirth in 1948.

> *Industrial growth has been especially rapid since 1990 in high technology, science-based industries such as electronics, advanced computer and communications systems, software,*

and weapons, and these have come to command the largest share of overall manufacturing output. Israel's diamond-cutting and polishing industry is the largest in the world and is a significant source of foreign exchange.[6]

The people of the Kingdom must come to grips with God's strategy behind the systematic order He spoke in Deuteronomy 8:7-9. These major capital markets have been speaking a foreign language to most of us because of many Christian's desire to vacate the planet instead of taking dominion over it. It takes the water industry to give access to foreign markets, which is vital for economic expansion. Remaining open to innovative ideas which produce scientific inventions, allows countries to develop economically and export profitably. The simple principle: If a nation exports more than it imports, there will be no balance-of-trade deficits—wealth will be built. No nation will successfully build wealth without one of the three wealth builders, or all three.

Historically, many unscrupulous individuals and ruthless cartels have taken advantage of the wealth possibilities connected to ports worldwide. Thus, we see the adversary working through people with anti-Kingdom objectives. What would happen if representatives from the Kingdom of God became the governing authority of port systems? After all, we do have the responsibility of managing all of God's estate on planet Earth. I have no doubt that dishonest gain would not be the common practice. A support structure could be created that would produce a culture of honesty rather than the den of iniquity individuals and companies have made them today. I cannot even begin to imagine the amount of wealth from illegal drugs and other contraband that now pass through ports annually. If we could possibly count the numbers from 70 or 80 major ports, the numbers would be astounding. That is why ports and all other dominion issues must come under the jurisdiction of the Kingdom of God.

There is another practical phenomenon with the water industry. Did anyone foresee other than the entrepreneurs what the drinking water industry would become in the modern world? Even in the developed countries, water companies are constantly springing up; and it seems more and more people are seeing the need for them. One would be hard pressed to go into any church building, office complex, or any other public facility and not find bottled water, or even soft drink machines carrying bottled water as one of their products. This is one more example that Father God knew the value of water to the human experience. Whoever can continue to provide the population with safe drinking water in a polluted world will build astronomical wealth.

Since God spoke to the children of Israel about the waters in the land first, it seems logical that if we can heal the Earth's polluted water supply, we'll take some gigantic steps toward healing the Earth of its problems. Chemists who unlock secrets in this arena will financially benefit. Even in a modernized nation like the United States, when a water line bursts the drinking water is compromised. Immediately the community is placed on alert to boil water to prevent water-borne diseases.

Lack of full production from a spiritual perspective is directly connected to a lack of water, or compromised water, which is a lack of spiritual life. The Bible tells about the transference of anointing from Elijah to Elisha, and one of his early miracles involves healing the waters and the barren land. Elisha was approached by the men of Jericho:

You can see for yourself, master, how well our city is located.
But the water is polluted and nothing grows. He said, bring

me a brand-new bowl and put some salt in it. They brought
it to him. He then went to the spring, sprinkled the salt into
it, and proclaimed, God's Word: I've healed this water. It will
no longer kill you or poison your land. And sure enough, the
water was healed - and remains so to this day, just as Elisha
said (2 Kings 2:19-22 TM).

The earth like the human body is at least 70 percent water. So to completely heal the waters of the earth would be like bringing forth almost three-fourths of the Earth's deliverance. The major natural problems in the developing world are: water shortages, droughts, floods, famines, forest fires, soil erosion, and loss of biodiversity. (Choosing a refrain from one more of Elisha's stories, 'there's death in the pot!' See 2 Kings 4:38-41.) Lacking these basic things diminish the carrying capacity for life support systems. What's needed? Without hesitation I will tell you a corporate man, like Elisha, with a creative word in his mouth. The waters heard the vibration of Elisha's voice and got on the same healing frequency from which he functioned. Oh! Let's not forget the salt! Salt is the natural symbol of the eternal covenant God has cut with creation. Salt reminds us that Father God has purposed to preserve us once we're healed. Elisha poured the salt into the spring (fountain or foundation) of the problem. A thing is healed when we heal it at the source of the problem rather than dealing with branches (extensions) of the problem.

Food Industry

For the Lord thy God bringeth thee into a good land,...a
land of wheat, and barley, and vines, and fig trees, and

The Kingdom—the Place of Production and Distribution

pomegranates; a land of oil olive, and honey; a land wherein thou shalt eat bread without scarceness, thou shalt not lack anything in it... (Deuteronomy 8:7-8).

The quality of a nation's food supply will directly determine the quality of life in that nation. Since Israel was God's representative nation, it wouldn't be delusional to think that Father God would give them a prime food supply to keep them at optimal level in health. Food provides fuel for the expense of energy for the body's muscular activities, maintenance for the skeleton, and revitalization of bodily fluids. If the children of Israel were going to be good stewards of the Promised Land, they also needed to be good stewards of their physical bodies. From what is listed as indigenous to the land, it seems that the Lord is presenting them with the opportunity to have a diet rich in fiber, soluble (fruit) and insoluble (grains). Many studies suggest that high-fiber foods help to maintain and stabilize the circulatory and digestive systems as well as other benefits.

Another important point is to contrast the food of Egypt against the produce of the Land. (See Numbers 11:5-6.) Egyptian foods consisted of six things; whereas the foods of the Promised Land are seven—the difference between human's carnal number and God's perfect, complete number. The food of Egypt keeps one pigging-out on lack and insufficiency; manna gives an unanswered generational question in an environment that promotes circularity; and the food of the Promised Land transports one into a place of prosperity with no shortages. Think of it—a nation in which everyone is well-fed with no indigence. As much as we mass produce in the USA, even we don't fit this description. We still have people who lack basic essentials as great as this nation is.

153

The foods listed as growing well in the land consisted of whole grains and fruits. Conspicuously absent in this listing is the wide variety of meat products we have come to enjoy in most nations. Without question, the children of Israel did have livestock, and they did partake of their meats, such as lamb, goats, rams. I would think vegetables, seeds, and nuts would have factored into their dietary habits as well. The real question is: What are the foods that will cause our human bodies to function best in this earth as we execute our dominion assignments? What will keep us healthy and clicking on all cylinders? The keys to wealth-building now and in the future are centered in these questions. As people in all nations become better informed about the human body and the proper fuel-producing foods it needs, more solutions will be available. Since cardiovascular disease and some forms of cancers are linked directly to some foods, how do we take what God spoke to the children of Israel and apply it to our own lives? How do we prepare these wonderful human bodies to live and function at the highest quality of life possible?

When it comes to answering these questions, those who receive broad, economically-feasible visions along with balanced strategies of implementation from God's wisdom will probably generate great amounts of wealth. The primary motivation cannot be greed – it must be service. All of God's children, as they execute the dominion mandate, need regular food replenishment. One of the most pressing problems is the present African food crisis. One could probably argue that the current situation is primarily the result of an interaction between blooming populations and a strong neglect of agriculture during the past decades. Even if this were the only reason, will anyone get a vision to bridge the widening gap between the domestic food supply and demand?

If we truly are our brothers' keepers, and we are, how do we help to better educate and temporarily supply their lack until more models can be developed that will enhance agricultural systems in developing nations? Many developing nations already have a vast array of fruits, nuts, and vegetables that will grow naturally because of geography and positive climate conditions. These are the foods I've read about that help to produce healthy diets. I look at them as powerful, wonderful opportunities for business provided home and foreign exploitation can be diminished. God spoke to the children of Israel about these things being in the land. If taken full advantage of, these foods could produce vast amounts of income in their organic form. There is a great move toward organic foods in this day. If one had the acreage to develop an organic farm, it would definitely become a great wealth producer, provided one honored the command of God to rest the soil every seventh year and resisted the temptation of overproduction.

The organic way was probably the way of the original Adam. Organic, for me, is that which is simple, basic, and in harmony with nature. "And God said, *Behold, I have given you every herb bearing seed, which is upon the face of all the earth, and every tree, in the which is the fruit of a tree yielding seed; to you it shall be for meat*" (Gen. 1:29). Since the human body was taken from the soil, foods directly connected to the soil would nourish it best. Things like fruits, nuts, seeds, and leaves, which would include a variety of vegetables, were common nutrition for the first Adam. Meat became a part of man's diet after the Flood in Noah's day. (See Genesis 9:3.) I cannot find proof positive evidence of a carnivore prior to this, not even other animals. (See Genesis 1:30.) The land wasn't suitable for agriculture immediately after the Flood; therefore, God granted Noah and his family the permission to partake of meat. Because Noah and his family carried the dominion assignment, only he could release this process in the earth. Afterward, other animals became carnivorous. Now, existing in the earth was the hunter and the hunted, with fear as the strongman behind this whole system. (See Genesis 9:2.)

I have my doubts that this will remain the pattern as we move more fully into the freedom of all creation. (See Romans 8:19-21.) However, as for now, we must filter everything through the teachings of the New Testament. It seems that some dietary restrictions of the Old Testament are permissible in the New Testament. (See Colossians 2:16; Romans 14:2-3; Mark 7:18-19; Acts 10:11-15.) Once again, the question I propose is what's going to give us the best quality of life as responsible Kingdom agents in the earth? Remember, that with authority comes responsibility. We have been delegated authority by our heavenly Father; now, we must be good stewards to keep the garden—our bodies.

Unfortunately, in this day there is also global terrorism. A powerful wealth producing idea would be for someone to present a solution to protect the food supply from bio-terrorism. This would be a huge undertaking with enormous costs to cover all nations; however, God can meet all needs. Media reports remind us daily of dangerous microbes lurking in the food supply with potentially mass genocide possibilities. What would happen if God downloaded into the mind of some saint a formula to purify the food and water resources of any pollutants, or an all-in-one inoculation against all viral infections? He can—are we listening?

With many men, women, and children in developing nations suffering violently from HIV/AIDS, how utterly life-giving would it be if someone heard God's voice and found a cure? Currently, entire villages in Africa are dying from the disease.

There is a desperate need for the children of God to come into their own. All of creation begs for His Church to take dominion for the hope and good of all people. (See Romans 8:19-22.)

Mining Industry

For the Lord thy God bringeth thee into a good land, . . . thou shalt not lack anything in it; a land whose stones are iron, and out of whose hills thou mayest dig brass (Deuteronomy 8:7-9).

I believe we need to discuss and explore the proper use of uranium and nuclear energy without compromising its integrity and its purpose for being on planet Earth. A peanut-size amount of uranium can do what it takes more than 100 gallons of oil and over 1,000 pounds of coal to produce energy. It can be converted into a safe source of energy with no pollution to the Earth's atmosphere—much cheaper than all the technology necessary to build a weapon of mass destruction.

What would happen if scientists could build diminutive uranium power cells to run vehicles instead of gasoline? Far less of it would be necessary to produce staggering, enormous amounts of energy for longer periods of time. What you don't see is far greater than what you see: Father God created the heavens (the invisible) before He created the earth (the visible). I don't believe Father God allowed physicists to unlock the secrets of this energy supply just to be enriched for destructive missiles, dirty bombs, and other explosives. That idea is an aberration and particularly barbaric.

Major population nations such as China, India, Indonesia, and other developing nations need more and better energy resources, which will create wealth-producing opportunities. Father God certainly knew the outcome of prolonged usage of fossil fuels when covetous, greedy men were in charge of production. It will be to our own peril with devastating consequences if we continue our same usage of fossil fuels. The opening of the atomic/nuclear world in the 1940s commenced at the right time—a time when the entire world was transitioning into the second major wave of the Industrial Revolution.

I envision the day when my wife and I will drive by production centers and tell our third generation grandchildren, "That's where they produce the energy cells to power our vehicles." We will retell the story of how we once used fossil fuels as our main energy source. I dream of the day when the world changes dramatically and enriched uranium is used only for a Kingdom purpose instead of a dastardly purpose. Instead of wondering if another weapon of mass destruction is on the robotic assembly line, we will confidently say, "The scientists and strategists are working for the good of humankind; if we in America don't need all the energy cells, we'll share them with less fortunate nations." There will be no more fears of subterranean silos with ICBMs or submarines carrying nuclear warheads; no concern for briefcases with dirty bombs. No need to be concerned about extremists getting their hands on these sophisticated weapons for counterproductive purposes! It will be as Isaiah the prophet stated: We will be drawn up into a reality of God that knows war no more.

> *And it shall come to pass in the last days, that the mountain of the Lord's house shall be established in the top of the mountains, and shall be exalted above the hills; and all nations shall flow unto it...And He shall judge among the nations, and shall rebuke many people: and they shall beat their swords into ploughshares, and their spears into pruning hooks: nation shall not lift up sword against nation, neither shall they learn war any more. O house of Jacob, come ye, and let us walk in the light of the Lord* (Isaiah 2:2,4-5).

BODY AND SOUL

The marriage of better medical technology and holistic alternatives would be another wealth producer. Both providers must stop competing and enter into an alliance to *complete* each other. Heath clubs, wellness centers, and exercise rooms and the amount of wealth they generate annually are proof more people are concerned about improving their quality of life. Even if bodily exercise profits little, it profits! Since the pre-Industrialized and Industrialized Ages and job markets have ended, many in the current workforce have become sedentary. Any movement and bodily activity help us to be better stewards of our bodies.

One of the most important books in my home is *Prescription for Nutritional Healing,*[7] a practical reference to drug-free remedies using vitamins, minerals, herbs, and food supplements. My wife and I own and use a treadmill and weights for good cardiovascular health and mild strength training. Major corporations value the importance of employees' health by providing fitness centers.

Because of the healing ministry of Jesus Christ, the church should be the biggest health center of all. When buildings are constructed, we should budget enough money for the fitness center as well. In the postmodern world, we must strategize differently: Isn't it better to teach preachers to become great healers as well as master orators? They need to know the power of God as well as the Scriptures of God.

FIRST THE NATURAL, THEN THE SPIRITUAL

The Scripture says, "First the natural and then the spiritual!" Each of the three avenues of wealth in the natural would have a spiritual application producing spiritual wealth today. It is clear from the Word of God that spiritual waters correspond to the Word of God. (See Ephesians 5:26.) Our inheritance is found in the Word. Inheritance comes from a father, and it is in the Word of God that we read about the lives of our fathers, the patriarchs. Also, it is in the Word that we read about the bread of God and the spiritual fruit He's growing in each of our lives. We become bread and fruit for the sake of others. Father God will empower and enrich others through what He grows in our lives. Finally, the true treasure is in earthen vessels. The apostle Paul summed it up beautifully, *"But we have this treasure in earthen vessels, that the excellency of power may be of God, and not of us"* (2 Cor. 5:7).

Sometimes all it takes is one God-idea to produce vast amounts of wealth. If we are open to Him, the heavenly Father may suggest one proposal leading to a witty invention that could transform society in general. It may not take three super initiatives.

A modern example is the Windows Operating System in computer technology. It immediately, with very few technical skills, allowed millions of people to use the computer who otherwise would have not learned the data operating system (DOS). I believe the Father wanted to share this technology with Kingdom citizens. When that download was being released from the heavens, most Christians were too busy dreaming about vacating the planet. We are now using the technology that unbelievers and agnostics accepted early on, and, by the way, made them rich.

It is my prayer that great adjustments will come to Christianity, particularly in the way we think. Right now, high-tech churches as well as some smaller, conservative churches are using with proficiency the technology supposedly the anti-Christ was going to rule the world with. What changed? Thankfully we became enlightened and finally disregarded the peddlers of panic. Thank God we are forsaking many of those concepts that spiritually duped us.

OVERPRODUCTION

A concern we must register in these days of great production and increased wealth is *overproduction*. Israel of old failed to listen to the Father and overproduced the land. Like Israel, the industrialized power of the modern world has caused us to overproduce the land, pollute the water sources, damage the ecosystems, lose biodiversity and forests, erode the topsoil, and deplete mineral and energy resources at alarming rates. Waste is counterproductive to the heavenly Father's restoration plan executed through Jesus Christ.

> *He was supreme in the beginning and—leading the resurrection parade—He is supreme in the end. From beginning to end He's there, towering far above everything, everyone. So spacious is He, so roomy, that everything of God finds its proper place in Him without crowding. Not only that, but all the broken and dislocated pieces of the universe—people and things, animals and atoms—get properly fixed and fit together in vibrant harmonies, all because of His death, His blood that poured down from the Cross* (Colossians 1:18-20 TM).

The Cross is the great reformer, the absolute equalizer, placing everything back into equilibrium. From the smallest atom to the most gigantic sea life, everything was restored and reconciled. Israel violated, through overproduction and dishonoring, 70 Sabbatical years which provoked the righteous indignation of their heavenly Father. He evicted them from the land for such flagrant violations. (See 2 Chronicles 36:15-21.) They became homeless vagabonds until their sentence was completed. Some of the minor prophets would have been unnecessary if Israel had honored the Lord's commandments. Since they didn't, they remained in Babylonian and Persian captivity until Jehovah refurbished His property. What discipline can we anticipate for our overproduction and over-consumption of global resources in general?

As long as the church as a whole believes God is going to give us a fire escape called the Rapture, we will fail to consider changes to our over-consuming ways. The church should be leading the conservation parade of earth's resources. The developing world, including countries in Africa, Asia, and South America, has 80 percent of the world's population and consumes only 20 percent of its natural resources. In the developed world, North American and European countries, the top 20 percent of the population consumes 86 percent of its resources.[8] It probably could be proven that the same rations are true with spiritual resources. Europe and the West have the technology and material resources; whereas, there is a greater dynamic of the power of God displayed in many of the developing countries. We need to synchronize the two to produce global equality.

We need to change our ways. I'm reminded of the prophet Haggai's admonition, *"Now therefore thus saith the Lord of hosts; consider your ways"* (Hag. 1:5,7). Our use of fossil fuels and human production of greenhouse gases exceeds the capacity of the earth's ability to absorb them. If the heavenly Father hadn't cut and kept a covenant with Christ, Abraham's seed, about the earth, we probably would have destroyed ourselves by now. Shall we be bold enough to tackle this problem along with the greed that produced it, knowing it will cause us to swim against the stream of opinion while most people are flowing with the tide of consumption? What about the problem of obesity? Is it another reflection of our overproducing, over-consuming problem? We must never forget that it is the will of God for us to be Kingdom producers of wealth and *good stewards* of the earth's resources.

Psalm 82 gives us a general analogy and tremendous depiction of what things look like when we fail to properly judge and steward the earth. Universally, there's a cry echoing from more than two-thirds of the earth's population. Daily their voices are resounding in the ears of a gracious and loving heavenly Father. The psalmist says,

> *God standeth in the congregation of the mighty; He judgeth among the gods. How long will ye judge unjustly, and accept the persons of the wicked? Selah. Defend the poor and fatherless: do justice to the afflicted and needy. Deliver the poor and needy: rid them out of the land of the wicked. They know not, neither will they understand; they walk on in darkness: all the foundations of the earth are out of course. I have said, ye are gods; and all of you are children of the Most High. But ye shall die like men, and fall like one of the princes. Arise, O God, judge the earth: for thou shalt inherit all nations* (Psalm 82).

Father God has the judges of the earth in lockdown in His courtroom. The issue: The judges on the earth have corrupted justice far too long by collaborating with the wicked and defiling the defenseless. Instead of justice, there's exploitation and wholesale disparity.

For example, it is easy to call someone evil without realizing how our actions may have contributed to another's evil behavior. The Righteous Judge corners the deputy judges by asking *"How long will you behave in this manner?"* Before they can respond, He makes it very clear that because of their actions everything is falling apart. The earthly judges have betrayed their commission. This strong rebuke was intended to detoxify the judges, liberating them to emulate the great Judge in judgment. Unless there is a commonwealth society with a Kingdom objective, great wealth will beget great exploitation of other pathological behaviors. Great producers of wealth will find ways to hoard all of it and repeat the knotty history of previous exploiters.

DISTRIBUTORS OF LAND AND CIRCULATORS OF WEALTH

Before distribution, there must be production. And, of course, before production, there was inheritance by design and newly established landholders. *Distribution* is "the act of dividing and giving out in portions." First, let us view how Joshua employed the principle of land distribution before we look at products distribution and circulation.

> *So Joshua took the whole land, according to all that the Lord said to Moses; and Joshua gave it for an inheritance unto Israel according to their **divisions** by their tribes. And the land rested from war* (Joshua 11:23).

> *And these are the countries which the children of Israel inherited in the land of Canaan, which Eleazer the priest, and Joshua the son of Nun, and the heads of the fathers of the*

*tribes of the children of Israel, **distributed** for inheritance to them. By lot was their inheritance, as the Lord commanded by the hand of Moses, for the nine tribes, and for the half tribe* (Joshua 14:1-2).

The words *divisions* and *distributed* are key words in these verses. The main consideration and implication behind distribution was the use of smooth stones for casting lots. Some of the other synonyms for this idea: to apportion or separate, to deal, to divide, and to break in pieces.

The division of the land by casting lots prior to its conquest expressed divine sovereignty, the principle of predestination. Also, Moses factored a sense of equitableness in his instructions. Inheritance would directly correspond with the size of each tribe. This principle anticipated greed and inheritance arguments; it kept the nation in a commonwealth mentality.

And the Lord spake to Moses, saying, unto these the land shall be divided for an inheritance according to the number of names. To many thou shalt give the more inheritance, and to few thou shalt give the less inheritance: to everyone shall his inheritance be given according to those that were numbered of him. Notwithstanding the land shall be divided by lot: according to the names of the tribes of their fathers they shall inherit. According to the lot shall the possession thereof be divided between many and few (Numbers 26:52-56).

Joshua and Caleb, prominent figures during the transition, received their inheritance as well. (See Joshua 19:49-51; Joshua 14:1-5.) They both moved from one age and administration into the grace of a new age. God also promised that *"little by little"* He would drive out the Canaanites. The gift would be inherited progressively by allotment. Once inhabited, the land was to be recognized as God's, and it was to be preserved as holy by sanctification, keeping it cleansed, and consecrating it to God. The inheritance would be kept perpetually contingent upon obedience to his law. It was conveyed through Joshua and Eleazer, a king/priest combination. The land differed in degrees of glory, indicating diversity in its scenery, landscape, and production capability.

All the tribes together are symbolic of the corporate inheritance of the new covenant, which was ratified by the death, burial, resurrection, and ascension of Jesus Christ. The unique son, Jesus Christ, is appointed heir of all things. (See Hebrews 1:2.) He, particularly, has an inheritance in the saints. (See Ephesians 1:18.) All of the overcoming saints will inherit all things, or God Himself as the blessing. *"He that overcometh shall inherit all things; and I will be his God, and he shall be My son"* (Rev. 21:7). *All things* can only be found in the reality of God. There is no greater inheritance than God Himself.

Now that the land has been taken out of the hands of the Canaanites and given to the families of Israel, a new administration begins for them. They have the good fortune to be landholders and property managers. As they labored and produced, each family would face the challenge of prosperity: learning how to remain spiritually alive in the midst of wealth. When there is massive wealth transference today, the children of God will face a similar quandary.

The solution would be in keeping the Lord's commandments, and learning to divide and to distribute portions of their harvests the way the Lord commanded them. It is important to remember what the Lord said the land would best produce, for therein lies the ability to generate wealth.

(See Deuteronomy 8:7-8.) Also, the economy of the Kingdom could be effected by their giving practices, which would test their national character.

> *And when ye shall come into the land, and shall have planted all manner of trees for food, then ye shall count the fruit thereof as uncircumcised: three years shall it be as uncircumcised unto you: it shall not be eaten of. But in the fourth year all the fruit thereof shall be holy to praise the Lord withal. And in the fifth year shall ye eat of the fruit thereof, that it may yield unto you the increase thereof: I am the Lord your God* (Leviticus 19:23-25).

The heavenly Father gave the children of Israel a five-year business plan. Five is the number representing the goodness of God's grace in the fullest measure. Grace is the true reason any of us succeed! There is, in addition, an anti-consumerism message in this plan, which prevents them from immediately consuming their fruitfulness, and thus qualifying them for richer harvest and profitability. How many people today destroy their businesses before they mount up because of undisciplined spending or foolish decision-making? It is important to note that this plan dealt strictly with what they planted or invested in the land, and not what was there when they entered. Immediately there is a powerful Kingdom principle of increase: Never eat your preliminary seed!

The Hebrew word for increase is *tebuwah*, which means "income, produce, fruit, gain, and revenue." Tebuwah is used 42 times with the highest occurrence in Leviticus, Deuteronomy, and Proverbs. Leviticus gives it a direct connection to the sanctuary; Deuteronomy to an overcoming, new generation; and Proverbs, as the wisdom from above given to a son of God.

Three statements can be made concerning the produce and fruit. First, priority must be given to the Lord who makes any yield possible. Without proper sunlight, water, soil conditions, environmental conditions, and seed, nothing grows. Father God is the only one capable of giving each of these proportionately, in right balance, and in the right season. I believe Paul captured this idea: *"Now He that ministered seed to the sower both minister bread for your food, and multiply your seed sown, and increase the fruits of your righteousness"* (2 Cor. 9:10). Israel was assured that even in the Sabbatical and jubilee year, the yield would be sufficient to meet every need. (See Leviticus 25.) God is praised for bringing about a fruitful yield because He promised blessing in the form of productivity.

Second, the ingathering of *tebuwah* was an occasion of celebration, which has a direct correlation to the three annual feasts.

Third, in both official and wisdom writings, the *tebuwah* belonged to the Lord. Once the Lord was honored with His portions of the harvest, then they had an obligation to circulate portions among others, namely those still in the totalitarian grips of poverty. Moses gave them specific guidance in this also.

> *And when ye reap the harvest of your land, thou shalt not wholly reap the corners of thy field, neither shalt thou gather the gleanings of thy harvest. And thou shalt not glean thy vineyard, neither shalt thou gather every grape of thy vineyard; thou shalt leave them for the poor and stranger: I am the Lord thy God . . . But the stranger that dwelleth with you shall be unto you as one born among you, and thou shalt love him as thyself; for ye were strangers in the land of Egypt: I am the Lord your God* (Leviticus 19:9-10,34).

And when ye reap the harvest of your land, thou shalt not make clean riddance of the corners of thy field when thou reapest, neither shalt thou gather any gleaning of thy harvest: thou shalt leave them unto the poor, and to the stranger: I am the Lord your God (Leviticus 23:22).

When thou gatherest the grapes of thy vineyard, thou shalt not glean it afterward: it shall be for the stranger, for the fatherless, and for the widow. And thou shalt remember that thou wast a bondman in the land of Egypt: therefore I command thee to do this thing (Deuteronomy 24:21-22).

Principles in the Kingdom are established after two or three witnesses. (See 2 Corinthians 13:1; Deuteronomy 19:15.) These verses of Scripture introduce us to the social responsibility of the children of the Kingdom, or what we would identify as *home missions*. In this type of giving, a person's return is the grateful heart of the recipient, the love lavished on us for almsgiving, and the open reward of the Father. People who produce without giving any portion of the gain reveal a covetous, greedy nature.

The great commandment that all the law and prophets hang on is love. When we walk in the royal command of love, we've walked in the whole law and a spirit of generosity. Father God beckons us to leave the edges of our fields for the disenfranchised, the disillusioned. Because poverty hasn't been eradicated from the earth, the New Testament teaches this same principle by commanding us to be given to *hospitality*, which means "to love strangers." Once again, the apostle Paul captures the full import of Moses' instructions when he says, *"distributing to the necessity of saints;*

given to hospitality" (Rom. 12:13). The writer to the Hebrews confirms the same message, *"Let brotherly love continue. Be not forgetful to entertain strangers: for thereby some have entertained angels unawares"* (Heb. 13:1-2). Part of the greater purpose in wealth distribution is to enable us to minister to needy brethren and foreigners whom we are commanded to love as ourselves.

In considering the Lord's commands, His children will either follow them, or they will be given over to the spirit of xenophobia, the fear of strangers. Part of the cultural war raging in the United States after 9-11-01 surrounds this issue. Will we continue to be a nation that welcomes strangers and love them as ourselves? Or will we become adversarial to one of the ideals that has made us great?

If we completely roll into a protectionist mode, we will miss important opportunities to impact the Kingdom of God. Some strangers entering our gates may become powerful Kingdom envoys when they return to their homeland. Some may come with dastardly intentions of terrorism; however, Father God may have orchestrated the plan to produce another apostle Paul, a former extremist. Who knows? Only God. I do know the people of the Kingdom cannot be manipulated by fear.

SUFFICIENCY IN ALL THINGS

Worldwide, with the gap widening daily between the rich and poor, I can clearly understand why the Lord desires to turn wealth over to uncompromisingly righteous people. Only a just person walking in the praxis of righteousness will avoid the pitfalls of newly acquired wealth. Many decades ago there existed only the rich and poor with no such thing as a middle class. Now that the former Industrial Revolution is history, it seems the middle class is being squeezed into poverty. This will create a new class of disenfranchised, especially when their most productive days have concluded.

The church, with a clear sense of mission, will become difference-makers, those capable of restoring dignity to people. Redistribution was purposed to make us effective in such circumstances. And for those who think they may be giving too much, the apostle Paul has some comforting words: *"For I mean not that other men be eased, and ye burdened: but by an equality, that now at this time your abundance may be a supply for their want, that their abundance also may be a supply for your want, that there may be equality: as it is written, He that gathered much had nothing over; and he that had gathered little had no lack"* (2 Cor. 8:13-15). There will always be enough for everyone. God's grace is sufficient! In the same epistle to the Corinthian church, Paul said: *"And God is able to make all grace abound toward you; that ye, always having all sufficiency in all things, may abound to every good work"* (2 Cor. 9:8).

God's resolve to remove us from being the world system's commodities and over-consumers to circulators of wealth is certain and sure. Just as the resurrection of Jesus Christ proved God's redemptive plan would work, wealth redistribution is one more statement in that line of thought. Sin impoverished humankind and left us feebly reaching to acquire more; whereas redemption allows us to reach, not to acquire, but to relinquish what we've been given.

Father God, in dismantling an antagonistic world system, will relieve them of their wealth and place it into more trustworthy hands—the mature hands of the church. The church is the safe harbor in which mystery, majesty, and money must confluence, the secure structure of community and righteousness where predictability based on the standards of

God's Word is uncompromised. The postmodern church will follow the guidance of the Holy Spirit and distribute and circulate wealth wherever He directs. And we will do it without a holier-than-thou attitude toward those in need.

I'll close this chapter with the musings of a young engineer, Eric Omohundro, as I taught on Kingdom distribution in Roanoke, Virginia, and a couple of contemporary examples of wealth builders. (These comments are used with written permission.)

At the conclusion of the meetings, over a plate of spaghetti, Eric shared his simple, yet profound thoughts:

> I was always interested in thermodynamics. It is a fascinating branch of physics, and I always did well in it somehow. One day while pondering Reaganomics, for no apparent reason, I thought about the accumulation of money in the top income bracket,s pooling there like stagnant waters. I thought that money might have more energy if it moves from the point of stagnation. Then, I had the idea that money/value transactions could be modeled like matter/energy chemical reactions—in the form of the free-energy equation. One of the easiest ways to explain it is to liken it to the tendency for a natural reaction, like putting baking soda with vinegar, which increases the entropy (a measure of the energy in a process that is unavailable for work), and lowers the free energy. So, say instead of matter to carry the energy and entropy, you have money to carry value and purchasing power and flexibility. I will stick to money and value for this analogy. Whenever there

is a money transaction, there is a transfer of value. You have bought something you value slightly more than the money you spent on it. The company gets more money than it used to produce what you bought. That is the value transfer. It is usually not a very large amount, but it moves enough value/energy to keep the economy moving. When money is given or donated freely, however, it is 100 percent value/energy. Then the transaction has all that energy driving it, and it can race around like a bullet doing amazing things.

I agree with Eric's conclusion. If we view this principle from what we freely distribute to God and to the disenfranchised, it will produce astronomical results. The value and energy released through no-strings-attached global circulation would ultimately break the backbone of poverty in all expressions. Some people may ask, "But what about accountability?" When people experience freedom from a purely righteous position, I don't think they are interested in hoodwinking or using anyone. I trust you are beginning see why Jesus said, *"It is more blessed to give than to receive"* (Acts 20:35). Paul used this as a foundational statement recognizing the underprivileged should be supported. He drew from our Lord's sayings in Luke 14:13-14: *"But when thou makest a feast, call the poor, the maimed, the lame, the blind: and thou shalt be blessed; for they cannot recompense thee: for thou shalt be recompensed at the resurrection of the just."* From the young engineer's analogy, this kind of giving is 100 percent value/energy. There's nothing about this transaction that is profit-making, which would become the friction to diminish the value/energy release.

Contemporary Wealth Builders

Traditionally over the last 300 years African Americans have been locked out of the marketplace and not given the opportunity to succeed. It has never been a problem of ability. The problem has been opportunity— opportunity for education and for access into the marketplace. It is clear that a paradigm shift has occurred and that opportunity is now available in many places. Many African Americans have now rejected the welfare mentality and understand that their greatest opportunity for success is not from the government but from their own latent potential to create wealth. Many African Americans are now learning the power of influence in the marketplace. The following are two excellent examples.

Jerome Edmondson[9] is an entrepreneur, multigifted international motivational speaker, lecturer, educator, advisor, business consultant, and founder and chief executive officer of CBN Entrepreneur Training Institute. He is also the senior partner of Edmondson Associates, an entrepreneur training and small business consulting firm based in Southfield, Missouri, and Atlanta, Georgia. He is the President of F.A.I.T.H.S. Restaurants, Inc., which formerly owned and operated Denny's and A&W restaurants and currently owns A&W Foods catering services.

Edmondson served four years in the U.S. Air Force as a law enforcement officer; he holds an associate degree in criminal justice from Arkansas State University and a Bachelor's degree in business finance from Cleary College. With these accomplishments he also serves as an executive trustee of the International Third World Leadership Association (ITWLA) chaired by Dr. Myles Munroe, a UN representative to the United Nations Headquarters in Geneva, and Board of Trustees for the Charles H. Wright Museum of African American History.

His restaurant career began in 1987 when he joined the Kentucky Fried Chicken team. After various promotions Edmondson led the nation in restaurant sales and profits as a market manager/director of operations. In 1994 his success came to an end as Edmondson was abruptly terminated. Edmondson endured a one-year battle with unemployment, which led him to six months of spiritual recovery through the Word of God. During his struggles with attorneys and civil rights organizations for wrongful discharge justification, Edmondson started his own restaurant consultant company, F.A.I.T.H.S. Restaurants, Inc. It was from this experience that he connected with the Denny's restaurant chain as the first graduate of the Fast Track Franchise Program. In July 1996, Edmondson made headlines as the Nations 1st Minority Denny's Franchise graduate owner. In November 1998, Edmondson also became the 1st Black A&W Restaurant franchise owner.

As a businessman, Edmondson understands how the current workforce's lack of talent and work ethic affects business growth. Edmondson founded Christian Business Network-Entrepreneur Training Institute in 1998 out of a need to compel business owners and leaders around the world to commit themselves and their business to Christ. His desire to deploy entrepreneurs led to the expansion of the CBN Entrepreneur Training Institute, which focuses on helping potential and existing entrepreneurs learn the skills needed to create, develop, and strengthen successful business ventures.

Edmondson often acknowledges that his wife, Alena, saved his spiritual and physical life. He consistently makes an effort to impart leadership and godly principles into the lives of young people through his Youth Protégé Program (Y2P).

Valerie Daniels-Carter[10] is another wealth builder. She is president and chief executive officer of V&J Holding Company, Inc., a company she started in 1982 with her brother John. V&J is an operator of Burger King and Pizza Hut restaurants with over 100 restaurants in four states. V&J is the largest African American-owned restaurant franchise operator in the U.S. with 137 restaurants that total $70 billion in sales.

As president and CEO of the country's largest African American-owned restaurant franchise, Valerie and her brother, John Daniels, a lawyer, own V&J Foods Holding Companies Inc., which controls 96 Pizza Huts, and 41 Burger Kings throughout the Midwest and New York.

She stated: "If you would have asked me in 1982, when I first started my application process, whether or not I thought I would have 98 restaurants in 1997, I would have said, 'heck, I'm just happy to get one.' But it's an evolving industry, and I don't ever say can't, never, or no."

In 1997, as President of the Minority Franchise Association of Burger King, which had 60 minority operators out of more than 6,300 franchises nationwide, Daniels-Carter says that having qualified employees has been her key to success.

> My faith in God has kept me with the wherewithal and the energy to move forward. I don't put my faith in money, I put my faith in God, because money can be here today and gone tomorrow. I recognize that I'm not where I am because I'm great, but I am where I am because God has just gifted me and blessed me, and I don't take that for granted.

Her company has a philosophy: "YOU ARE THE STANDARD OF EXCELLENCE." An entrepreneur well-known in Milwaukee business circles, she is a determined woman of tight focus, who learned the value of clear-cut goals early in her life. "Negativity wasn't part of my childhood," she recalled during a December 1997 interview with the *Milwaukee Journal Sentinel*. "We grew up with our parents telling us, "You can achieve anything you want to achieve.""

Along with a determination to succeed, Daniels-Carter intensely studied fast-food industry. As she told *Black Enterprise* magazine in August of 1998: "You have to have a true understanding of the industry you're entering. And you have to surround yourself with a circle of key advisors, accountants, attorneys, and counselors."

Daniels-Carter believes fervently that successful people must give something back to the community that has helped them on their way. She feeds the hungry from her restaurants every Thanksgiving and allows her restaurants to be used for fundraising purposes. She also staffs her restaurants with local residents.

She has been instrumental in the development and implementation of numerous community projects, several of which are: Daniels-Carter Youth Center; Jeffrey A. Carter Sr. Center for Community Empowerment and Family Reunification; HR Senior Housing Complex; CH Mason Health Clinic; HR Educational Complex; No Child Left Behind Christmas, Purchase of Christmas presents for children of employees, church members, and other persons in the community.

Ms. Daniels-Carter was recognized as one of *Essence* Magazine's Trailblazer in the Top 40 Inspiring African-Americans (2003). She is also a recipient of the Top 10 Black Female Entrepreneurs (1999 & 2000); *Black Enterprise* magazine's Women of the B.E. 100; The Heritage Award from Spiritual Perspective (1999); and many others. Her company, V&J has received awards such as the Top 500 Women-owned Businesses (*Working Woman* magazine); Top 200 Restaurants in the U.S. (*Restaurant Finance*

Monitor); Top 100 Black-owned Businesses (*Black Enterprise* magazine); and numerous other accolades, both locally and nationally.

Jerome Edmondson and Valerie Daniels-Carter serve as models of what can happen when education and industry come together in people who were once disenfranchised by a broken economic system. The grace of God will lift us up. He will help us accomplish things others thought were impossible.

ENDNOTES

1. Ben Franklin quote source Virginia Ely, *I Quote* (New York: George W. Stewart Publishers, Inc., 1947), 356.

2. http://www.israports.org.il/, accessed 2/3/08.

3. China port statement List of world's busiest ports by cargo tonnage, years 2002-2005: http://en.wikipedia.org/wiki/World%27s_busiest_ port_by_cargo_tonnage, accessed 2/15/2008.

4. "U.S. Customs Container Security Initiative Guards America, Global Commerce From Terrorist Threat"; http://www.cbp.gov/xp/cgov/ newsroom/news_releases/archives/legacy/2002/112002/11012002_4.xml, accessed 2/3/08.

5. Israel. (2007) In *Encyclopedia Britannica*. Retrieved August 22, 2007, from Encyclopedia Britannica Online: http://www.britannica.com/ eb/article-23092.

6. Ibid., http://www.britannica.com/eb/article-23093.

7. Phyllis A. Balch, *Prescription for Nutritional Healing* (New York: Avery Publishers, 2006).

8. http://www.nativevillage.org/Messages from the People/21st poverty_facts, 21st Century Poverty Facts and Stats.

9. Edmondson Associates, http://www.edmondsonassociates.com/Portal/desktopPages/JE_Bio.htm.

10. Valerie Daniels-Carter, http://www.exodusnews.com/Religion/Religion032.htm.

Chapter 6

THREE HISTORICAL UNDERSTANDINGS OF FIRSTFRUITS

Thou shalt not delay to offer the first of thy ripe fruits, and of thy liquors: the firstborn of thy sons shalt thou give unto Me. Likewise shalt thou do with thine oxen, and with thy sheep: seven days it shall be with his dam; on the eighth day thou shalt give it Me (Exodus 22:29-30).

It has been established in previous chapters the astounding strategy of God to bring about a transference of wealth, from the wicked to the righteous. Perhaps part of His plan encompasses bringing many wicked into the salvation experience. What a tremendous idea from a Kingdom and Great Commission perspective! It is incumbent upon Kingdom citizens, then, to begin preparations for this gradual transfer.

Once we're settled in the unbending reliability of the sovereign end of this plan, how do we participate to maintain a constancy of its flow? This chapter deals with the human level of participation, what I call the proactive side for us. There must be a point of entry, a plausible place to begin. It's extremely important that we consider what the Lord said to do first.

In my early years of intense Bible study, I presumed the Lord first challenged the children of Israel with giving opportunities connected with the Tabernacle of Moses. Theoretically, this would seem the most accurate train of thought since the Tabernacle was built before they entered the Promised Land. How wrong I was!

FIRSTFRUITS

The first offering the Lord spoke to them about was the *firstfruits*, and not building construction offerings or tithes as we understand and practice them today. This amazed me! But, it made sense. Since God is a God of priorities, He will speak about first things first. God was casting vision, preparing them for days ahead. It is also important to realize that the Book of Exodus accounts for their beginning days and months of transition, from Egypt to the Promised Land; so most of their instructions were transitional and transformational by nature. It would be impossible to fulfill what the Lord was commanding them to do without productive efficiency in the Promised Land. Since the wilderness wasn't their inheritance, the commands of God had to be implemented later.

As I reread Exodus chapters 22 and 23 for contemplative purposes, I was pleasantly surprised. There were certain Scriptures I had overlooked. What really arrested my attention was when the Holy Spirit, like a laser, zeroed in on *"the first ripe fruits"* and *"the first of the firstfruits"* in these chapters. At that point, I realized there must be at least two parts or more to this idea called *firstfruits*. Perplexed for a moment, I wondered how I missed this for almost four decades. I am now traveling a path I've never been on before; in fact, one less traveled by most Christians. I set out to discover what the first of the firstfruits were. If I could determine exactly what it was, then the remainder of the firstfruits would certainly be revealed.

First, I needed to biblically define firstfruits. According to Strong's Concordance, the Old Testament employs two particular words for first-fruits: *reshiyth* and *bikkuwr*. Both basically mean "the first, in time, place, order or rank: the beginning, the chief, the first part, or principle thing." This definition is broad enough to cover a great expanse of ideas. Israel was to bring *the first* as the beginning of a series of offerings to God's house.

I will limit our study to production rather than the first of many other things. What was the first release of their production? Only when they began to produce could they enact this principle. The Lord required the children of Israel to participate in this arena on the corporate level and the individual level. It was the establishment of the corporate level that would make the individual so much more meaningful.

FEAST OF FIRSTFRUITS OF THE BARLEY HARVEST

And the Lord spake unto Moses, saying, speak unto the chil-dren of Israel, and say unto them, when ye come into the land which I give unto you, and shall reap the harvest thereof, then ye shall bring a sheaf of the **firstfruits** *of your harvest unto the priest: and he shall wave the sheaf before the Lord, to be accepted for you: on the morrow after the Sabbath the priest shall wave it* (Leviticus 23:9-11).

Israel experienced two distinct grain harvests: barley and wheat. The Lord had spoken concerning how the land would be a land of wheat and barley. (See Deuteronomy 8:8.) In terms of harvest order, barley came first and afterward wheat. Along with their commemoration and celebration of the Passover lamb, the Feast of Firstfruits was observed at the beginning of the barley harvest, when the first grain came in. The first sheaf of the new crop, together with a sacrifice, was presented as a wave offering before the Lord on the day after the Passover Sabbath. They were waved before the Lord in their natural state.

The importance of this observation was more than ceremonial, in the sense that it reminded them of God's involvement in their harvest. The words of Jesus to His disciples could be supplemented here as well: *"I am the vine, ye are the branches: he that abideth in Me, and I in him, the same bringeth forth much fruit: **for without Me ye can do nothing**"* (John 15:5). The sheaf of firstfruits acknowledged that all came from God and belonged to Him. If God wasn't involved with the intangibles, there would be no harvest period. Nothing was to be used for food until this ceremony had been performed. It was the noteworthy acknowledgement of divine providence. (See Leviticus 23:9-14.)

Some 1,500 years later, Jesus Christ became the antitype of all that this ceremony represented. For us, no truth has relevance until we understand the Christological revelation. We must always interpret the pictures of the Old Testament under New Testament light. What happened to Jesus had a direct correlation to the Scriptures, beginning with Moses and procedures like the sheaf of firstfruits. (See Luke 24:27.) When Christ was raised from the dead the third day, He became the firstfruit of all who slept and were awaiting general resurrection. Someone may ask: "Didn't Jesus raise people from the dead before He was raised from the dead?" Yes, but not exactly. All the people Jesus called forth from the dead died again. That's a fact of history. However, in the case of Jesus, once He was raised, death could no longer touch Him. (See Romans 6:9.)

This event was so phenomenal that the disciples thought the women, the first clarions of His resurrection after the angels, were speaking idle tales. Years after our Lord's resurrection, Paul wrote beautifully: *"But now is Christ risen from the dead, and become the **firstfruits** of them that slept. For since by man came death, by man came also the resurrection of the dead. For as in Adam all die, even so in Christ shall all be made alive. But every man in his own order: Christ the **firstfruits**; afterward they that are Christ's at His coming"* (1 Cor. 15:20-23).

The truth of harvest allows us to see the power of life over death. There's a starting point, or someone who is first in order and rank to experience this as a seed corn. His name is Jesus. It's equally important to note that His resurrection indicates we will be raised as well. The great sixteenth century reformer, Dr. Martin Luther, said, "Our Lord has written the promise of the resurrection, not in books alone, but in every leaf in springtime."[1]

On the Cross, Jesus suffered, bled, and died the most gruesome, dishonoring death as the Son of God. His experience was horrific, but only to the extent in which He agreed as *"the Lamb slain from the foundation of the world"* (Rev. 13:8). The pre-existing covenant cut between the members of the Godhead predetermined and settled eternally this direction. God's wisdom kept this information away from men until His plan could be executed; otherwise they would have aborted it. Jesus lived out in His earthsuit what He said yes to as the eternal Word in the timeless zone of spirit. In resurrection, Christ was victoriously waved before the heavenly Father as the sheaf of firstfruits. It was now permissible for the rest of the harvest—a different genesis—to begin. Seven weeks later the beginnings of the bulk of the harvest commences.

Feast of Pentecost Firstfruits

*And thou shalt observe the feast of weeks, of the **firstfruits** of wheat harvest, and the feast of ingathering at the year's end* (Exodus 34:22).

Fifty days after the completion of the sheaf of firstfruits were waved before the Lord, a new kind of firstfruits were offered. Again, as Passover dealt with the barley harvest, Pentecost occurred at the completion of the wheat harvest. The first of the wheat was to be brought to the Lord at this time. This wheat was to be baked into two wave loaves in which leaven was to be used. (See Leviticus 23:17,20.) The loaves of Pentecost were presented to the Lord by simply waving them before Him, with no portion of the loaves burned.

The Feast Day of Pentecost gives us an ecclesiological perspective to the firstfruits ideal. By revelation, the two wave loaves represent the Jewish loaf, and then the Gentile loaf later. (See Acts 2 and Acts 10.) God's order is first the Jewish people, and then the Gentiles. (See Romans 1:16.) Previous moves of God are afforded the opportunity to respond to the new thing God is doing first! The two loaves would eventually become one bread. Paul said: *"For we being many are one bread, and one body: for we are all partakers of that one bread"* (1 Cor. 10:17). The Church of Jesus Christ, with all its variety and diversity, is one bread. I can visualize the priest waving the two loaves from a point of separation to a point of togetherness. Various groups of people helped to create the firstfruits of the New Testament harvest.

Paul even further said: *"For He is our peace, who hath made both one, and hath broken down the middle wall of partition between us; having abolished in His flesh the enmity, even the law of commandments contained in ordinances; for to make in Himself of twain one new man, so making peace"* (Eph. 2:14-15).

Five times in the New Testament the term *firstfruits* is in reference to the Church. First, the apostle Paul stated, *"For if the firstfruit be holy, the lump* [SC #5445. Phurama, which means "to mix a liquid with a solid through the idea of swelling in bulk: to knead a mass of dough"] *is holy: and if the root be holy, so are the branches"* (Rom. 11:16). Apparently, the apostle Paul draws from the analogy of the *dough firstfruits* in Numbers 15:17-21. These cakes were actually pierced cakes, which reveal the Church does fellowship the sufferings of our Lord by being pierced. Men wounded Him for us; and men will wound us because of Him.

From a holy and righteous perspective, the whole Church is appraised on the basis of the firstfruit and the root. Applying proper interpretation, Jesus is the firstfruit and the root; His Church is the lump and the branches. (See John 15:5.) The heavenly Father judges us strictly on His view of Christ. We are now reconciled through the death of Jesus and presented as holy, unblameable, and unreproveable in the sight of Father God. (See Colossians 1:21-22.)

Second, the apostle James said, *"Of His own will begat He us with the word of truth, that we should be a kind of **firstfruits** of His creatures"* (James 1:18). A new creation came to planet Earth in the person of Jesus Christ. The Word of Truth, as incorruptible seed, was planted into the womb of the human experience. Out of the confluence of divine and human interaction comes a byproduct totally new and different in nature and quality. This was definitely a divine act, one of God's own choosing. The first-century church, as James said, became as a wheat firstfruits of what God was creating, which would increase in latter generations and more perfectly mature.

To further amplify this principle, the apostle Paul writes, *"Likewise greet the church that is in their house. Salute my well beloved Epaenetus, who is the firstfruits of Achaia unto Christ"* (Rom. 16:5). It seems that he speaks of the same group in First Corinthians 16:15-16: *"I beseech you, brethren, (ye know the house of Stephanas, that it is the firstfruits of Achaia, and that they have addicted themselves to the ministry of the saints,) that ye submit yourselves unto such, and to every one that helpeth with us, and laboreth."* We can safely conclude that people form the highest kind of firstfruits unto God.

Third, the apostle Paul describes the measure of the Holy Spirit in earthen vessels presently: *"And not only they, but ourselves also, which have the **firstfruits** of the Spirit, even we ourselves groan within ourselves, waiting for the adoption, to wit, the redemption of our body"* (Rom. 8:23). In this context, two concepts are synonymous: *the firstfruits and the earnest payment*. We all experience the Holy Spirit by measure *(earnest)* until the appointed time when we all experience Him without measure *(fullness)*. The first measure is called firstfruits or earnest portion. An earnest pledge of anything equates to a down payment. God's pledge to the human race to complete His initiatives starts with an earnest payment. Many times, when we buy large capital purchases they begin by our commitment to give a down payment, which suggests we will complete the payment process.

When we received the baptism of the Holy Spirit, it was God's powerful statement of also producing a final outcome. The end result is in the firstfruit statement. By law, then, the first is in the last and the last in the first. *"In whom ye also trusted, after that ye heard the word of truth, the gospel of your salvation: in whom also after that ye believed, ye were sealed with that Holy Spirit of promise, which is the earnest of our inheritance until the redemption of the purchased possession, unto the praise of His glory"*

(Eph. 1:13-14). From a forensic viewpoint, the mortal world that the first Adam created was swallowed up by the immortality and incorruptibility of the last Adam. The baptism of the Holy Spirit is the guarantee, the sign or token, that our natural bodies will catch up to what has happened in our spirit. (See 2 Corinthians 5:4-5.) In fact, it is like the old fashioned canning process I observed with my parents—where the sealing of the jar was the final step of preservation. Sealing guaranteed that the contents would stay within and corruption would stay without. The Holy Spirit is the insurance Christ will stay within us until God has finished His work. And as we yield to Him, the corrupting influences of the old Adamic world will stay without.

INDIVIDUAL OFFERING OF FIRSTFRUITS

*The first of the **firstfruits** of thy land thou shalt bring into the house of the Lord thy God. Thou shalt not seethe a kid in his mother's milk* (Exodus 23:19; 34:26).

When I first read this Scripture, it somewhat baffled me! The context shows that God was speaking to the children of Israel as families and individuals. God, through Moses, was laying out all the principles of how to function as a Kingdom culture, a holy nation, and a peculiar people just before he ratified the covenant with blood. Why would the Lord direct Moses to place what appears to be two disjointed thoughts together to form important instructions?

As I meditated on and pondered this verse, the Holy Spirit gave me some incredible light. Most civilized nations frown upon and prevent animal cruelty. In fact, a person could end up incarcerated or paying a stiff fine if convicted. If I weren't convinced of the sanctity placed on human life, I would think the judicial system cares more for felines and canines than people. It would be inhumane to boil (seethe) a young goat (kid) in his mother's milk. Quite frankly, it is unthinkable and unconscionable to cook anything or anyone in that which has been purposed to nurture and feed them.

Then I had a *kairos moment*—a heavenly download! If to treat a young goat in this manner is cruel, then it would be cruel not to bring the firstfruits of the land into the house of the Lord. This thought stayed with me as I studied the concept of the firstfruits.

Individual firstfruits were brought into the house of the Lord as a part of family worship *after* harvest times. It is safe to conclude that harvests precipitate giving. Through the Passover sheaf, and by the Pentecostal loaves, the nation of Israel fully acknowledged God as Lord of the harvest. Every family and each individual specifically acknowledged the Lord by the yearly presentation of the firstfruits. An attitude of gratitude was conveyed in this act of worship, submitting to the fact that God's hands bountifully supplied the harvest as a blessing, and for their enjoyment.

Rabbis established sophisticated rules for the exact time of the year, as well as for the stage of growth, when produce was to be given. "Generally, the people began to bring firstfruits to Jerusalem after the Feast Day of Pentecost until December."[2] Because they were to be heaved and waved before the Lord, the Scriptures spoke of the firstfruits and the heave offering in the same breath.

In Deuteronomy 26:1-11, Moses gave us a notable glimpse of what a firstfruits worship ceremony was like. What an auspicious occasion—a moment of reflection, an observance of joy. In a most persuasive display,

God is recognized as title holder and benefactor of all, and His people the recipients of His bequest, dependants on His blessing, and the custodians of His property. As time passed, the people developed creative ways of identifying the firstfruits. Usually, they were marked from the onset of the most promising portion of the harvest before the harvest was actually gathered in order to preserve its integrity and to present the best to the Lord. Thus, each time someone would enter the field, he would be continually reminded of the ownership of the Lord until the full harvest. The head of the household would go among the fruit trees and the vineyards, and stopping at each *best* tree, tie a rush around the stem, and say: "*Lo, these are the firstfruits!*"[3]

"The fundamental idea behind any giving in the Scriptures is that of substitution."[3] Webster defines *substitution* as "somebody or something that replaces another and has equal value." Any type of firstfruit giving would be considered as though one gave everything to God. The agricultural firstfruits stood for the whole produce in the fields. The firstlings of the flock are as though one gave the entire flock. The redemption money was necessary for each firstborn son who could not be offered on the altar of sacrifice. And the life of the sacrificial victim, which is in its blood (see Lev. 17:11), actually stood for the life of the one sacrificing.

So how important is this firstfruits matter? It stands to satisfy that desire in every true child of God to give their Lord and Master everything. When we hastily without delay bring God firstfruits, Heaven records this as the gift of all that we are and can be.

Concerning individual firstfruits, the Lord did not leave it to the imaginations of the people to determine what they were. He said, "*All the **best** of the oil, and all the **best** of the wine, and of the wheat, the firstfruits of them* *which they shall offer unto the Lord, them have I given thee. And whatsoever is first ripe in the land, which they shall bring unto the Lord, shall be thine; every one that is clean in thine house shall eat of it. Every thing devoted in Israel shall be thine*" (Num. 18:12-14). From these verses, it is evident that firstfruits consisted of grains and ripened fruit from the trees and the vintage. Grains ripened in early spring and early summer and fruits through the summer and into the fall of the year.

Why give the best? Prophetically it reminds us of Father God giving His best to humanity in the person of Christ. Because of this, the final Scripture with the concept of the firstfruits in the New Testament directly relates to the oil and wine firstfruits mentioned in the Book of Numbers. Oil and wine were connected to the Feast of Tabernacles just as barley was to the Feast of Passover and wheat to the Feast of Pentecost. Since Tabernacles was the end of the agricultural year, it speaks to us of the completed firstfruits harvest at the end of the age.

Most of the canonized New Testament speaks of the firstfruits from an ecclesiological viewpoint; whereas the Revelation of Jesus Christ speaks to us from an eschatological viewpoint. The former being the early development of the church primarily because of the Pentecostal experience; the latter being the maturing of the Body of Christ in the end of the age because of the Feast of Tabernacles. The apostle John captures this overcoming company with this metaphor: "*These are they which were not defiled with women* [the carnal realm]; *for they are virgins. These are they which follow the Lamb whithersoever He goeth. These were redeemed from among men, being the* **firstfruits** *unto God and to the Lamb*" (Rev. 14:4).

Obviously, we can not literalize this Scripture, for in doing so married people would be excluded. I define spiritual virginity as the quality of life that completely follows Jesus regardless. This group is an end-time harvest like no other harvest in New Testament times. The heavenly Father brings conclusion to a long process in a virgin company. Because of that fact, they are likened to the oil and wine firstfruits of Numbers 18:12. Note the full dedication of these redeemed men and women; regardless, they follow the Lord implicitly. When the apostle John mentions the oil and wine in another text, we get a feel for this idea of full commitment. He said, *"And I heard a voice in the midst of the four beasts say, a measure of wheat for a penny, and three measures of barley for a penny; and see thou hurt not the oil and the wine"* (Rev. 6:6). Wheat and barley are measured and valued; however, the oil and wine have no measurements or particular values placed on them. Why can't the oil and wine be hurt?

If we consider how oil and wine are extracted, the revelation is simple. We get oil and wine through crushing olives and grapes. Jesus encountered Gethsemane (the oil press) before He went to Calvary. The apostles and disciples experienced the bruising darkness of the soul before receiving the new wine of Pentecost. One can no longer injure what has been absolutely squashed. Oil and wine represent the life-blood of things that were once in another form.

I already see a people in this new apostolic reformation who have suffered the crushing press of the Lord—a death to selfishness like no other generation. Starting in the form of the first Adam, the blow of the Cross brings people to a place of being conformed to the image and likeness of the last Adam. They lose their individual identity as single olive berries and grapes and form a corporate expression of oil and wine. The identifying markers in them will be the nature and character of the Lamb, for they are His firstfruits.

TIME OF CAPTIVITY

*And the first of all the **firstfruits** of all things, and every oblation of all, of every sort of your oblation, shall be the priest's: ye shall also give unto the priest the first of your dough, that he may cause the blessing to rest in thine house* (Ezekiel 44:30).

The events in the Book of Ezekiel were recorded during the time of Israel's captivity in Babylon. Most of the children of Israel were in either stubborn denial or despondency about what had happened. Portions of Habakkuk's prophecy dared to voice his opinion about the way God was conducting His business just prior to Israel's deportation into Babylon. Habakkuk started with, "God how could you?" His puzzled befuddlement and God-accusations have been repeated century after century by someone almost every day. How could God use violent, wicked people to discipline people more righteous than they? How could God allow any despot or despotic nation to prosper? (I have found myself asking the same question regarding some of the more recent world events.) However, Habakkuk comes to a place of love and resolve, knowing that trusting God produces something wonderful in the end. If we wait on God long enough, the things producing bewilderment will come to an end.

Ezekiel chapter 44 deals with the priesthood during the time of captivity and their allegiance to the principles of God. There were priests who remained faithful and those who were unfaithful. Certain promises are made to both groups. The Lord elaborates concerning the responsibilities of the faithful priest during the latter discourse of Ezekiel chapter 44. Instructions were given concerning the presentation of the firstfruits unto the priest. It had been established that firstfruits were the primary support structure for priests. (See Deuteronomy 18:4.) The Message Bible gives us a strong rendering of what God said about the priests:

> *As to priests owning land, I am their inheritance. Don't give any land in Israel to them. I am their land, their inheritance. They'll take their meals from the grain offerings, the sin offerings, and the guilt offerings. Everything in Israel offered to God in worship is theirs. The best of everything grown, plus all special gifts, comes to the priests. All that is given in worship to God goes to them. Serve them first. Serve from your best and your home will be blessed* (Ezekiel 44:28-30).

While the people are in the throes of captivity, the Lord speaks with them about the firstfruits principle, which they had more than likely violated just as they had overproduced the land, thus breaching its Sabbath laws. Whenever contravention occurred, the land failed to produce as guaranteed by the covenant.

> *The field is wasted, the land mourned; the corn is wasted: the new wine is dried up, the oil languisheth. Be ye ashamed, O ye husbandmen; howl, O ye vinedressers, for the wheat and for the barley; because the harvest of the field is perished. The vine is dried up, and the fig tree languisheth; the pomegranate tree, the palm tree also, and the apple tree, even all the trees of the field, are withered: because joy is withered away from the sons of men* (Joel 1:10-12).

Joel revealed that all the harvest items that constituted firstfruits were non-existent; therefore Israel was a joyless, empty society. One cannot bring firstfruits, provide gleanings for the poor, or anything else if there is no harvest. I see the same susceptibility in the modern church; we attempt celebrations, revivals, and feasts without harvests of people. Widespread crop failure happens when God's people violate His commandments and principles. Humiliating captivity serves as an incarceration period as they purify their hearts. Obviously, greed was one of the reasons they were in this condition.

The Lord reminded them in the midst of their despair not to forget the verdict He had established for the priests. He didn't speak to them about tithes or any of the other offerings at this point. There was a necessity to re-establish the order of first things. It is fruitless to speak of other giving commands when people fail to walk in primary financial literacy.

REFORMATION AND RESTORATION

During times of revival, restoration, and reformation, the people abundantly brought firstfruits to the priests. One of the most extraordinary examples is during the reign of King Hezekiah. He was distinguished as one of Judah's greatest kings when it came to displaying his faith, though he wasn't renowned for great spiritual gifts. Sincere and devout, Hezekiah was admirable when considering his family background. His father, Ahaz, provided no virtuous preparation, for he was a wicked and despicable king. His heritage was one of spiritual weakness, moral failure, and everything that could embarrass a future king. However, the sovereign hand of God, through the encouragement of the prophet Isaiah, caused Hezekiah to excel in the things of God. His simple, uncomplicated faith in God was the key to his success. He recognized that if the nation was to be prosperous the priests and Levites must have their appropriate portions.

> *Moreover he [Hezekiah] commanded the people that dwelt in Jerusalem to give the portion of the priests and the Levites, that they might be encouraged in the law of the Lord. And as soon as the commandment came abroad, the children of Israel brought in abundance the firstfruits of corn, wine, and oil, and honey, and of all the increase of the field; and the tithe of all things brought they in abundantly. And concerning the children of Israel and Judah, that dwelt in the cities of Judah, they also brought in the tithe of oxen and sheep, and the tithe of holy things which were consecrated unto the Lord their God, and laid them by heaps. In the third month they began to lay the foundation of the heaps, and finished them in the seventh month* (2 Chronicles 31:4-7).

The people of God responded to the command of the king concerning the firstfruits and the tithes. If you'll notice, firstfruit and tithe are distinct in these writings for the purpose of establishing differentiation.

When people are in a perpetual state of joy, they give uninhibitedly from their production and incomes. No one has to twist arms or play games with people's minds to get them to give in these conditions. Abundant giving directly links to abundant production and prosperity. As a former pastor, I understood that lack, need, fear, and greed prevented people from encouragement giving because they were discouraged about their financial condition. Most people are motivated to do what they do either out of fear or faith, both are strong emotional forces.

Judah and Israel responded in faith and brought so much it had to be stacked in heaps. Note carefully the extended time period it took to gather their charitable generosity. Instantaneously, I see the period of time between the Feasts of Pentecost (third month) and Tabernacles (the seventh month). Can you imagine today's church doing this? In fact, it would be quite shocking and captivating to receive an offering of this magnitude, which took three months to count!

NEHEMIAH

Another powerful season of reformation giving was during the days of Nehemiah, the seasoned soldier and statesman. Although born a refugee, he demonstrated priceless patriotism and steadfast faith for Israel's God. When permitted to return to the Promised Land, he fearlessly labored for the wholesomeness of public worship, the veracity of family life, and the inviolability of the Sabbath.

After captivity, the returnees to Jerusalem covenanted with him to give the firstfruits and tithes faithfully to the house of God. It would have been difficult at best to rebuild without a sound support structure established upon the principles of God's Word. When it came to firstfruits and tithes, Nehemiah made sure they were distributed to the priests in a systematic manner.

*And we cast the lots among the priests, the Levites, and the people, for the wood offering, to bring it into the house of our God, after the houses of our fathers, at times appointed year by year, to burn upon the altar of the Lord our God, as it is written in the law: and to bring the **firstfruits** of our* *ground, and the **firstfruits** of all fruit of all trees, year by year, unto the house of the Lord: also the **firstborn** of our sons, and of our cattle, as it is written in the law, and the **firstlings** of our herds and of our flocks, to bring to the house of our God, unto the priests that minister in the house of our God: and that we should bring the **firstfruits** of our dough, and our offerings, and the fruit of all manner of trees, of wine and of oil, unto the priests, to the chambers of the house of our God; and the **tithes** of our ground unto the Levites, that the same Levites might have the **tithes** in all the cities of our tillage. And the priest the sons of Aaron shall be with the Levites, when the Levites take **tithes**: and the Levites shall bring up the **tithe of the tithes** unto the house of our God, to the chambers, into the treasure house* (Nehemiah 10:34-38).

Nehemiah understood the meticulousness of the law concerning firstfruits and tithes. He doesn't leave one stone unturned, nor does he get confused. In this stage of reformation, it is important to understand the properly blended life of what we call the sacred and the secular. Nehemiah, the secular leader, was a very spiritual man; though today we would call his primary occupation a building contractor. Because people attempt to categorize these two (secular and sacred) into separate distinctions, they sometimes miss the entirety of life God determines for us to live. A gratifying, lucid life must be a balance of the two. I'm not exactly sure when people began to separate sacred and secular other than to appease some carnal agenda. It certainly isn't a Bible position at all.

One of the great fallacies enveloping the culture in the United States centers on this separation idea. Because of the narrowness of some Christian points-of-view, I can sense the heavenly Father's safety by allowing this thing to be for now. However, when this separation is left in tact without Kingdom adjustments, we see a damaged life in our application of daily Kingdom work. For instance, I'm a teacher of the Gospel, and my work is considered sacred. A businessperson, government worker, and educator are considered by society as secular employees. Both groups need to understand we are conducting Kingdom business, but in different genres. My labor is no more important to the Kingdom than a garbage man, provided we both understand whom we're laboring together with. (See 1 Corinthians 3:9.) Nehemiah is a wonderful example of a leader who was able to bridge the great divide between what is labeled sacred and secular. Along with Ezra, a scholar and teacher, they did great exploits for the nation of Israel during the reformation process.

One further observation: there must be a responsible structure established in this realm once we discern the move and flow of the Holy Spirit. It is what I call an *operating organism*. Moves of God start in the Spirit realm traveling to the earthly domain. Spirit and earth touching one another creates a birthing zone. The birth takes place in the earth, which is the realm of containers without, necessarily, the spirit of containment.

In order to prevent what I call "crazy kingdom," one of the metaphors for the Spirit of God moving is a river. Every river has banks or boundaries. People become containers or borders of God's glory without the ruse of trying to control Him or His movements. Now that Nehemiah had reestablished the necessity of the firstfruits and the tithes, he also provided wise stewards, or containers, for His grace. The instructions were a God-idea; the leadership implementation was men responding to God's idea. Men were commissioned as overseers to assist Israel in the nation's responsibilities.

> *And at that time were some appointed over the chambers for the treasures, for the offerings, for the firstfruits, and for the tithes, to gather into them out of the fields of the cities the portions of the law for the priests and Levites: for Judah rejoiced for the priests and for the Levites that waited. And both the singers and the porters kept the ward of their God, and the ward of the purification, according to the commandment of David, and of Solomon his son. For in the days of David and Asaph of old there were chief of the singers, and songs of praise and thanksgiving unto God. And all Israel in the days of Zerubbabel, and in the days of Nehemiah, gave the portions of the singers and the porters, every day his portion: and they sanctified holy things unto the Levites; and the Levites sanctified them unto the children of Aaron* (Nehemiah 12:44-47).

These verses exude with the spirit of dedication and interdependence, or what we would call a *one another spirit*. All of Israel contributed the daily allowances of the singers and security guards; and they also set aside portions for the Levites, and the Levites did the same for the priests. It seems no one is motivated by covetousness, greed, or selfishness. Nehemiah was an unselfish leader and the people modeled his example. When people can become unselfish long enough to rejoice over the success of someone else, something holy and unadulterated happens in the realm of the Kingdom. Such was the case in Nehemiah's day. Israel was

201

filled with blithesomeness, mirth, a spirit of glee; no one is complaining about what they are giving. The same may be true of us in the postmodern world if we will allow the Holy Spirit to fill us with His unmodified agenda rather than our own alternate one.

When Nehemiah had faithfully executed his assignment, he closed his memoirs with a very apposite statement.

> *All in all I cleansed them from everything foreign. I organized the orders of service for the priests and Levites so that each man knew his job. I arranged for a regular supply of altar wood at the appointed times and for the **firstfruits**. Remember me, O my God, for good* (Nehemiah 13:30-31 TM).

Nehemiah had accomplished many things in reforming God's people to the principles of His Word. High on the list was His commitment to the order of the firstfruits. Obviously, in God's mind, this was also extremely important. For which, he asked the Lord to keep him in mind *for good*.

ENDNOTES

1. R. Daniel Watkins, *An Encyclopedia of Compelling Quotations,* (Peabody, MA: Hendrickson Publishers, Inc., 2001), 625.

2. Alfred Edersheim, *The Temple—Its Ministry and Services Updated Edition,* (Peabody, MA: Hendrickson Publishers, Inc., 1994), 303.

3. Ibid, 306.

4. Ibid, 76.

Chapter 7

JESUS AND THE FIRSTFRUITS IDIOM

Lay not up for yourselves treasures upon the earth, where moth and rust doth corrupt, and where thieves break through and steal: but lay up for yourselves treasures in heaven, where neither moth nor rust doth corrupt, and where thieves do not break through nor steal: for where your treasure is, there will your heart be also. The light of the body is the eye: if therefore thine eye be single, thy whole body shall be full of light. But if thine eye be evil, thy whole body shall be full of darkness. If therefore the light that is in thee be darkness, how great is that darkness! No man can serve two masters: for either he will hate the one, and love the other; or else he will hold to the one, and despise the other. Ye cannot serve God and mammon (Matthew 6:19-24).

Matthew chapter 6 places us diametrically in the middle of Jesus teaching what some scholars call the "constitution of the Kingdom of God." He discusses two major temptations we all face as believers that distract us from our relationship with our heavenly Father.

The first temptation deals with a need in most religious people for public approval by peers for their accomplishments instead of doing things covertly before our Father. The examples that He used to clearly communicate this point are alms giving, prayer, and fasting. Because most people battle with rejection and identity issues, what others think of them is highly important. They refuse to wait for the open reward from the heavenly Father. When we are square about whom Christ is in us, these things subside.

The second temptation spins out of the first one. People often place value in things they think will gain them acknowledgement before others. So often we place our treasures into something ridiculous knowing full well the outcome. We seek security with temporal things, trusting them to fill the vacuum and empty wastelands in our souls. These conditions come from lusts ambushing and circumventing our relationship with our heavenly Father. Both of these temptations must be identified and conquered.

Where do we begin? First, it is very important to understand that Jesus Christ's public ministry was at the end of the Law Dispensation. He even said, "*I am not sent but unto the lost sheep of the house of Israel*" (Matt. 15:24). Jesus had no gaffe about His mission. He was ending, transitioning, and introducing something new all at once. Therefore, He was well acquainted with all the patterns of thinking in people of His day. He demonstrated for them that He came to fulfill the Law without desecrating it.

Also, He modeled for the people the principle of inward purity concerning the matter of money, storing up treasures, and serving God. Matthew, Mark, Luke, and John could be the memoirs of Jesus' life and ministry as He brought closure to the Law economy and permanently inaugurated the Kingdom.

Many things that Jesus taught and practiced were misunderstood, though His listeners could probably identify some of His metaphors, idioms, and figures of speech. He did not evade any subject which had a direct affect on the Kingdom expressed in our daily lives. He focused first on how things would affect people's hearts—the wellspring of all human behavior. He didn't even avoid the subject most spiritual people consider too taboo to discuss: money. As he tackles the temptation surrounding the fear of lack and the anxiety connected to need, He deals with the force behind them both: *a lack of trust in the integrity of our heavenly Father.*

People's fear of not having enough money,or their fear of losing money stashed away, reveals an inordinate trust in the material rather than the spiritual. Jesus taught us that when we're steeped in eternal realities, sovereign initiatives, and God-provisions, we'll find all our daily human concerns met. The Message Bible says it powerfully: *"Give your entire attention to what God is doing right now, and don't get worked up about what may or may not happen tomorrow. God will help you deal with whatever hard things come up when the time comes"* (Matt. 6:34 TM).

Laying Up Treasure in Heaven

I have often thought about how to lay up treasure in Heaven. Certainly Heaven doesn't need any natural money or treasures since it is the resplendent realm of spiritual realities. How do we accomplish this feat then? If I were laying up monies for the future, I would place it into some type of managed account guaranteeing at least some type of successful return. Where is Heaven's account? Let's explore.

First, our treasures amount to deposits—wealth or words. The word treasure translated from the Greek language is *thesaurus*. A thesaurus is a storehouse or treasury, also a book of related word groups. Are we storing up words, money, or both? Based on the definition of thesaurus, it should be both. When we speak, we send words out as seeds stored up for an appointed time. Our words may penetrate the heavens in prayer or dialogue with the Father as a masterful treasury of the heart; however, that doesn't solve the money dilemma. Since the Heaven of heavens has no money depository, where is Heaven's depository in the earth?

Before we go there, Jesus equally taught that if treasures are placed in the wrong place, corruption, or worse burglary, would occur. Fine clothing was a mark of prosperity in the first century. The best clothes were made of wool and often suffered from moths eating them. Another sign of wealth was barns filled with grain. Rust, or, literally, *an eating*, could consume the store. This perhaps referred to rodents and insects eating away at those storehouse grains. And, of course, thieves were attracted to the amassing of material things by the wealthy, which caused them to break in and steal. Each illustration speaks of something or someone aggressively and illegally violating a person's possessions. If a person's heart was tied up in possessions, any of these things could produce disillusionment.

Jesus also said that our monies will always determine the location of our hearts. In other words, where we devote our treasure will determine where we place our affections. For example, my wife and I invest monthly in our son's education. Certainly, we care about his success or failure as if our sweat-equity has gone into a good cause. If our affections are on things above or heavenly, our treasures will also be there. But if we're focused on self, then we will become greedy and self-indulgent.

I often tell people that if they give me five minutes with their checkbook I can tell them exactly what their hearts are like by examining their spending patterns. People take a vested interest in any project, ministry, or mission they allocate funds to; and they sense part ownership, expressed or not. I personally experienced this with large contributors to our ministry in bygone years.

So how do we lay up deposits in Heaven? It is very important to allow the Scripture to interpret the Scripture. Read carefully.

> *And a certain ruler asked Him, saying, Good Master, what shall I do to inherit eternal life? And Jesus said unto him, why callest thou Me good? None is good, save one, that is, God. Thou knowest the commandments, do not commit adultery, do not kill, do not steal, do not bear false witness, honour thy father and thy mother. And he said, all these have I kept from my youth up. Now when Jesus heard these things, He said unto Him, yet lackest thou one thing: sell all that thou hast, and distribute unto the poor, and thou shalt have treasure in heaven: and come, follow Me. And when he heard this, he was very sorrowful: for he was very rich* (Luke 18:18-23).

This wealthy young man must have been quite awed with the ministry of Jesus. There's no indication of how often he listened to Jesus teach or minister to broken humanity; however, something touched him, provoking him to ask Jesus, "What is it going to take to be like you?" Being that he was rich, he was use to dealing in terms of how much does something cost? Those who are wealthy based upon this world's standards often misunderstand what it takes to follow Christ wholeheartedly.

In profit-making societies, some people assume everything and everyone have a price. They figure if the price is right, anybody or anything can be purchased. Then we meet someone like Jesus who has already sold out to the heavenly Father; therefore, He has no price, nor can He be impressed by our accomplishments. Jesus had successfully passed this test when the adversary offered Him the kingdoms of this world for a price.

Many young ministers will listen to seasoned Gospel veterans and ask, "How can I be like you?" I have personally had this question asked of me more times than I care to discuss. Or, someone may say, *"When I grow up, I want to be just like you!"* Whether question or statement, what they are asking is: *"What is it going to cost me?"* You should be prepared with an answer if this situation arises. The answer: everything! If we reduce Jesus' response down to simple terms: *"Every person must die to the thing that matters the most to them; anything that gives you identity, security, or a sense of worth outside of a relationship with the heavenly Father must be sacrificed."*

People must understand that in the Kingdom everyone begins at ground zero. Everything we've achieved with our human identity must eventually go. It doesn't matter if you're a Hebrew of Hebrews or listed among *Who's Who*, we all must enter the Kingdom as children totally dependent upon the love, grace, and goodness of our heavenly Father.

Performance-based religion will never merit acceptance into the Kingdom; it is solely a grace matter. Jesus challenged this rich official at the level he understood before raising the bar. This young, successful businessman had no idea it takes more than money to make one rich. This man had kept the relational, horizontal commandments without breaking them from the age of accountability. He was squeaky clean in his obedience. I'll acknowledge that's a pretty impressive resume, except it is the works of flesh apart from the overwhelming, accomplishing power of grace. Imagine the amount of willpower it took not to tell a lie from adolescence!

Jesus lastly dealt with this man in a realm in which he had no performance history. What He spoke to the young man exposed his nakedness. He suddenly had no feeble garments or accomplishments to wrap himself in for comfort. Jesus commanded him to sell everything, step into the law of Kingdom distribution to the poor, and then follow him unreservedly. Jesus equated this level of benefaction and dedication to *"having treasure in heaven."* The one relational commandment the young ruler had not kept was the prohibition against the infection of covetousness. Thus, we can perceive Jesus' wisdom and logic behind commanding him to sell everything.

Our query is answered! When any of us give to the poor, we have found Heaven's primary depository in the earth. The Lord's command and our responsiveness to missions produce several things. First, we are uniting to the Lord and positioning ourselves for full loan repayment by giving to the poor. Second, generosity will never leave us lacking; it prevents a gauntlet of curses connected to selfishness and carries the currency of blessing. Third, giving to the poor is a great equalizer in that, when done from a heart of love, it removes the wretchedness of prideful feelings about wealth. A wealthy station in life gives no man the right to rule and oppress another man. Some of the greatest diatribes and atrocities in human history occurred because the poor felt abused and disrespected by the rich. Every major governmental revolution was filled with carnage because of this.

He that hath pity upon the poor lendeth unto the Lord; and that which he hath given will He pay him again (Proverbs 19:17).

He that giveth unto the poor shall not lack: but he that hideth his eyes shall have many a curse (Proverbs 28:27).

The rich ruleth over the poor, and the borrower is servant to the lender (Proverbs 22:7).

After reading these verses, can you see the premium placed on missions? The propagation of the Gospel of the Kingdom may be summed up in one word: *missions*! If you are searching for a core objective behind wealth redistribution, it's missions, not bigger and better toys for covetous hearts. What the young man had never acknowledged about himself, or anyone else, was how deep-rooted covetousness was embedded in his heart. It was acceptable because the whole culture in Jesus' day was avaricious and materialistic, including the pernicious priests. (See Luke 16:14-15.) This young man, who trusted in his wealth, wouldn't be any different, for he, like the Sadducees and Pharisees around him, looked religious while serving money rather than God. Therefore, he left what was supposed to be an encounter of spiritual enrichment with great sadness of heart. Strong's Concordance suggests he was gloomy through and through; a potentially bright, sunny and uplifting day suddenly turned sour and downcast.

This story teaches us that we should be cautious about what we ask the Lord. He'll analyze each request and answer us in His time. We may even get replies we're not ready to process, though our souls yearn for greater truth, and greater growth in the things of God. Like most people, I have asked questions or made commitments to the Lord that I wasn't ready to live out. I thank God for His tender mercies. I remember saying to the Lord, "I'll go wherever you send me!" I hadn't considered the full ramifications of my statement; He might send me to a state or country I'd rather not live in. I needed to comprehend God's stipulations and supply given with each assignment; He always gives the grace, vision, and provision for the assignment.

If we initially don't like the assignment, we tend to fall back into carnal reasoning in a vain attempt to abort God's instructions. We fail to realize the Lord has given us the keys to the next dimension of spiritual growth. Just like the rich young ruler, we may leave a God-encounter distressed, and fall away into oblivion because we are challenged to give up where we are, to get to where we need to be.

QUALITY OF LIGHT IN A PERSON

The second aspect of Jesus' discourse became the supporting details for the main idea of the heart's condition in giving. He said, *"The light of the body is the eye: if therefore thine eye be single, thy whole body shall be full of light. But if thine eye be evil, thy whole body shall be full of darkness. If therefore the light that is in thee be darkness, how great is that darkness!"* (Matt. 6:22-23). For many years when I studied these verses, I was a bit baffled about why Jesus used this illustration when He was obviously talking about trusting the heavenly Father, the heart's condition in giving, and the proper view of material possessions, which all relate directly to the way we view and use our money. Jesus actually used similar sayings connected with firstfruits giving in which those listening understood clearly. Those who voluntarily gave firstfruits had heard the priests use these terminologies many times. Then, it was revealed and confirmed to me that He was differentiating between generous people and stingy, covetous people.

In regard to the firstfruits, it is said that a *"fine eye"* or *"eye full of light"* (a liberal man) gives one-fortieth or two and one-half percent, *"an evil eye"* (a covetous person) one-sixtieth or one and two-thirds percent, while the average rate of contribution *"a middling eye"* gives one-fiftieth, or two percent of the produce.[1] Since the firstfruits offering was a heave offering, the

Hebrew word *Terumah* was connected. *Terumah*, the Hebrew word for heave offering, was built from the concept *Terei Mimeah*, which means "two out of a hundred or two percent."[2]

The message is clear. Everyone will give, based upon the revelation, not the information, they've received from the Holy Spirit. People devoid of spiritual revelation give very little; whereas, people full of revelation give much! When Christ isn't the light of our lives, we tend to respond to life's circumstances out of darkness, including giving. It isn't a question of how great is that darkness; but, the startling reality *that darkness is greater than I ever thought!*

From my many years of leadership, I'm profoundly aware that every person gives, either bountifully or sparingly, based on the amount of light or revelation they have. As in the natural, the higher one ascends the clearer one's vision becomes. The apostle Paul said, *"Set your affection on things above, not on things on the earth. For ye are dead, and your life is hid with Christ in God"* (Col. 3:2-3). Revelation from the heavenly Father promotes understanding. In revelation, God has a masterful way of unlocking what has been enclosed with the greatest sublimity. Revelation enables us to see what others only hope to see. Revelation permits us to have single-minded devotion to God, which absolves the heart of divided loyalties. Years ago, when I worked in a military warehouse, I would often engage one of the truck drivers in conversation. Often we would have spiritual discussions. Because I had received the spirit of revelation at the age of 17, I would share some insight the Holy Spirit had given me. The driver would say, "Why can't I see that when I read the same Bible?"

The Lord was distinguishing for me the differences between revelation and information. Being older men, the drivers had more information due to longevity and experience; however, being a spiritual man, I had more revelation of their information. Revelatory light really does make a difference. Wherever and whenever it is present, darkness or ignorance has to flee. The light one holds about giving will indeed determine to what degree one gives.

To illustrate my point, I remember one of the ministers from my childhood days reading from Malachi chapter 3 concerning tithes and offerings with emphases on certain words. The question; "Will a man rob God?" captured my immature attention. Thinking to myself, I said, "If men will rob men whom they see, certainly they will rob God whom they do not see." Of course, at that time, I didn't have the courage to voice that opinion; besides, my mother would have ministered unto me numerous corrections regarding being mannerly. The minister read further and told us how we were robbing God—in tithes and offerings!

The vast majority of people in that church didn't give tithes and offerings, though they heard the same Scripture every other Sunday. Most working people gave a few dollars at best; and children gave the coins their parents gave them when the candy man wasn't getting them. What was lacking? We desperately needed revelation! Like the Ethiopian eunuch, we were calling words but we had no revelation of the words. (See Acts 8:26-40.) Without a question, everyone in that church gave based upon the light they had. And most of our light was darkness.

THE SINGLE-EYED PERSON

Jesus used two metaphors to describe the revelation of trusting God and free-will giving: *"the single eye"* and *"the evil eye."* Like a skillful, ingenious tactician, He communicated to prepare His listeners for functioning in the alternate society called the Kingdom of God. What is He reintroducing, only in an organic form, which embellishes life and does away with strong-arm religious tactics from the old regime of money-lovers? Do we have clear, unfettered vision, or blurred, distorted vision? We need to answer these questions.

Through my studies, I discovered that the metaphor *single-eyed* primarily means "a liberal or generous person." It is the eye of the new person in Christ; it's the dove's eye of an unwavering lover; it's the face of flint of someone resoundingly committed to God's purposes.

The way I was able to deduce this was through observing three Greek words in the New Testament from the same word *family*. The words are *single*, *liberal*, and *liberally*. As I give you the words in the Greek language, perhaps you'll notice what I noticed.

- *Single* is #573 in the Strong's Concordance. It is the word *haplous*, from #1 (as a particle of a union) and the base of #4120; *folded together*, i.e. single (figuratively clear):—single.

- *Liberal* is #572 in the Strong's Concordance. It is the word *haplotes*, which translates as singleness, sincerity (without dissimulation or self-seeking), generosity, (copious bestowal);—bountifulness, liberal (ity), simplicity, singleness.

- *Liberally* is #574 in the Strong's Concordance. It is the word *haplos*, an adverb from #573; bountifully:—liberally.

I see a quality of vision so enhanced with the nature of God that it has no room for ulterior motives. From this place, we can be utterly clear in our understanding about what Jesus was teaching because of clear eyesight. We are also in union life with Him, hearing from the same frequency He's speaking from. That constitutes being single, unmixed, and full of revelation, but yet, not alone. The Christ-life delivers us from the symptomatic problems of greed, love of money, and an independent life from God. This life can be so fulfilling it will prevent us from self-seeking; we are removed from the clutter that occupies so many worldly hearts. In the end, it manifests as a generous, bountiful heart awaiting opportunities to give.

Scriptures describe a generous person in these terms.

> *The liberal soul* [the soul of blessing] *shall be made fat: and he that watereth shall be watered also himself* (Proverbs 11:25).

> *He that hath a bountiful eye shall be blessed; for he giveth of his bread to the poor* (Proverbs 22:9).

> *Moreover, brethren, we do you to wit of the grace of God bestowed on the churches of Macedonia; how that in a great trial of affliction the abundance of their joy and their poverty abounded unto the riches of their liberality* (2 Corinthians 8:1-2).

> *For the administration of this service not only supplieth the want of the saints, but is abundant also by many thanksgivings unto God; whiles by the experiment of this ministration they glorify God for your professed subjection unto the gospel of*

Christ, and for your liberal distribution unto them, and unto all men (2 Corinthians 9:12-13).

THE EVIL-EYED PERSON

What about *"the evil eye"*? Was Jesus describing something that was profoundly immoral, deliberately harmful, malicious, devilish, and characterized by misfortune? Emphatically, yes! An evil eye is a metaphor for the covetous, stingy, and sparing seed-planter. Once again the Greek words connected with this concept establish a clear definition from the word family.

- *Evil* is #4190 in the Strong's Concordance. It is the word *poneros*; from a derivative of #4192; hurtful, diseased, derelict, vicious, facinorous: bad, evil, grievous, harm, lewd, malicious, and wicked.

- Evil is the derivative #4192 is the word *ponos*; from the base of #3993; toil, (by implication) anguish:—pain.

- The base word of #4192 is #3993 is the word *penes* from *peno*, (to toil for daily subsistence); starving, indigent:—poor.

The *evil eye* is the "diseased-eye" consistent with poverty and lack because that's all one can see based on environmental stimuli. It's what Adam's eye became once he fell into duality by entertaining the wrong information from the serpent. It is the gateway to every repulsive and sadistic humankind experience. There's no deliverance from it except in

Christ. We all must eventually heal our diseased eye by asking: *What am I concentrating on?* Am I distracted by the cares of this life more than the reality of my heavenly Father's person and care?

People controlled by poverty believe that if they acquire certain temporal things they will be set for life; if they refuse to give freely, it will mean more for them. Begrudgingly, they hold on to everything that comes into their hands, thinking it will never escape them. What a mistake! This is like sand; the tighter it is squeezed, the more it slips away. They seek to find security and satisfaction in possessions instead of the heavenly Father. Because I was born into poverty, I understand this position.

The Kingdom addresses our distorted-image world by challenging us to move into the world of generosity. It's the only world that truly represents the nature of God, which is love and always giving. It begins when God gives us a penetrating revelation of His Son that changes the landscape of our spiritual myopia. We move from the vicious, beastly cycle of toiling for daily subsistence and barely surviving, to God's world of more than enough. Every time Jesus entered a situation of lack or penury, He manifested the reality of the Father, which is abundance. Money was never an issue or a god to Him because He never hedged on His relationship with His Father. The Scriptures speak of the evil eye in this manner:

He that hasteth to be rich hath an evil eye, and considereth not that poverty shall come upon him (Proverbs 28:22).

But they that will be rich fall into temptation and a snare, and into many foolish and hurtful lusts, which drown men in destruction and perdition. For the love of money is the root of all evil: which while some coveted after, they have erred from the faith, and pierced themselves through with many sorrows (1 Timothy 6:9-10).

This know also, that in the last days perilous times shall come. For men shall be lovers of their own selves, covetous [lovers of money]... (2 Timothy 3:1-2).

The covetous, evil-eyed person will seek money instead of God, attempting to fill the empty void caused by lusts. Covetousness surges out of a twin operating system: grabbing and grasping followed by a spirit of withholding. The covetous person snatches for more and more, usually more than he/she can handle responsibly out of a spirit of greed. Covetousness is also the spirit of withholding when it is within the power of one to give generously. Adam snatched knowledge; Achan seized material possessions; and Ananias and Sapphira chose to withhold money. All of these were covetous acts.

A modern example of the uncontrollable operation of covetousness is revealed in the following personal experience. My wife and I traveled to Henderson, Nevada, to visit with friends. We also visited Las Vegas, as well. As beautiful as that desert city is, there is something sinister lurking in the spirit realm over it, drawing in people and feeding the spirit of covetousness. I was astonished at what covetous astigmatism can do to people. Many were watching their money disappear in slot machines hoping for a big payoff. Some people would debate me saying, "I do it just for the fun of it!" However, history has proven otherwise.

Gamblers don't gamble just for the fun of it, nor do they keep money attained from gambling—those are facts! There's always a bigger jackpot, a bigger thrill, than the previous one. Therefore, they keep going back, riding in the vehicle of greed, coursing down the boulevard of avariciousness.

There is only one remedy for this financial deathtrap—trust God instead of mammon. Also a fact: If we seek God's Kingdom and His righteousness, He has committed Himself to add to us whatever we need.

In summary, when it comes to the firstfruits or any type of giving, individuals must determine how liberal or stingy they will be based upon what revelation they have. No person has the right to dictate that to another. It is not about the percentage, necessarily, that a person gives; it's about the heart of generosity with which a person gives. Percentages are acceptable minimums, points-of-entry to begin giving. Nothing about percentages speaks of maturity because they are impositions rather than heart convictions. Since we are no more shiftless vagabonds in Adam's world of need, our lives can be defined by the liberality of the in-Christ world, which exudes extravagant giving because of no identification with lack.

I love the way The Message Bible states Proverbs 11:24: *"The world of the generous gets larger and larger; the world of the stingy gets smaller and smaller."* Jesus was giving us the antidote for increase in His teachings. We increase in our economic strength in order to minister effectively to our families, our ministries, and the poor. Again, the Message Bible speaks powerfully on this subject: *"Generous hands are blessed hands because they give bread to the poor"* (Prov. 22:9). Finally, the apostle Paul made it clear that dire straits have very little power over people who have chosen to be generous because they are moved by the extravagance of God in their lives.

WHO ARE WE SERVING?

The pivotal point of Jesus' discourse was in the third portion of His deliberation. Who are we serving? He states, *"No one can serve two masters; for either he will hate the one and love the other, or else he will hold to the one, and despise the other. You cannot serve God and mammon"* (Matt. 6:24). This verse deals with the epic struggle in the hearts of men in yielding either to God or the spirit of money. Strong's Concordance defines mammon as "wealth, confidence, and avarice deified." Another way to say this: You cannot serve God and covetousness personified in all its trappings and manifestations. Since Jesus came at the close of the old covenant, the principle opposing duality was still in effect. The Law said, *"Thou shalt have no other gods before me"* (Exod. 20:3). Literally, you're not to have other gods before "My" face. Anytime something enters the window of the soul greater than our heavenly Father, it is idolatry. In effect, whatever and whomever we place before Him in our hearts actually govern our lives.

In keeping with the overall theme of this book, wealth redistribution and the order of first things is paramount when thinking about what Jesus taught. Our heavenly Father must be enthroned in our lives when He releases trillions of dollars into our hands; otherwise we will commit the same financial mayhem of the past. We will spend without conservation. A few questions to think about: Do you give regularly to charitable situations? Have you grown in your giving since conversion? Are you punctual in taking care of your financial obligations? What does your credit score look like if you have one? Are you investing? Do these questions matter? Absolutely!

Financial mismanagement reveals what spirit is dominant in a person's heart. With that said, without a thorough working of the Holy Spirit, many Christians find themselves in a tenuous position. If a person has failed to demonstrate fiscal responsibility with little, how can the same be made ruler over much? This cuts to the core. God wants us in a position to do Kingdom business without delay. If we are in debt to every company that has bombarded us with opportunities for credit, we have a different obligation—regardless of the call of God on our lives. We must pay our debts to show there's integrity in the Kingdom.

Who we are serving matters! If we are serving God, our money is involved in the things of God, such as local ministry and missions. We really won't have an issue with giving, whether it's alms, firstfruits, tithes, missions, vows, etc. If we are serving mammon, worldly stuff has our money. God isn't against us having things; however, the things shouldn't have us. Remember, credit card companies are in business to make a profit—period. It has nothing to do with helping their clientele; it's about profit. If you are in financial trouble and believe this message is true, seek counsel quickly from Kingdom financial advisors. Our heavenly Father desires to bring us back to the place where we can serve Him freely— where our hearts are no longer questioned, our treasures are in the right place, and the revelation within us is clear.

ENDNOTES

1. Alfred Edersheim, *The Temple—Its Ministry and Services Updated Edition* (Peabody, MA: Hendrickson Publishers, Inc., 1994), 303-304.

2. Ibid, 304.

Chapter 8

NEW TESTAMENT PRINCIPLE OF KINGDOM DISTRIBUTION

*And Jesus took the loaves; and when He had given thanks,
He **distributed** to the disciples, and the disciples to them
that were set down; and likewise of the fishes as much as
they would. When they were filled, He said unto His disciples, gather up the fragments that remain, that nothing be
lost. Therefore, they gathered them together, and filled
twelve baskets with fragments of the five barley loaves,
which remained over and above unto them that had eaten
(John 6:11-13).*

JESUS AND DISTRIBUTION

Jesus Christ taught New Testament principles, although He lived
during the end of the Old Testament. His teachings provoked paradigm
shifts. He provided many teachable moments when He instructed and
illustrated the Kingdom of God to His followers. The Master continued to
teach them, though they, like most students did not immediately catch the
intent behind every lesson. Some of the greatest lessons came when the
trainees were confounded and perplexed, almost dazed by some of the

circumstances. At times they would panic and show their disapproval through anger, demonstrating their insecurities.

We must all remember our Master saying, *"What appears to be an impossibility to man is total possible with God!"* Jesus, on every occasion, illustrated the measures a Son of God should take. When you live in the sphere of peace and are uninfluenced by the lack of dominion around you, nothing rattles your world. The things that are impossible in Adam's environment are nothing more than possibility opportunities in the anointed world of Jesus.

The principle of distribution is very powerfully demonstrated in John chapter 6. Jesus and His disciples were in the season of Passover, which represents a time of new beginnings and accessing new dimensions in the Spirit. Israel's first Passover experience established precedence. As previously mentioned, it was the time of the barley harvest or the firstfruits of grain. During this time, a multitude of people followed Jesus to His next training station. Jesus challenged Philip to purchase bread to feed the multitude—bread is a staple of life. He responded to Jesus' request from a position of shortages and paucity, *"Two hundred pennyworth of bread is not sufficient for them, that every one of them may take a little"* (John 6:7). With a penny being the average day's wages, 200 would represent about two-thirds of a year's wages. Jesus wasn't subject to their lack of resources or mental insufficiencies. He already knew what He would do in response to this need.

It is delightfully dynamic, something captivatingly incredible about Jesus' use of a little boy's lunch. The disciples could only use their logical, carnal reasoning, rather than accept Jesus' vision that says, *"Come and create with me out of the illimitable world of energy—the world in which miracles are always common in the spoken word!"* Five thousand men along with the women and children are staring down the portal of a miracle. Jesus took the loaves and blessed them, invoking the law of rapid reproduction. I have watched something similar with vegetables under direct sunlight during the summer months in places like Alaska.

Jesus, the Son of God, places the fishes and loaves under the direct Son-light of Himself and they increased. He then distributes the gain. He releases the blessed meal into the hands of His trainees, who in turn, release what they received to the people. The law of distribution is simple: *Release what you hold in your hands for distribution.* The lad was at the highest level of blessing in all of this because he gave Jesus all that he had, precipitating the next law of distribution.

The second law of distribution centers around this thought: *If we are faithful to distribute, the law of exponential growth is released almost immediately. Exponential* means "to rapidly increase in size." We can execute our assignments easily and experience growth when we align with what God is doing in a particular season. Note the results of this lesson on distribution: *"When the people were filled, Jesus said unto His disciples, gather up the fragments that remain, that nothing be lost. Therefore they gathered them together, and filled twelve baskets with the fragments of the five barley loaves, which remained over and above unto them that had eaten"* (John 6:12-13).

We can ill-afford to waste the fragments of a miracle attesting to the power of dominion in what appeared to be an impossible situation. Sometimes, the very next challenge in life demands the sustainable substance of the previous miracle. All of the remains, which are described as *over and above*, are the outward indicators that Jesus functioned at all times out of a spirit of prosperity at the highest level.

Miraculous signs are indicators Father God desires to teach us something greater than the obvious. Further in John chapter 6, the miracle of the barley bread progressed to Jesus, the spiritual barley bread, referring to Himself as the bread of life. *"And Jesus said unto them, I am the bread of life: he that cometh to Me shall never hunger: and he that believeth on Me shall never thirst"* (John 6:35). Most of us need concrete objects to perceive spiritual truth. Clearly, you cannot think of literal bread in the final part of His teachings. The idea is simple: The moment we receive Jesus Christ into our lives we have taken in the quality of His life, which is eternal.

Jesus spoke of eating His flesh and drinking His blood. Certainly, He is not speaking of cannibalism. Again, revelation is important. His flesh is His Word and His blood is His Spirit. We must receive His Word and Spirit to maintain true life. Otherwise, we are no different from the fathers who ate temporary food, manna, and died in the wilderness. An important axiom comes from these teachings: *The quality of what we eat will determine the quality of the life we live!* We must learn to forego that which does not satisfy to gain what does satisfies.

WHAT IS DISTRIBUTION?

There are four key words used in the New Testament to describe distribution: (1) koinonia, (2) diadidomi, (3) merizo, and (4) eumetadotos. With each of them varying just a little, we could create a list of ideas with nouns such as partnership, participation, benefaction, communion, fellowship, and social intercourse.

- *Partnership* is cooperation between people or groups working together.

- *Participation* means "to take part in an event or activity."

- *Benefaction* is a good deed, especially a donation given to a charitable cause.

- *Communion* is a relationship, one in which something is communicated or shared.

- *Fellowship* is sharing common interests, goals, experiences, or views.

- *Social intercourse* is the exchange between people or groups, especially conversation or social activity.

The New Testament church operated in each of these ideals. (See Acts 2:42.) They shared their lives together in practical, meaningful worship and in spiritual and social intercourse. From just a giving basis, *distribution* means "to get money or other gifts out of your control before they get into your heart"! Many people struggle with giving because they don't understand the dynamics of distributional increase. The moment something leaves our hands it leaves as seed. *"Now He that ministered seed to the sower both minister bread for your food, and multiply your seed sown, and increase the fruits of your righteousness"* (2 Cor. 9:10). Righteous harvests are always greater than the seeds planted! We all minister *seed* singular and reap *fruits* plural. I remember planting gardens at home with my parents and siblings during my adolescence years. We planted various seeds and vegetables in the garden. We always gathered a whole lot more than we planted. And my parents always shared some of our increase with our neighbors, teaching all of us the importance of benefaction and selfless action.

There are a number of New Testament Scriptures corroborating the development of the principle of distribution. Each of them gives us clues as to how the church took this concept and applied it.

Distributing to the necessity of saints; given to hospitality (Romans 12:13).

*For the administration of this service not only supplieth the want of the saints, but is abundant also by many thankgivings unto God; whiles by the experiment of this ministration they glorify God for your professed subjection unto the gospel of Christ, **and for your liberal distribution unto them, and unto all men*** (2 Corinthians 9:12-13).

*Let him that is taught in the world **communicate unto him that teaches** in all good things* (Galatians 6:6).

*Now ye Philippians know also, that in the beginning of the gospel, when I departed from Macedonia, **no church communicated with me as concerning giving and receiving, but ye only**. For even in Thessalonica ye sent once and again unto my necessity* (Philippians 4:15-16).

*Charge them that are rich in this world, that they be not high-minded, nor trust in uncertain riches, but in the living God, who giveth us richly all things to enjoy; that they do good, that they be rich in good works, **ready to distribute, willing to communicate**; laying up in store for themselves a*

228

good foundation against the time to come, that they may lay hold on eternal life (1 Timothy 6:17-19).

By Him therefore let us offer the sacrifice of praise to God continually, that is, the fruit of our lips, giving thanks to His name. ***But to do good and to communicate forget not:*** *for with such sacrifices God is well pleased* (Hebrews 13:15-16).

Five of the seven references use the word *communicates*. In the early 16th century when the King James Version of the Bible was developed, *communicate* meant "common share." Saints shared when necessary or they met necessities when essential. When compelling circumstances created need, those without the need felt an obligation to meet the need willingly.

I witnessed this type of sharing as a young boy. Unfortunately, my daddy fell on some difficult times that affected the whole family. Various members in the two local churches brought poundings to our home. *Pounding* was when neighbors would bring a pound of any type of food during a time of charitable distribution. I remember my mother being extremely thankful; for once again, we had food in the house to feed hungry children. Those who sacrificed and came to our aid did something God was well-pleased with, and this carried eternal value. In the words of the apostle Paul, they each *"laid up for themselves a good foundation against the time to come."*

OPENING CHAPTER OF THE CHURCH

And all that believed were together, and had all things common; and sold their possessions and goods, and parted them to all men, as every man had need (Acts 2:44-45).

And the multitude of them that believed were of one heart and of one soul; neither said any of them that ought of the things which he possessed was his own; but they had all things common. And with great power gave the apostles witness of the resurrection of the Lord Jesus: and great grace was upon them all. Neither was there any among them that lacked: for as many as were possessors of lands, or houses sold them, and brought the prices of the things that were sold, and laid them down at the apostles' feet: and distribution was made unto every man according as he had need (Acts 4:32-35).

After the birth of the church, we are introduced to a model of giving and distribution that has not been since duplicated with the integrity we read about in the Book of Acts. There was a purity in this operation because of the pure hearts of a leadership function. Socialist governments and some church groups have tried, only to pale in comparison of the ideal we read about in the early church.

The New Covenant started at the level of what I call "Kingdom distribution." A spirit of sharing was imported from the heavens at the same time the people received the baptism of the Holy Spirit. There's no indication the apostles compelled or coerced people to give. As they thrived in the new life and nature, the Christ life, they were empowered and motivated in their giving. This is actually an elevated dimension of what was illustrated in the wilderness wanderings, in which the gatherers of much manna would share with those who gathered less so there would be no lack. As the wilderness gives us a glimpse of what is to come in Christ, the New Covenant church lives out this principle fully.

The prudent purpose behind Kingdom distribution is to firmly deliver the hearts of individuals from covetousness, consumerism, and greed—the three sources of containment. The purpose is to promote openhandedness and the spirit of generosity. The apostle John saw three frogs, or unclean spirits, coming out of the beastly culture. Covetousness, consumerism, and greed could easily, from a modern context, fulfill these descriptions. All of us live life with either an open hand or a clenched fist; depending on whether we live out of Adam's diabolical nature or Christ's dazzling nature.

As the early church launched, the particular season they were in initially demanded the spirit of distribution. Everyone did not sell everything they possessed, as some people think. This action would have produced an empty, communistic society with very few resources. Those who had more than they needed became distributors. The church body trusted the integrity of the apostles' leadership and brought the extra to them which the apostles distributed. Eventually, many had to go back to production in order to maintain this level of distribution. The apostle Paul said, *"If you do not work, you do not eat."* (See 2 Thessalonians 3:10.)

JOSEPH BARNABAS, SON OF CONSOLATION

And Joses [Joseph], *who by the apostles was surnamed Barnabas, (which is being interpreted, the son of consolation,) a Levite, and of the country of Cyprus, having land, sold it, and brought the money, and laid it at the apostles' feet* (Acts 4:36-37).

Joseph Barnabas is one of the most beautiful, venerable models of exemplary distribution in the New Testament. He's the kind of person we

231

should want to emulate. If we combine his given name (Joseph) and his spiritual name (Barnabas), we create Joseph Barnabas. Joseph is a noble name in Israel's economy, which means *"He will add."* (See Genesis 30:23.) Many individuals bore this name among the sons of Israel. Barnabas means *"son of consolation or comfort."* He is an archetype of the Holy Spirit, which Jesus called the Comforter. (See John 16:8.) The combined name, Joseph Barnabas, speaks to us of the productive, empowering, and comforting nature of the Holy Spirit. He essentially has a nature that gives away power, which makes room for others. Though we don't read much about his apostolic experiences, we can see greatness in the few opportunities the Scriptures speak of him. His single-eyed giving established precedence in Kingdom distribution that has been copied many times since. He laid money at the apostles' feet, further empowering them to be the diplomats with full authority that they were called to be in Kingdom business. Men like Barnabas epitomize the right attitude in Kingdom distribution.

Several details in these verses reveal some special characteristics about Barnabas. He was from the tribe of Levi whose birth place was an island country in the eastern Mediterranean Sea. He was also a member of the upper crust from the former paradigm in Israel's history. Being a Levite, he was knowledgeable of the financial setup supporting priests and Levites. Barnabas experienced conversion and actively involved himself in the new order of God's Kingdom, which was led by apostles rather than priests. So he knew something about the strategies necessary for sacrificing what he had in order to gain that which he didn't have.

Barnabas stepped beyond the forbidden law of the old governing the antiquated Levitical structure: *"And if a man purchase of the Levites, then the house that was sold, and the city of his possession, shall go out in the year of jubilee: for the houses of the cities of the Levites are their possession among the children of Israel. But the field of the suburbs of their cities may not be sold; for it is their perpetual possession"* (Lev. 25:33-34).

Something may be eternally yours in one order and may be relinquished for an order that's greater. When Barnabas sold his property, he renounced a privileged position, forsaking it through the law of benefaction. He voluntarily agreed with the heavenly Father to take away the Law for him to enter grace. Grace opens a wealthy place, a pool of blessing unimaginable. He demonstrates a generous, magnanimous heart (grace personified) that ultimately led to his commission as an apostle himself. (See Acts 13:1-3.) Though the Bible says very little about his latter apostleship, with the type of heart he had, Barnabas was probably very effective.

GROWING IN KINGDOM DISTRIBUTION

How does one grow in a fuller expression of Kingdom distribution? Are there strategies we can learn in the postmodern world?

We all must come to understand the full benefits package that we have in Christ Jesus, and then move on to benefaction. Realizing that we lack in no benefit accelerates us in our giving disposition. However, if we remain in the position of always receiving benefits, it is a great indication of spiritual immaturity, causing us to clutch to personal possessions. The psalmist David writes: *"Bless the Lord, O my soul: and all that is within me, bless His holy name. Bless the Lord, O my soul, and forget not all His benefits"* (Ps. 103:1-2). Benefits are advantages that have a good effect and promote well-being. The spiritual benefits we have received through the redemptive power of Jesus are:

- Forgiveness of all our iniquities.

- Healing of all our diseases.

- Redemption from destruction.

- A crown with loving-kindness and tender mercies.

- Renewal of youth, like the eagle's renewal.

We have forgiveness, healing, mercy, and constant renewal of our lives through Jesus Christ. The apostle Paul said, *"In whom we have redemption through His blood, the forgiveness of sins, according to the riches of His grace"* (Eph. 1:7). We are Abraham's seed, and therefore, the beneficiaries of that entire promise God guaranteed him. If we go back to the original promise, it speaks to the fact that we will receive benefits; but we must turn them into a spirit and nature of benefaction. The Father said to Abraham:

> *And I will make thee a great nation, and I will bless thee, and make thy name great; and thou shalt be a blessing; and I will bless them that bless thee, and curse him that curseth thee: and in thee shall all families of the earth be blessed"* (Genesis 12:2-3).

When the apostle Paul was considering this same promise, he said

> *And if ye be Christ's, then are ye Abraham's seed, and heirs according to the promise* (Galatians 3:29).

Very simply, God blesses us and expects us to bless others. The means by which this can be accomplished is Kingdom distribution.

THREE INGREDIENTS

There are three necessary ingredients essential to produce a shift in our concepts of benevolence. First, we must have *new information*. It is impossible to change your mind about anything without different and/or better information. Change becomes hopeless, empty-headed dreaming without our information systems improving.

Second, we must ask the heavenly Father to grant us a *"hearing ear"* and *"a seeing eye"* (see Prov. 20:12.). These two spiritual senses heighten our perception faculties. We can only see the things we first hear.

Third, know that distribution can never be from an assessment or imposition mentality. New Testament distribution must *come from the heart*; otherwise, it becomes an injudicious corruption. If someone must tell us what to give, more than likely we never intended to give it anyway. The Old Covenant imposed rules, regulations, and requirements because of the blighted, heart conditions of its worshipers. The writer of the Book of Hebrews summed up the Old Covenant in these words, *"Which stood only in meats and drinks, and divers washings, an carnal ordinances, **imposed on them** until the time of reformation"* (Heb. 9:10). As Isaiah said, most people worshiped God with their mouths and not with their hearts.

When the apostle Paul spoke to the Corinthian church, with enthusiasm he summarized the spirit of distribution that can work in any congregation. The Message Bible's contemporary language, helps us to hear the zeal and zest in which he communicated this idea.

Now, friends, I want to report on the surprising and generous ways in which God is working in the churches in Macedonia province. Fierce troubles came down on the people of those churches, pushing them to the very limit. The trial exposed their true colors: they were incredibly happy, though desperately poor. The pressure triggered something totally unexpected: an outpouring of pure and generous gifts. I was there and saw it for myself. They gave offerings of whatever they could—far more than they could afford!—pleading for the privilege of helping out in the relief of poor Christians. This was totally spontaneous, entirely their own idea, and caught us completely off guard. What explains it was that they had first given themselves unreservedly to God and to us. The other giving simply flowed out of the purposes of God working in their lives . . . (2 Corinthians 8:1-5 TM).

Paul witnessed in Macedonia the selfless generosity of the churches. What a pleasing sight this must have been! People had caught the vision, the true spirit of the gospel—a spirit that turns people from voracious consumers to big-hearted contributors; even the message that allows us to move into the second half of the Abrahamic promise. The thing that makes it truly special is when people are motivated by a spontaneous spirit of cooperation. If I pondered this passage of Scripture for the first time without any previous bias, I would have to conclude that the Corinthian church walked in the *grace of giving*. There was nothing legalistic about their giving. Leaders don't have to be triggers, coaches, or catalysts when people are motivated by grace. The people's success was based on unadulterated and wholehearted commitment that they had given themselves to God and the leadership.

GIVING DISPOSITIONS

I have discovered four giving dispositions essentially important to the spirit of distribution in the New Testament: (1) willingness or intentionality, (2) regularity or systematically, (3) cheerfully or rejoicing joyfully, and (4) bountifully and plenteously. I have equally discovered the seeds of each ideal in the Old Covenant. Though the Old Covenant required many different types of gifts, yet the true spirit of giving our heavenly Father conveyed was the same. All gift-giving is to be worship, which comes from the hearts of worshipers.

1. *Give willingly*. The simple idea of *willing* means "to volunteer (as a soldier), to present spontaneously, to offer willingly."

> *Moreover, brethren, we do you to wit of the grace of God bestowed on the churches of Macedonia; how that in a great trial of affliction the abundance of their joy and their deep poverty abounded unto the riches of their liberality. For to their power, I bear record, yea, and beyond their power they were willing of themselves* (2 Corinthians 8:1-3).

Note the construction of the Tabernacle of Moses in the wilderness. The only giving tolerated in the project was freewill, from-the-heart charitableness.

> *And the Lord spake unto Moses, saying, speak unto the children of Israel, that they bring me an offering [heave offering]: of every man that giveth it willingly with his heart ye shall take my offering* (Exodus 25:1-2).

And all the congregation of the children of Israel departed from the presence of Moses. **And they came, every one whose heart stirred him up, and every one whom his spirit made willing,** *and they brought the Lord's offering to the work of the tabernacle of the congregation, and for all his service, and for the holy garments. And they came, both men and women,* **as many as were willing hearted,** *and brought bracelets, and earrings, and rings, and tablets, all jewels of gold: every man that offered an offering of gold unto the Lord* (Exodus 35:20-22).

The children of Israel brought a willing offering unto the Lord, every man and woman, whose heart made them willing *to bring for all manner of work, which the Lord had commanded to be made by the hand of Moses* (Exodus 35:29).

Note the construction of the Temple of Solomon in the Promised Land. The leadership modeled willing hearts in giving and the people followed their example.

Then the chief of the fathers and princes of the tribes of Israel, and the captains of thousands and of the hundreds, with the rulers of the king's work, **offered willingly** *... Then the people rejoiced,* **for that they offered willingly, because with perfect heart they offered willingly to the Lord;** *and David the king also rejoiced with great joy ... But who am I, and what is my people,* **that we should be able to offer so willingly after this sort?** *For all things come of thee, and of thine own* *have we given thee . . . I know also, my God, that thou triest the heart, and hast pleasure **in uprightness. As for me, in the uprightness of mine heart I have willingly offered all these things**: and now have I seen with joy thy people, which are present here, **to offer willingly unto thee** (1 Chronicles 29:6,9,14,17).*

Note the reconstruction of the Temple once the remnant returned to the Promised Land after the captivity:

*Then rose up the chief of the fathers of Judah and Benjamin, and the priests, and the Levites, with all them whose spirit God had raised up, to go up to build the house of the Lord which is in Jerusalem. And all they that were about them strengthened their hands with vessels of silver, with gold, with goods, and with beasts, and with precious things, beside **all that was willingly offered** (Ezra 1:5-6).*

*They kept also the feast of tabernacles, as it is written, and offered the daily burnt offerings by number, according to the custom, as the duty of every day required; and afterward offered the continual burnt offering, both of the new moons, and of all the set feasts of the Lord that were consecrated, and of **every one that willingly offered a freewill offering unto the Lord** (Ezra 3:4-5).*

Forasmuch as thou art sent of the king, and of his seven counselors, to inquire concerning Judah and Jerusalem

according to the law of thy God which is in thine hand; **and
to carry the silver and gold, which the king and his counselors have freely offered unto the God of Israel,** *whose
habitation is in Jerusalem, and all the silver and gold that
thou canst find in all the province of Babylon,* **with the
freewill offering of the people, and of the priests, offered
willingly for the house of their God which is in Jerusalem**
(Ezra 7:14-16).

*And the rulers of the people dwelt at Jerusalem: the rest of the
people also cast lots, to bring one of ten to dwell in Jerusalem
the holy city, and nine parts to dwell in other cities. And the
people blessed all the men,* **that willingly offered themselves**
to dwell at Jerusalem (Nehemiah 11:1-2).

The cardinal principle that must govern apostolic and prophetic distribution is a willing heart: *"For if there be first a willing mind, it is accepted*
according to that a man hath, and not according to that he hath not"
(2 Cor. 8:12). This is what I call *ability* "benevolence" The preponderance
of the evidence in the Old Covenant proves that a willing heart and mind
are the only requirements connected to building programs. Some of the
methods used in the modern church are unscriptural and deplorable. As
always, the best results come when we use the principles accurately established in the Scriptures. We cannot achieve a greater extravagance in giving
beyond the promptings of a willing and ready heart.

*Charge them that are rich in this world, that they be not
highminded, nor trust in uncertain riches, but in the living*

God, who giveth us richly all things to enjoy; that they do good, that they be rich in good works, ready to distribute, **willing to communicate** [liberal] (1 Timothy 6:17-18).

One of the most powerful displays of willing communication I bore witness to was my mission to South Africa in October 2006. I had been invited as one of the speakers in an apostolic school of ministry. Before arriving at the school, I asked lead apostle Thamo Naidoo, who would be my host, "What is the theme of the school?" Being under authority, my desire was to speak from the frequency established by the Holy Spirit for that convocation. Thamo said, "There is no theme—be open to the Holy Spirit!" As I sought the Lord for accuracy, He made it very clear to me to speak on Kingdom distribution. Actually, I had some misgivings; however, God is little concerned about our reservations and doesn't, necessarily, speak to us only about comfortable subjects. Sometimes He commands us to do the things we'd rather not do.

After I arrived in South Africa, it was immediately clear that the theme of the school was Kingdom economics. What a joyous week we experienced! Each of the speakers spoke on the overall same material without previously collaborating with one another. The teachings during that week triggered a spirit of distribution that would have pleased the early apostles. People gave without coercion or frustration. All week long, brethren cheerfully shared their resources. Various needs were met; individuals were ministered unto without ulterior motives. Father God allowed us to participate in the principle of *willing giving*, of which we all began to understand a little better the power of God-motivated ideas. Unprecedented giving power is released when we do things God's way.

241

2. ***Give regularly or systematically.*** *Systematically* means "orderly, not varying, constant, methodical, and purposefully regular."

> *Upon the first day of the week let every one of you lay by him in store, as God hath prospered him, that there be no gatherings when I come* (1 Corinthians 16:2).

> *Three times a year shall all thy males appear before the Lord thy God in the place which He shall choose; in the feast of unleavened bread, and in the feast of weeks, and in the feast of tabernacles: and they shall not appear before the Lord empty: every man shall give as he is able, according to the blessing of the Lord thy God which He hath given thee* (Deuteronomy 16:16-17).

Have you ever thought about the Kingdom spirit behind tithing, or have you been primarily caught up in the frustration of it, considering it legalism? How about almsgiving? I have pondered both many times over the years, though both practices are no real issues with me. Certainly, the academic debate lingers as theologians and laypeople attempt to determine the legitimacy of tithing in a New Testament culture. There are those who believe tithing is legalism and has no real place in New Testament life. Citing references from the early church leaders, such as Irenaeus and Epiphanius, many believe there should be freedom in Christian giving without any outside pressure.

Conversely, I believe it is important that we grasp the Father's heart behind this principle since He is the one who permitted it in the beginning. Our Father does not speak vain, purposeless words. All of His words are full of purity and purpose because they reveal something about His heart before people taint it with their misrepresentations.

One of the ways to promote systematic giving is the principle of the tithe, which was the second aspect of firstfruits giving. "The Hebrew root *sr* is related to the Arabic verb *ashara*, which means "to form community, or a group." It is in the family with the Arabic noun *ashirat*, meaning "tribe," and *mashar*, assembly. Because of ten fingers, the semantic development was ten equaled collection or union."[1] As I studied the Strong's Concordance, the base word (#6237 = *asar*) means "to grow or make rich." The primary idea behind systematic tithing is to accumulate wealth.

Tithe is one of the establishing points of our participation in a covenant in which the Father has promised us the ability to get wealth. Thus, from these definitions, the tradition of giving a tenth part of income, produce, and the spoils of war to priests and kings was common among the nations of the ancient Near East.

The tithe was one of the economic means by which the community came together to form a support structure, and also to model systematically the culture of interdependence upon one another. This is why structurally tithing was a covenant with a person and not with an organization or institution. For example, Abraham tithed to Melchizedek; or, the corporate nation of Israel tithed to Levi. Levi was in Abraham tithing to Melchizedek. Do you see the principle? Then, it's up to the one receiving the tithes to become a conduit of distribution in the midst of the community and in missions. Distribution is the one principle to illustrate the man of God has been delivered from the love of money. I have discovered three different tithe in the Old Covenant, with each one dedicated to a distinguishable purpose.

The first is the *Levitical tithe*. It amounted to a systematic support account for the Levites and not an institution or church. If we modernized the Levite, we're speaking of the associate ministers and support personnel in churches and ministries. The heavenly Father made sure there was provision for those who labored in the sanctuary. Apostle Paul used this same principle for support for those in fulltime ministry in the New Testament, which enabled them to concentrate on prayer and the Word of God.

> *And, behold, I have given the children of Levi all the tenth in Israel for an inheritance, for their service which they serve, even the service of the tabernacle of the congregation* (Numbers 18:21).

> *Say I these things as a man? Or saith not the Law the same also? For it is written in the law of Moses, Thou shalt not muzzle the mouth of the ox that treadeth out the corn. Doth God take care of oxen? Or saith He it altogether for our sakes? For our sakes, no doubt, this is written: that he that ploughed should plough in hope; and that he that thresheth in hope should be partaker of his hope. If we have sown unto you spiritual things, is it a great thing if we shall reap your carnal things? If others be partakers of this power over you, are not we rather? Nevertheless we have not used this power; but suffer all things, lest we should hinder the gospel of Christ. Do ye not know that they which minister about holy things live of the things of the temple? And they which wait at the altar are partakers with the altar? Even so hath the Lord ordained that they which preach the gospel should live of the gospel* (1 Corinthians 9:8-14).

Let him that is taught in the word communicate unto him that teaches in all good things (Galatians 6:6).

The second tithe was the *festival tithe.* It allowed the person giving to actually share in the consumption of the tithe. This amounted to *an annual savings plan* in preparation for the feasts. Many churches or fellowship groups have annual convocations or assemblies encouraging participation from their affiliates. Most people save in order to participate during those times. This law went into effect to keep people from mooching off of others. But to carry this thought a bit further, it is a sound economic principle to save ten percent of what you harvests for a year. Think of how much debt could be cancelled if all people would practice this principle.

Thou mayest not eat within thy gates the tithe of thy corn, or of thy wine, or of thy oil, or the firstlings of thy herds or of thy flock, nor any of thy vows which thou vowest, nor thy freewill offerings, or heave offering of thine hand: but thou must eat them before the Lord thy God in the place which the Lord thy God shall choose, thou, and thy son, and thy daughter, and thy manservant, and thy maidservant, and the Levite that is within thy gates: and thou shalt rejoice before the Lord thy God in all that thou puttest thine hands unto. Take heed to thyself that thou forsake not the Levite as long as thou livest upon the earth (Deuteronomy 12:17-19).

Thou shalt truly tithe all the increase of thy seed, that the field bringeth forth year by year. And thou shalt eat before the Lord thy God, in the place which he shall choose to place his name there, the tithe of thy corn, of thy wine, and of thine oil, and the firstlings of thy herds and of thy flocks; that thou mayest learn to fear the Lord thy God always (Deuteronomy 14:22-23).

The third aspect of tithing was the increase tithe, which was equivalent to *a modern mission fund* (social responsibility) established to minister to the Levite and the underprivileged. Some scholars believe that every third and sixth year the festival tithe became the increase tithe. Whether that's true or not, it is clear that there is an increase tithe, which was given systematically every three years in the economy of Israel. Again, let's modernize this concept. What would happen if people today would give an increase tithe every three years from investment portfolios strictly for home and foreign missions? I believe the church would be much more efficient and effective in accomplishing the Great Commission. Of course something like this could never become obligatory or compulsory.

At the end of three years thou shalt bring forth all the tithe of thine increase the same year, *and shalt lay it up within thy gates: and the Levite, (because he hath no part nor inheritance with thee,) and the stranger, and the fatherless, and the widow, which are within thy gates, shall come, and shall eat and be satisfied; that the Lord thy God may bless thee in all the work of thine hand which thou doest* (Deuteronomy 14:28-29).

When thou hast made an end of **tithing all the tithes of thine increase the third year,** *which is the year of tithing, and hast given it unto the Levite, the stranger, the fatherless* *and the widow, that they may eat within thy gates, and be filled; then thou shalt say before the Lord thy God, I have brought away the hallowed things out of mine house, and also have given them unto the Levite, and unto the stranger, to the fatherless, and to the widow, according to all thy commandments which thou hast commanded me: I have not transgressed thy commandments, neither have I forgotten them: I have not eaten thereof in my mourning, neither have I taken away ought thereof for any unclean use, nor given ought thereof for the dead: but I have hearkened to the voice of the Lord my God, and have done according to all that thou hast commanded me. Look down from thy holy habitation, from heaven, and bless thy people Israel, and the land which thou hast given us, as thou swarest unto our fathers, a land that floweth with milk and honey (Deuteronomy 26:12-15).*

More needs to be clearly communicated about the priority of missions and the principle of third-year tithing in the postmodern world. Missions must be presented as a venerable alternative—an attractive lifestyle that objects to materialism's clutches. If we live in an affluent society, a land that flows with milk and honey, we have been lavished with incredible opportunities to succeed in the Great Commission with much financial backing.

We must begin to visualize beyond the hedonistic culture driven by the spirit of greediness that we live in. Few things control the behavior of human beings like finances and economic conditions in general. It seems the more money we have the more we are distracted from what is really important. Money becomes a determinant of everything we do. Whether a person lives in the ghetto, suburbs, or a gated community depends on economics. What would happen if the more strength we have economically the more missions-conscious we became? Instead of condemning other cultures, we could persuade young people into becoming missionaries because of the beauty of the calling and the elation it would generate in their lives.

I am convinced that attitudes must change in the West and most of the world's industrialized societies! We are overindulged and overwhelmed with materialism. We equate being blessed with the kinds of status symbols we possess. For instance, our culture screams, "A blessed person drives a Mercedes Benz rather than a Ford Taurus." What a person drives is a matter of preference and does not gauge what degree someone is blessed. I will never forget that one of the richest men in Jacksonville, North Carolina, always drove an old Plymouth station wagon. He certainly was financially positioned to purchase anything he desired.

The second thing I'd like to know is *"Who came up with the criterion with which we appraise ourselves?"* Some of the world's billionaires would rather drive a Chevrolet than a million-dollar Bugatti. We are blessed because the heavenly Father declared us blessed in Christ— period! (See Ephesians 1:3.)

I agree with the great reformer, John Wesley, when he proposed this quadrilateral thought: "A person should earn all they can, save all they can, invest all they can, and then, give all they can." One of the four areas of giving he encouraged was giving to the needy, even though some may not be believers. History records that Wesley thought correctly and practiced what he preached. When he died, he owned only a few miscellaneous items—had given everything away.[2] This reminds me of what Jesus challenged the rich young ruler to do. Today's postmodern apostles must challenge the rich young rulers of our day to do the same; therefore, they lay treasure up in Heaven in the process.

3. *Give cheerfully*. *Cheerful* comes from Strong's Concordance word

entry #2431; *hilaros*, which means "propitious or merry (hilarious), prompt or willing: -cheerful."

> *Every man according as he purposeth in his heart, so let him give; not grudgingly, or of necessity: for God loveth a* **cheerful giver** *(2 Corinthians. 9:7).*

> *I want each of you to take plenty time to think it over, and make up your own mind what you will give. That will protect you against sob stories and arm-twisting. God loves it when* **the giver delights in the giving** *(2 Corinthians. 9:7 TM).*

> *But when ye go over Jordan, and dwell in the land which the Lord your God giveth you to inherit, and when He giveth you rest from all your enemies round about, so that ye dwell in safety; then there shall be a place which the Lord your God shall choose to cause His name to dwell there; thither shall ye bring all that I command you; your burnt offerings, and your sacrifices, your tithes, and the heave offerings of your hand, and all your choice vows which ye vow unto the Lord:* **and ye shall rejoice before the Lord your God**, *ye, and your sons, and your daughters, and your menservants, and your maidservants, and the Levite that is within your gates; forasmuch as he hath no part nor inheritance with you (Deuteronomy 12:10-12).*

Joyful giving is one of the most refreshing things to be around. Nothing is more disheartening and annoying than attempting to persuade stingy or ungrateful people to give. During offering time, I've watched people reach into their wallets or purses and give the smallest bill they could find. God loves a cheerful, prompt-to-do-it giver, not a stingy-on-notice, holding-back giver. I have been in many churches when precious time was spent cleverly convincing the doubtful and arm-twisting the spiritually illiterate to give. People's faces often reveal the conditions of their hearts—they hadn't planned on giving abundantly.

There is no reason to waste spiritual gifts on people unconvinced that they should give. Such actions may border manipulation and witchcraft. People should already be prepared to give when they come together, which isn't asking too much. When people give freely, they usually give joyfully. Henry Ward Beecher said: "The test of your Christian character should be that you are a joy-bearing agent to the world."[3] Joy-bearing should be most reflective in our giving. The apostle Paul said: "*Rejoice in the Lord always; and again I say, rejoice*" (Phil. 4:4). I simply believe joy in giving is one of the proofs of the efficacy of our Christianity.

4. **Give bountifully**. *Bountifully* comes from Strong's Concordance word entry #2129; *eulogia*, which means "elegance of language; commendation, reverentially adoration; benediction; consecration; benefit or largess:—blessing (a matter of) bounty (x - tifully), fair speech."

> *But this I say, He which soweth sparingly shall reap also sparingly;* ***and he which soweth bountifully shall also reap bountifully*** *(2 Corinthians 9:6).*

> *Remember: A stingy planter gets a stingy crop; a lavish planter gets a lavish crop (2 Corinthians 9:6 TM).*

> *And Moses gave commandment, and they caused it to be proclaimed throughout the camp, saying, "Let neither man*

*nor woman make any more work for the offering of the sanc-tuary." So the people were restrained from bringing. **For the stuff they had was sufficient for all the work to make it, and too much*** (Exodus 36:6-7).

*And when Hezekiah and the princes came and saw the heaps, they blessed the Lord, and his people Israel. Then Hezekiah questioned with the priests and the Levites concerning the heaps. And Azariah the chief priest of the house of Zadok answered him, and said, "**Since the people began to bring the offerings into the house of the Lord, we have had enough to eat, and have left plenty**: for the Lord hath blessed his people; and that which is left is this great store* (2 Chronicles 31:8-10).

It is my conviction that every principle the apostle Paul espoused in the New Testament can be seen in seed form in the Old Testament. Paul says: *"All Scripture is given by inspiration of God, and is profitable for doc-trine, for reproof, for correction, for instruction in righteousness: that the man of God may be perfect, thoroughly furnished unto all good works"* (2 Tim. 3:16-17). What Scripture was Paul speaking about? From a first-century perspective, it had to be the Old Testament because the New Tes-tament hadn't been canonized as Scripture yet. However, it is fair to say that not all Old Testament Scriptures apply in the New Testament. The question must always be asked: "Does the New Testament sanction, main-tain, amend or abolish the Old Testament practice?"

Father God highly rejoices over His children when they practice giv-ing principles according to the apostolic pattern. There is an elegance of grace when we follow His time-tested design. These four principles form a beautiful tapestry of truth for freehearted people. It is spiritual excellence combined with divine DNA, which reveals something amazingly marvelous about the nature of God. When we follow divine initiatives, we don't have to fret over being trapped into human tomfoolery.

STALWARTS IN THE PRACTICE OF DISTRIBUTION

Before closing this chapter, it would be worthwhile to hear from a few of the people who processed Kingdom distribution. In the early church, Joseph Barnabas and the Macedonia churches were singled-out as trendsetters in the principle of Kingdom distribution. They each rose to the heavenly mandate of giving without necessarily expecting any return from God or others. They left a legacy for the modern church stalwarts of distribution who were faithful in the early years of the Protestant Reformation. From that time, we see the new pacesetters and pathfinders of truth. The following extraordinary individuals, with remarkable intuition, saw and walked in the principle of Kingdom distribution:

1. *He who bestows his goods upon the poor shall have as much again, and ten times more.* —John Bunyan, Puritan writer and preacher[4]

2. *He who is not liberal with what he has, does but deceive himself when he thinks he would be liberal if he had more.* —W.S. Tulner[5]

3. *Be charitable before wealth makes thee covetous.* —Sir Thomas Browne, English writer[6]

4. *Without a rich heart wealth is an ugly beggar.* —Ralph Waldo Emerson, American writer[7]

5. *I have watched hundreds of Christians in my time become financially blessed then develop an acquisitiveness that makes their souls as metallic as the coins they seek.* —Selwyn Hughes, English pastor and author[8]

6. John Wesley, an 18th-century reformer, was another powerful model. When he first became a believer in Christ, He had a salary of 30 pounds per year. He lived on 28 and gave two to the church. His salary increased to 50 pounds per year. He lived on 28 and gave 22 to the church. When his salary was increased to 100 pounds per year, he lived on 28 and gave 72 to the church. At first, Wesley used 93 percent of his income and gave 7 percent to the ministry.

   Does that sound like tithing to you? As he received a raise, he used 56 percent of his income and gave 44 percent to the ministry. And finally, Wesley used 28 percent and gave away 72 percent of his funds to the ministry. He said, "Money never stays with me. It would burn me if it did. I throw it out of my hands as soon as possible, lest it finds its way into my heart."[9] John Wesley was never bound by the law of tithing; rather, he walked faithfully in the principle of Kingdom distribution. In the greatest year of his earning power, Wesley gave away a purported 98 percent of his income.

7. Andrew Carnegie was another powerful example of dis-
    tribution. By the time he died in 1919, he had given away
    $350,695,653. At his death, the last $30 million was given
    way to foundations, charities, and pensioners. With the
    devaluing of today's dollar, Carnegie's gift could easily be
    currently worth $100 billion. He expressed his trustee-
    ship of money in terms he called the gospel of wealth
    penned in 1889. I offer this abridged statement of that
    document.

> This, then, is held to be the duty of the man of wealth:
> To set an example of modest, unostentatious living,
> shunning display or extravagance; to provide moder-
> ately for the legitimate wants of those dependent
> upon him; and, after doing so, to consider all surplus
> revenues which come to him simply as trust funds,
> which he is called upon to administer, and strictly
> bound as a matter of duty to administer in the man-
> ner which, in his judgment, is best calculated to pro-
> duce the most beneficial results for the
> community—the man of wealth thus becoming the
> mere agent and trustee for his poorer brethren, bring-
> ing to their service his superior wisdom, experience,
> and ability to administer, doing for them better than
> they would or could do for themselves.[10]

8. American businessman, and mega-millionaire industrialist,
    R.G. Letourneau understood the principle of distribution

in his concept of *God's shovel is bigger than mine*. In an interview, Mr. Letourneau shared his thoughts on why he gave away ninety percent (or reverse tithe) of his income. He believed that we are all stewards of God's money. In other words we are money managers for God. God's will is not for us to horde the money he gives us but to use it to God's good. If we are good managers and we at least tithe, and help others, then God will give us more money to manage. All Mr. Letourneau did was shovel money to charities, churches, and organizations that needed help.[11]

In maintaining the theme of this book, redistribution and the transference of wealth, it is extremely important to consider what these men said and how they lived. The problem in any age is the proper administration of wealth from a Kingdom perspective that binds humanity together in an affable relationship. We're living in a rapidly shifting world, much more so than what the previous industrialists faced. Our world is driven by accessible information altering almost every day. Wealth is changing hands rather quickly, and more people possess the necessary information on how to accrue wealth.

How do we prevent ourselves from returning to the universal squalor of greed and selfishness? I believe there's a master key to aid us. We must observe the strictest principles of empowerment. One of the means of empowerment is to contribute charitably anytime possible. Intense individualism will only drive us back to the accumulation practices of the past. As Mr. Carnegie said, beyond personal responsibilities, fortunes are amassed for prudent distribution.

It is highly commendable when we listen to the voice of the Holy Spirit long enough to discover where our surplus should go. God is well pleased when we do!

ENDNOTES

1. R. Laird Harris, Gleason L. Archer Jr., and Bruce K. Waltke, *Theological Wordbook of the Old Testament, Volume 2* (Chicago, IL: The Moody Bible Institute, 1980), 702.

2. http://www.generousgiving.org/page.asp?sec=72&page=427: Stewardship Sermon Illustrations, accessed 2/18/08.

3. R. Daniel Watkins, *An Encyclopedia of Compelling Quotations* (Peabody, MA: Hendrickson Publishers, Inc., 2001), 394.

4. Brian Kluth, *Quips and Quotes on Finances, Money and Generosity Giving.* (http://www.Kluth.org/church/quips&quotes.htm.), May 2007.

5. Virginia Ely, *I Quote* (New York: George W. Stewart Publisher, Inc., 1947), 143.

6. Brian Kluth, May 2007.

7. Ibid.

8. Ibid.

9. Ibid.

10. Adapted from R. Bannis' publication of Andrew Carnegie's writing, *Wealth,* http://www.Swarthmore.edu/SocSci/rbannis1/AIH19th/Carnegie.html, May 2007.

11. Brian Kluth, May 2007.

Chapter 9

PRACTICAL APPLICATION OF DISTRIBUTION

The Lord shall increase you more and more, you and your children. Ye are blessed of the Lord which made heaven and earth. The heaven, even the heavens, are the Lord's: but the earth hath He given to the children of men (Psalm 115:14-16).

All that I have written thus far brings us to this most imperative moment. The intent was to establish the theology and hermeneutical support of wealth redistribution, Kingdom distribution, and the order of biblical first things from a historical and practical viewpoint. In so doing, everything traces back to the seed plot of the original dominion mandate in Adam, and corporately, in the nation of Israel as a sound Kingdom theocracy and economy.

The psalmist captures the order of God concerning first things in Psalm 115. In the beginning, the first of all first things must come from God, establishing that first things in every generation of humankind will belong to Him. Afterward, humanity, whose assignment it is to rule and manage the earth, must assist in the production and distribution of first things. As Adam apprenticed under the tutorship of the heavenly Father, he learned how to administrate his domain and the wealth consisted in it. He learned what, when, how, and where to release things. His success determined the quality of fellowship for all people and would become the tie that binds us together. Failure would create unparalleled consequences—hardships affixed to life inconceivable.

Two catalysts prompting success is obedience and industry. Humankind must obey the Creator; and the Creator stimulate our mind, growth, and development through sanctified labor. Our labor allows us to routinely unearth the wealth in our environment. Inevitably, we achieve a place of awesome wealth, but not without our Creator as our guide.

We have seen glimpses of people in history experiencing each of these concepts (wealth redistribution, Kingdom distribution, and the order of first things), such as the patriarchs and some of the prophets, priests and Levites, apostles of the first century, and the industrialist. Each subject discussed has some obscure aspects which makes it difficult to totally reconstruct its history perfectly. However, one thing is unchallengeable: Over and over we see the unparalleled blessing of seeking God first, and the dire consequences of failure to do so. No one will go wrong by choosing to honor the Lord in this manner.

In light of this, law and grace are distinct principles and must not be mixed together. People err, in my opinion, by making the spiritual law from God's mouth equivalent to legalism and people's traditions based upon their interpretations of the law. Only 1,500 of the 4,000 years of Old Testament history were considered the Law years. That gives us 2,500 years of Kingdom activities in which we see wealth redistribution, distribution, and the order of first things operating outside of the Law economy, which constitutes about 63 percent of all Old Testament activity. Consider it this way: Nearly two-thirds of the Old Testament had nothing to do with the Law of Moses.

It is essential to understand the differences between the Old and New Covenants when considering the plan of God, especially concerning giving. A challenge we face as teachers of the Word that is sure to provoke a red-hot argument is, *"How many Old Testament giving practices do we bring across the covenantal divide?"* If I may take up an apologist role for a moment, and focus on the great debate about tithing, it becomes a simple matter to me. The Old Testament is form and the New Testament is substance. What lesson did God want us to learn from the form?

When Father God breathed through Moses the principles of firstfruits and tithes in Numbers chapter 18, He knew the Old Covenant would end through the death, burial, and resurrection of Jesus Christ. He also knew the apostles would reach back to draw from this text to establish biblical proof for apostolic financial support. The most important question would be, "Did we hear what the Father was saying, and why He said it?" If we heard clearly, there is no way we could transport across the great covenantal divide one means of supporting ministry and neglect the other as though it does not exist. We do an injustice to the Scriptures by carrying tithing across the divide and leaving firstfruits behind.

Another injustice is the attempt to make them synonymous, just as we erred in the past attempting to make the baptism in the Holy Spirit and the New Birth synonymous. Either they both come across or they both stay behind. There is one thing for sure: We can ill afford to cherry pick either one at the expense of the other.

Some will argue that the New Testament confirms tithing while it does not confirm firstfruits giving. (See Matthew 23:23-24 and Hebrews 7:4-10.) I will counter that statement by saying, "The New Testament has more to say about firstfruits than it does tithing." First, Jesus came at the end of the Law Dispensation. The activities of His ministry are all Old Covenant activities. So Jesus was not opposed to tithing, though we do not read one recorded instance in which He tithes. It would be unreasonable to believe one can responsibly fulfill the law and oppose it at the same time. Jesus may have resisted the methodology of the existing priesthood, but He did not resist the holy laws of His Father. However, Jesus literally became a living manifestation of what the tithe was about—something wholly unto the Lord. Jesus lived the spirit of total giving, which is whole-life giving.

In the case of Abraham tithing to Melchizedek, this occurred once; and it is very different from production tithing. The principle we practice in the modern church is tithing off our regular income, or production tithing. Abraham tithed from the spoils of war. Obviously, these two are different. Once again, I appeal to the spirit of what the heavenly Father was teaching us. If Abraham, our father, saw unsolicited tithing as a necessity of expressing one's love, so should we. It indicates we are learning the principle of trusting God as our resource and not our money. Spiritual people give and do not cherry pick in the process. They simply heed the voice of the Master. As one matures, greater giving becomes a Kingdom cultural behavior.

GIVING YOUR BEST

At the heart of Old and New Testament giving is Kingdom distribution and breaking the backbone of covetousness. Basically there is nothing wrong with giving ten percent of one's income; however, that should only be a starting point if we bring discipline to our finances. Since the Book of Hebrews calls the New Covenant a better Covenant, giving should significantly improve under the auspices of grace. All of us should be sensitive to the Holy Spirit's directives and sensitive to the needs of others in a responsible, scriptural manner. God's gift to all of us in the person of Jesus

Christ remains the compelling distinctive for giving. God gave us His best and we should give our best at all times. The order of first things is all about giving one's best.

When we understand these principles, we *move away from frustration giving* and *compulsory giving*. All of our responses will flow out of a desire to fulfill the dominion mandate. It is only as I give freely that I master money rather than having money master me. Rather than struggling with biblical interpretations, we will manage our affairs with better execution and with a greater sense of Kingdom stewardship. Whether we like it or not, people will always give based upon what they have decided in their hearts to give. Though we teach them all the giving Scriptures, they will follow the impulses of their hearts.

I encourage all believers to get a greater revelation of grace, and then be willing to steward money wisely. We will better distribute money based upon biblical priorities. Those priorities:

1. Our covenant with God.

2. Our covenant with the immediate family.

3. Our covenant with the extended family.

4. The relief of needy Christians.

5. The relief of unbelievers.

If we'll follow this pattern, we will spiritually mature and grow in a genuine partnership with Christ in grace giving.

Resource Living

The primary question before each of us is: "Do we desire to live by a restricted source, or do we desire to live out of a never-ending resource?" When we consider everything theoretically, no one qualifies to be our resource but God. Adam traded God, the ultimate resource, for a very limited source of information, which led him into a land of devastation. In view of this, it's very important to define *source* and *resource*.

Webster defines *source* as "a point of origin, or one that causes, creates, and initiates. One that supplies information." Source comes from the Old French word *sourde* meaning "to rise" and the Latin word *surgere* meaning "to surge." One of the important meanings of *surge* is "*to increase suddenly.*" A source is someone in your life who causes you to surge ahead; they are instruments of empowerment; those who supply you with whatever you may be lacking. The nature of their assistance is temporary and not permanent. From parents to other helpful people, we all have had a number of sources in our lives. Whether help is in the realm of information, money, or other vitals, sources do what they can out of the limited supply they possess.

A *resource*, on the other hand, is unlimited. That's the reason God is the only One who qualifies as our resource. Even if a source has several billion dollars, they are still limited to what several billion can produce. God, as a resource, is an accessible supply who can be withdrawn from when necessary. By adding *re* to *source*, the word comes from the Old French word *resourdre* meaning "to rise again." When others who have been wonderful sources of aid exhaust their support, our heavenly Father will always have another source waiting. That's the reality of a resource.

Sometimes He will make sure circumstances cut off some relationships to prevent us from becoming too dependent upon one person. Or, some-one may develop a negative attitude and withdraw their support. Either way, it's the hand of God making sure His children remain dependent and connected to Him. Although there may be people God will use to pour into our lives causing us to surge ahead, don't ever forget God, the Resource, is behind each source. There's a powerful principle mentioned several times in the Scriptures that boldly declares God's intentions to be our main resource.

> *And, behold, I am with thee, and will keep thee in all places whither thou goest, and will bring thee again into this land;* ***for I will not leave thee, until I have done that which I have spoken to thee of*** *(Genesis 28:15).*

> *And the Lord shall give them up before your face, that ye may do unto them according unto all the commandments which I have commanded you. Be strong and of a good courage, fear not, nor be afraid of them:* ***for the Lord thy God, He it is that doth go with thee; He will not fail thee, nor forsake thee*** *(Deuteronomy 31:5-6).*

> *There shall not any man be able to stand before thee all the days of thy life:* ***as I was with Moses, so I will be with thee: I will not fail thee, nor forsake thee*** *(Joshua 1:5).*

> *And David said to Solomon his son, "Be strong and of good courage, and do it: fear not, nor be dismayed:* ***for the Lord God, even my God, will be with thee; He will not fail thee,***

nor forsake thee, until thou hast finished all the work for the service of the house of the Lord" (1 Chronicles 28:20).

I have been young, and now am old; yet have I not seen the righteous forsaken, nor his seed begging bread (Psalm 37:25).

And Jesus came and spake unto them, saying, "All power is given unto Me in heaven and in earth. Go ye therefore, and teach all nations, baptizing them in the name of the Father, and of the Son, and of the Holy Ghost: teaching them to observe all things whatsoever I have commanded you: and lo, I am with you always, even unto the end of the world." Amen (Matthew 28:18-20).

Let your conversation be without covetousness; and be content with such things as ye have: for he hath said, "I will never leave thee, nor forsake thee." So that we may boldly say," the Lord is my Helper, and I will not fear what man shall do unto me" (Hebrews 13:5-6).

From the times of the patriarch Jacob to the sterling epistle to the Hebrews, God makes a categorical guarantee to each vessel during a time of transition. Though transition may be unsettling, one of the most comforting thoughts on earth is the sense of security we get from the abiding presence of our Father. Proper alignment with our assignment produces the overwhelming support of the heavenly Father. Because of this, there is an overriding clause to each divine commission: *Father God commits to be the resource to anyone He calls, whether corporate or individual.* This principle establishes the foundation for abundant life.

FIRSTFRUITS AND THE ABUNDANT LIFE

The thief cometh not, but for to steal, and to kill, and to destroy: I am come that they might have life, and that they might have it more abundantly (John 10:10).

Jesus makes it clear that thieves have prevented us from living the abundant life. In relationship to the abundant life, why is the principle of firstfruits and first things so important to us? Science tells us that the firstfruits, like sprouts, are the most biologically alive plants. They have the fullest life potential with the full chemical composition for the beginning and the end of its life unlike any other time in the life cycle of the plant. Abundant life is quality life, and the best quality is in the seedling of the firstfruits.

This concept connects with the *finished work of Christ*, though it may be the initial form of a new genesis of humankind; yet it's a statement of what the completion will be as well. Isaiah the prophet shared the same thought in these powerful words: *"Declaring the end* [full harvest] *from the beginning* [firstfruits], *and from ancient times the things that are yet done, saying, 'My counsel shall stand, and I will do all my pleasure'"* (Isa. 46:10). Father God sees the full abundant harvest of a new humanity from the quality that is in Christ, the firstfruits. Therefore, everything about the new creation is evaluated based upon Him. Christ is everything God is! To me, that's a profound definition of abundant life—*everything that God is which makes it unlimited and replete.*

Jesus Christ declared Himself to be the fullness of life, the beginning and the end, the first and last, and the Alpha and the Omega—abundant life. (See Revelation 1:8, 11; 21:6; 22:13.) Based on the Kingdom law of circularity, the alpha and the omega are the same points on a circle or sphere. For example, my wedding ring is in the form of a circle. Any point I choose to start a rotation of my ring would also be the finishing point. Physicists discovered that the universe is designed in this same manner. If we could release a light beam from a certain point in the universe, it would move at the speed of light in an elliptical until it reached its original starting point. Father God built the universe and life itself to have no dead-end streets. Paul captures this idea: *"For of Him, and through Him, and to Him, are all things: to whom be glory for ever. Amen"* (Rom. 11:36).

The firstfruits are a substitutional statement that says, "All that came from God must return to God; and it begins by becoming proactive in the culture of firstfruits giving." For instance, would it not be laudable to focus on God at the beginning of every year rather than bills, needs, and other obligations? Because my life came from God, it must return to God. My biological life has measured time, which eventually must be swallowed up into a higher grade of life. Since life, time, and money are all interconnected, it is rather simple to see why God implemented this order of the first and last as being the same unique point with which to start. And if we merge the two together, we establish precedence for the abundant life. There is no finer time than January 1st every year to begin planning firstfruits giving.

One other thought that brings the first and last together is in the word *truth*. Truth is always the key to an abundant life since thieves use lies to rob each of us of quality life. Jesus said *"I am the truth."* (See John 14:6.) The Hebrew word for truth is *emeth*. Since Hebrew words are spelled with consonants and not with vowels, truth begins with the first letter and ends with the last letter of the Hebrew alphabet. Whatever is truth in the beginning is also truth in the end.

Concerning the firstfruits, it was truth in the beginning with Cain and Abel, with Israel as a Kingdom culture, and it will be truth in the end with the church as the final installment of a Kingdom culture on earth.

CAIN AND ABEL AND THE FIRSTFRUITS

It is highly important to study the embryo of Kingdom activities in the Book of Genesis to understand completely the practical application of distribution. The first acceptable offering to God by men involved the order of first things. It takes us back to the story of Cain and Abel. Both men engaged in *heart response* giving. Father God taught Adam and Adam taught his sons. Each man vigorously responded to God based on his perception of what God was saying. Sometimes we filter things correctly and other times we do not. All in the postmodern world can learn from both men.

> *And in process of time it came to pass, that Cain brought of the fruit of the ground an offering unto the Lord. And Abel, he also brought of the **firstlings** of his flock and of the fat thereof. And the Lord had respect unto Abel and to his offering: but unto Cain and to his offering he had not respect. And Cain was very wroth, and his countenance fell. And the Lord said unto Cain, "Why art thou wroth? And why is thy countenance fallen? If thou doest well, shalt thou not be accepted? And if thou doest not well sin lieth at the door. And unto thee shall be his desire, and thou shalt rule over him"* (Genesis 4:3-7).

By faith Abel offered unto God a more excellent sacrifice than Cain, by which he obtained witness that he was righteous, God testifying of his gifts: and by it he being dead yet speaketh (Hebrews 11:4).

The story of Cain and Abel is poignant. They represent the extremes of the same tree, good and evil. Remember, they weren't born until after the infamous decision was made to eat and receive knowledge from the wrong tree. In time, Cain and Abel presented the Lord with an offering, indicating some type of communication had occurred. Cain brought a generic offering (*minchah* #4503; to apportion, bestow a donation, a sacrificial offering [usually bloodless and voluntarily]: gift, oblation, offering, sacrifice, and present); Abel brought firstlings (*bekorah* #1062; that which burst the womb first of man and beast) and the fat (*cheleb* #2459; the richest and choicest part: the best, the finest). Obviously, from the different Hebrew words, there's a sharp, distinct difference in what each man thought God deserved. Why did God have respect for Abel's offering and none for Cain's? This question can best be understood by looking at the Septuagint, or the old Greek translation of the Hebrew Scriptures.

*And the Lord God said to Cain, wherefore didst thou become vexed, and wherefore did thy countenance fall? If thou **didst rightly offer**, but **didst not rightly divide**, didst thou not sin? Hold thy peace* (Genesis 4:6).

I thought for years that Cain's offering was unacceptable to the Lord because it was not a blood sacrifice, or proper approach offering. Thoughtfully, I have had to reconsider this. Cain had information he didn't apply. It was good to offer, but his attitude didn't allow him to rightly divide the Lord's portion. Obviously, Cain failed to identify the crops that ripened first, and then, willingly present them unto the Lord. His stance was that any offering would be acceptable and appreciated by the Lord. Many people today in the spirit of Cain still think God will accept anything, which is a grave error.

One of the major keys to understanding this scenario is to understand Abel offered by *faith* and Cain didn't. Faith comes by hearing the Lord's instructions. (See Romans 10:17.) The writer to the Hebrews helped me to process what was going on. Father God had given them the same instructions concerning what was acceptable to Him if they desired to present gifts in due order. Abel mixed what he heard with faith. The order of first things was the proper way to approach God. Further, the writer to the Hebrews declared that a firstling spirit is an excellent spirit, or a spirit of prosperity. Cain was everything in the embryo form that a covetous person could be; and Abel models for us the generous, liberal giver. To prove this, the Book of Jude places Cain, Balaam, and Korah in the same category of selfishness and greed. They are examples of apostates—men of immense shame, involved in something for what they could get out of it.

> *Woe unto them! For they have gone in the way of Cain, and ran greedily after the error of Balaam for reward, and perished in the gainsaying of Core. These are spots in your feasts of charity, when they feast with you, feeding themselves without fear: clouds they are without water, carried about of winds; trees whose fruit withered, without fruit, twice dead, plucked up by the roots; raging waves of the sea, foaming out their own shame; wandering stars, to whom is reserved the blackness of darkness for ever* (Jude 11-13).

JERICHO—FIRSTFRUIT CITY

The city of Jericho was one of the most urban civilizations known to man in the ancient world. It had excellent architectural technique consisting of large dwellings and public buildings, in addition to the great wall it was known for. Though standing as a formidable obstacle, Jericho was to be a confidence builder in the infallibility of God's strength. The entire city was to be a firstfruit of all their conquest; therefore, everything that wasn't devoted to the Lord was to be destroyed.

> *And the city shall be accursed, even it, and all that are therein, to the Lord: only Rahab the harlot shall live, she and all that are with her in the house, because she hid the messengers that we sent. And ye, in any wise keep yourselves from the accursed thing, lest ye make yourselves accursed, when ye take of the accursed thing, and make the camp of Israel a curse, and trouble it. But all the silver, and gold, and vessels of brass and iron, are consecrated unto the Lord: they shall come into the treasury of the Lord* (Joshua 6:17-19).

Everything in Jericho belonged to the Lord. The order of first things is clearly revealed in this passage from Joshua. If it wasn't exterminated, it was to be dedicated. In the Kingdom, there are times when whole cities became firstfruits of the Lord's dealings. That's why Achan's thievery of the devoted things troubled the entire nation. God viewed Achan's problem as Israel's problem; thus, placing a corporate identity to the problem. Once again, the spirit of covetousness and greed is uncovered in the midst of the nation of Israel. Several generations died in Achan's egregious violation of

God's word. This story proves how valuable the firstfruits were in the economy of God. They may either bless a man and his family or trouble them. After we have received revelation from the Spirit of God, we have a responsibility to walk in the truth.

I believe the United States of America was intended to become a firstfruit nation under God. For example, Germany was a firstfruit nation of restored Passover truths under Dr. Martin Luther. As the church moved into the second major wave of reformation, the U.S.A. became a Pentecostal firstfruit nation. In the panoply of reformation, God wanted to demonstrate His great power as a sign to all in the U.S.A. Covetousness, greed, and debt have hindered us just as Achan hindered the nation of Israel. We have stated on our money *"in God we trust,"* but actually, it is our money we really trust. If it was really about God, we wouldn't have bungled our responsibility to steward a land filled with milk and honey the way we have. Other nations have saved money, but we have spent with a vengeance. The federal and state governments are as guilty as the people.

In the May 29, 2007, issue of *USA Today*[1], an article states that taxpayers are now on the hook for a record $59.1 trillion in liabilities, which is a 2.3 percent increase from 2006. This amount is equal to $516,348 for every U.S. household. By comparison, U.S. households owe an average of $112,043 for mortgages, car loans, credit cards, and all other debt combined. Federal and state governments are $400,000 more in debt than the average household. Unfunded promises made for Medicare, Social Security, and federal retirement programs account for 85 percent of taxpayer liabilities. State and local government retirement plans account for much of the rest.

This hidden debt is the amount taxpayers would have to pay immediately to cover government's financial obligations. Like a mortgage, it will cost more to repay the debt over time. Every U.S. household would have to pay about $31,000 a year to do so in 75 years. According to King Solomon, this makes the USA the servant to all our creditors. Without experiencing a year of Jubilee, in which all debt is excused, the debt is expected to grow to unimaginable sums. Also, this doesn't include the $3 trillion budget recently introduced by the president—plunging the United States even further in debt.

Elijah and the Firstfruit Operation

The order of first things was in operation during the prophetic period. Some prophets were also priestly in nature because of corruption in the Kingdom, and especially the Levitical priests. The prophet Malachi's stinging rebuke was written primarily to the priests of his day. He dealt with their abuse of the storehouse tithe, which should have been placed there for the high priestly family. Elijah employed the firstfruits principle with the widow woman of Zarephath during the time of famine, thus launching her into a prosperous, wealthy place. Because Elijah moved by the word of the Lord, what he did was a faith act rather than one of presumption.

> So he arose and went to Zarephath. And when he came to the gate of the city, behold, the widow woman was there gathering sticks: and he called to her, and said, "Fetch me, I pray thee, a little water in a vessel, that I may drink." And as she was going to fetch it, he called to her, and said, "Bring me, I pray thee, a morsel of bread in thine hand." And she said, "As the Lord thy God liveth, I have not a cake, but a handful of

meal in a barrel, and a little oil in a cruse: and, behold, I am gathering two sticks, that I may go in and dress it for me and my son, that we eat it, and die." And Elijah said unto her, "Fear not; go and do as thou hast said: but make me thereof a little cake first, and bring it unto me, and after make for thee and for thy son. For thus saith the Lord God of Israel, the barrel of meal shall not waste, neither shall the cruse of oil fail, until the day that the Lord sendeth rain upon the earth." And she went and did according to the saying of Elijah: and she, and he, and her house, did eat many days. And the barrel of meal wasted not, neither did the cruse of oil fail, according to the word of the Lord, which he spake by Elijah (1 Kings 17:10-16).

The words of the prophet had released dearth and deprivation, collapsing the economy of the nation. At this point, the famine in the land was grievously painful. Though there was great lack in the land, God had sent two commands to sustain the prophet in the midst of it; thus, revealing the Lord's provision in difficult seasons.

Carnal people fear recessions and depressions; however, they do not limit a son of God operating in Kingdom order, speaking only the words of the King. Zarephath became the second place of purification and enlargement in Elijah's life. The story of the widow conveys the extreme conditions and a panoramic view of life itself for the average person during the famine. Most people lived on a simple supply until it ran out; and then they died. Elijah's meeting with the widow would be a most unusual day for her and her son. She was thinking in terms of finality; the prophet had the words of life in his mouth.

People prosper when they believe the words of prophets sent by God. He employed the principle of the firstfruits. When the widow gave Elijah food first in response to the word of the Lord, it was as though she gave it to the Lord Himself. In fact, she gave what represented all for her, thus, showing that total release and an unlimited supply are in the same place. This act opened an unlimited supply of God's abundance in her life that didn't lift until the Lord sent visitation to the earth. Once again, this confirms the power of the firstfruits offering in compliance to the word of the Lord.

At first, this may have appeared to be a very selfish act on the prophet Elijah's part; however, it was far from that. God had already commanded the widow to minister to Elijah before he approached her. (See 1 Kings 17:8-9.) Today, many people of God stand in the valley of decision, facing either command or coercion. Commands are simple: *The Lord said it and that settles it!* With coercion, people must scheme and almost sedate others with an inundation of false promises to get them to comply with their wishes. Coercion is despicable.

Once again, when we're speaking of billions of dollars to come into the church, it's going to take free people to avoid the trap of placing others under duress to collect funds from them. The church, throughout her long history, has faced a glut of these types of unscrupulous, deceitful ministries. As we all face our Zarephath, our times of extreme cleansing by the fire of the Holy Spirit, the heavenly Father will purge us of any desire to fleece and defraud people. Our words will be exactly what the Lord is saying and nothing more. We will not be guilty of the same mistake that Balaam made, which was prophesying for money.

I am personally acquainted with men and women who started honorably in God but became overwhelmed by the desire to get wealth. Instead of maintaining integrity in the principles of God's Word, they chose to sell out for the color green. It is my prayer that these individuals will return to their first love. Also, I am praying daily that no ministry would ever use the order of first things to selfishly build their bank accounts or portfolios. It would be a terrible shame that such a powerful tool of economic reformation became an opportunity for greater intemperance in the minds of irresponsible priests.

ELISHA AND FIRSTFRUITS FROM THE TREBLED ZONE

Elisha was the attendant of Elijah and his successor as the primary prophet to Israel. When Elisha received a double portion of Elijah's anointing, it was indicative he was Elijah's firstborn prophetic son. He received firstfruits and used them as an opportunity to distribute, thus walking in the law of benefaction. This was one of the many miracles Elisha was best remembered for. The miracle of the firstfruit loaves anticipated the miracle of Christ feeding the multitude with the fishes and loaves. He was motivated by a deep compassion as he responded to pleas for help on various occasions. As he relinquished the loaves of firstfruits, he released faith for the miraculous, squelching any prospect of covetousness and greed.

> And there came a man from Baal-shalisha, and brought the man of God bread of the firstfruits, twenty loaves of barley, and full ears of corn in the husk thereof. And he said, "Give unto the people, that they may eat." And his servitor said, "What, should I set this before a hundred men?" He said again, "Give the people, that they may eat: for thus saith the Lord, they shall eat, and shall leave thereof." So he set it

before them, and they did eat, and left thereof, according to
the word of the Lord (2 Kings 4:42-44).

I found this to be a most interesting passage in considering the principle of firstfruits or the law of first things. First, there is no suggestion of
social intercourse between Elisha and the man from Baal-shalisha. He
clearly practiced the principle of firstfruits as he brought them to the
school of the prophets in Gilgal. Baal-shalisha was a fertile valley in
Ephraim conducive to growing crops.

Second, when we look closely at the name Baal-shalisha, we find some
interesting facts, understanding that names carry purpose. *Baal* is a
generic term for master, husband, or lord. *Shalisha* means "trebled land; to
be or made triplicate (by restoration, in portions, strands, days, or years):
do the third time, three (days, -fold, parts, years old)." This story prefigures
a man coming from the third dimension with firstfruits transporting them
to the prophetic order, who chooses to feed the people with them.

Much can be said about this. Obviously Jesus was a man from the third
dimension, transporting bread from Heaven to a dying world. Each time
He would feed the multitude He engaged in the principle of unselfish distribution; furthermore, it was a prophetic precursor of who he was. Even,
today, Father God is elevating a prophetic and priestly people who will
minister from the trebled zone.

There's a third wave of reformation flooding the earth. Some of the
bread that was fresh during the first two waves of reformation has grown
stale. It was very appropriate for the past seasons in God, but not for now.
Bread baked in the third dimension is the only bread capable of satisfying
God's children in all dimensions. Three ingredients are essential to make
this bread: *mercy, unconditional love,* and *simplicity.* Like Elijah's servitor,

there are those incapable of seeing the possibility of great things in something, apparently, so simple. The spirit of distribution is always larger than it seems.

Firstfruits giving will increase as more people discover the revelation and the power of this principle. In doing so, the church is embarking on a new journey. We will find out what kind of heart postmodern apostles and prophets have as this increase takes place. True men and women of God are always seeking ways to bless people. Additional income from a principle like firstfruits will provide the opportunity to do so. The praxis of this principle will lead us to a place in which we can model extravagant grace giving in the Kingdom. May we receive such a heart of humility and understanding from the heavenly Father that we seek out opportunities to give as He does.

WHAT HAPPENS WITH FIRSTFRUITS?

And this shall be the priests' due from the people, from them that offer a sacrifice, whether it be ox or sheep: and they shall give unto the priest the shoulder, and the two cheeks, and the maw. The firstfruit also thy corn, of thy wine, and thine oil, and the first of the fleece of thy sheep, shalt thou give him. For the Lord thy God hath chosen him out of all thy tribes, to stand to minister in the name of the Lord, him and his sons forever (Deuteronomy 18:3-5).

When the Lord was establishing firstfruit giving, it was a part of the total culture being reformed. In fact, Israel was in the final stages of constructive preparation in order to inhabit the Promised Land. It is important that people understand exactly the destination of the firstfruits. Moses wrote in the Book of Deuteronomy that all firstfruits belonged to the priest, who was the primary spiritual leader in the nation. His direct words were: *"This shall be the priests' due from the people, from them that offer a sacrifice."* It is noteworthy to see the word *priests* is plural, preventing any selfishness from one individual. The Hebrew word for "due" is Strong's Concordance #8189, *mishpat,* which means "a verdict (favorable or unfavorable) pronounced judicially, especially a sentence or formal decree as divine law."

Imagine the Father, Son, and Holy Spirit discussing this matter. Within this Kingdom judicial forum, a decision will be made that's binding and lasting. There's no further court of appeals to go to change their decision. The foresight of the Godhead knew this would be the best plan for the sake of Kingdom integrity.

In the New Covenant, the apostle Paul established apostolic prerogative concerning economic support for ministry gifts. His words were: *"Do ye not know that they which minister about holy things live of the things of the temple? And they which wait at the altar are partakers with the altar? Even so hath the Lord ordained that they which preach the gospel should live of the gospel"* (1 Cor. 9:13-14). It is clear Paul used Numbers chapter 18 as a backdrop for his statements. Numbers chapter 18 deals directly with the subjects of firstfruits and tithes. The thing that prevents any of this operation from becoming witchcraft is the willingness of the person who is freely offering. Our responsibility as ministers of the gospel is to teach the people and empower them with proper information and revelation. From that point, it is the job of the Holy Spirit to persuade them whether to give or not.

I would like to close this book with a testimony of a privileged observance of a firstfruits worship service in February 2007. It was one of the most beautiful experiences I've witnessed. Because the groundwork had been properly laid, most of the congregation participated that day. I watched people come with joy, even some with tears of joy and thankfulness to present their gifts to the Lord. One particular single mother came without money. She shared with the man of God that she had no money but could give of herself. I watched him embrace her and bless her just as though she had given like anyone else.

When the final family had presented their gift, the man of God called the young lady back up and gave her money from his personal funds. As she was about to return to her seat, the man of God called her again and gave her a second offering. At that point, the young lady prostrated herself at the altar, expressing much gratitude to God. The Holy Spirit spoke to me to take note of what was about to happen. The congregation flooded that altar with more gifts for that young lady. They ministered love to her and her children like I've rarely seen.

The Holy Spirit spoke to me, "Now, you have witnessed in just a few moments the things you have taught and practiced." This young lady who had nothing to give received of the gleanings of the congregation's monetary harvest. As stated earlier in the book, the firstfruits and gleanings were set apart before people began to tithe. I am grateful to God for allowing me to witness these things. It is one thing to teach a principle; it is quite another to watch the principle caught, embraced, and lived right before my eyes.

As we continue in the process of reforming the church apostolically, we will be challenged to practice and teach new things. Some of them will be just for a season while others will have a more permanent quality to them. We must discern the prophetic registry of the season we're living in.

We are boldly moving toward the final conquest. Anything less than a culmination mentality is too small.

God is raising up a people in the earth who will become the converging point of many decades of Kingdom activities. They are a firstfruits unto God and the Lamb. Remember, God's objective is to bring conclusion to the matter He began in Himself before the foundation of the world. Firstfruits and the order of first things are idioms proclaiming God finished the same way He started—*in victory!*

ENDNOTE

1. Dennis Cauchon, "Taxpayers on the hook for $59 billion," *USA Today*, May 28, 2007, http://www.usatoday.com/news/washington/2007 -05-28-federal-budget_n.htm?loc=interstitialskip.

Epilogue

As you finish this book, it is extremely important to read afresh Deuteronomy 26:1-11. This is the portion of Scripture that details the personal worship observance connected with the release of firstfruits, thus sanctifying the order of first things. There are several keys to understand in this text regarding then and now.

- The firstfruits blessing was only applicable to people who were producing and fruitfully engaged on their property. People came on their own and humbled themselves before the heavenly Father.

- Some of the produce of the harvest was placed in a basket and brought to the house of the Lord as a preemptive statement of a greater commitment in giving.

- It is important to know who serves as a priest in your life, and recognize the place the Lord has placed them in.

- You must approach the high priest, or leader, and profess that you and your family have come into the Kingdom that the Lord swore unto our fathers.

- The priest will receive the offering without prejudice from the presenter, and place it upon the altar for consecration and dedication.

Some people may choose not to participate in something like this, citing Galatians 4:9—*"But now, after that ye have known God, or rather are known by God, how turn ye again to the weak and beggarly elements, whereunto ye desire again to be in bondage? Ye observe days, and months, and times, and years. I am afraid of you, lest I have bestowed upon you labor in vain."* Bear in mind, the most important truth is that whatever one does it must be by the leading of the Holy Spirit; and second, with a conviction of the heart.

I wrote a small confession, or statement of acknowledgement, for former descendants of American slavery.

> *Slaves ready to perish were our fathers, who came into this great country, this land of abundance. At first they were thousands who were members of the African Diaspora, but now we are millions, great, mighty, and very populous. At first we were evilly entreated in this great nation, afflicted, and had hard bondage laid on us.*
>
> *When our fathers cried unto the Lord our God, You heard their voice, looked upon their affliction, their labor, and their oppression. Lord, You brought forth our fathers out of slavery with a mighty hand, and with an outstretched arm, with awesomeness, with signs, with wonders; and You have brought us into this blessed place in the Kingdom of God, and have given us the competence*

to get wealth, wealth itself, and the resources of the King and His Kingdom. Your Kingdom is a place of milk and honey—a place of the double portion.

I not only confess the double portion, but also position myself for this principle to work a thousand times more in my life. And now, behold, I have brought the firstfruits of my increase, which You, O Lord, have given me. As I place this before You, I worship and rejoice in every good thing in which You have given unto me, unto my house, the ministry, and the strangers among us.

This confession certainly may be adapted for others. It serves as a means of remembering where the Lord has brought us from and His goodness and mercy. *"But thou shalt remember the Lord thy God: for it is he that giveth thee power to get wealth, that he may establish his covenant which he sware unto thy fathers, as it is this day"* (Deut. 8:18). We must remember the Lord's favor and blessings while we forget the injustice of others.

Remembering and forgiving are important because of the principle of "prophetic enactment." My dear friend, Clarice Fluitt, has been a vital instrumental in pioneering this activity within the Body of Christ. Because most people must have their senses stimulated to really learn, drama and ceremony are not necessarily evil in themselves. In fact, with the proper motivation, many things become tools of instruction in the Master's hands. Many of Clarice's meetings are filled with prophetic enactment that generates corporate involvement and provides the correct frequency of the Holy Spirit. Many commit to sharing the life of Christ within them.

During the firstfruits dedication, your expression may be similar to the following:

The man of God, the priest, has the responsibility of waving [Strong's Concordance #5130; νψωπη; to quiver (i.e. vibrate up and down, or rock to and fro); to lift up and wave] the firstfruits before the Lord, thus causing the blessing to rest in each person's home. After the minister has received the firstfruits, it is up to that person to be nobler in character than previous generations. Great honor will come to the Kingdom of God if ministers follow the example of Christ.

As mature sons, we are possessors of all things and in need of nothing. Because of that, distribution is like a Kingdom insurance policy, which understands and abides in the truth of no lack. The more we freely distribute, the more we alleviate the concern of some brethren that this will be just one more good scriptural principle gone awry. The heavenly Father factored into the culture that some would have abusive tendencies. People have abused everything Jesus said, proving that the Kingdom of God has come.

For instance, the baptism of the Holy Spirit and the gifts of the Holy Spirit have been greatly abused. Regardless, we continue to encourage people to receive the baptism of the Holy Spirit. Abuse should not cause us to abandon the truth as though we must protect God. Our responsibility is to bring integrity to truth by living within the structure of that truth. Father God is honored and the Kingdom of God is magnified when we do so. In the end, if this principle becomes just another means of collecting money, it has become a corrupted practice. This isn't about any of us *getting*; it's about all of us *learning to give more generously and effectively* in the post-modern reformation.

Author Contact Information

DR. STEPHEN EVERETT

3227 S. W. 1st Avenue

Cape Coral, FL 33914-5000

USA

E-mail: newcman@aol.com

Additional copies of this book and other
book titles from DESTINY IMAGE are
available at your local bookstore.

Call toll-free: 1-800-722-6774.

Send a request for a catalog to:

Destiny Image® Publishers, Inc.

P.O. Box 310
Shippensburg, PA 17257-0310

*"Speaking to the Purposes of God for this
Generation and for the Generations to Come."*

**For a complete list of our titles,
visit us at www.destinyimage.com.**